To Julian

With best wishes for a very Happy Birthday and my love

Grannie -

2nd May 1988

Staff Officer

STAFF OFFICER

THE DIARIES OF WALTER GUINNESS (FIRST LORD MOYNE) 1914–1918

Edited by
BRIAN BOND and SIMON ROBBINS

LEO COOPER
LONDON

First published 1987 by Leo Cooper
Leo Cooper is an independent imprint of
the Heinemann Group of Publishers,
10 Upper Grosvenor Street, London W1X 9PA.
LONDON MELBOURNE JOHANNESBURG AUCKLAND

ISBN: 0-85052-053-3

Printed by Butler & Tanner Ltd,
Frome and London

Contents

Foreword

By Lord Moyne

It is appropriate that I should express my great appreciation of the work of the two editors in selecting what is of interest from a military historian's point of view from my father's account of his experiences in the First World War, and in collating it with letters written to my mother, from which they have quoted in appropriate cases. I would also like to pay tribute to Brian Bond for his introduction which puts so well into perspective the interest of these day-to-day records.

As the same person as the small boy who watched my father ride by on his mare Butterfly in 1914 on his way to parade with the Yeomanry on a sunlit morning in Suffolk, it fills me with sadness to think of the horrors of trench warfare he was so courageously to face, in spite of my pride in his two DSOs. If I was at home from my prep school he never failed in his kindness to me during his brief spells of leave. But, though he never speaks of his feelings in the Diaries, it was not for years after the war that I felt him to be free from the strain of what he and so many others had undergone.

Editors' Introduction

Some words of explanation and justification are perhaps required for the decision to publish yet another British army officer's contemporary account of the First World War after the passage of so many years. The importance of these memoirs lies partly in the personality and distinguished public career of their author, Walter Guinness, Conservative Member of Parliament for Bury St Edmunds from 1907 to 1931 and later to hold high political office and be created first Baron Moyne.

Even more significant, however, is the comparatively rare standpoint in the military hierarchy from which Guinness recorded his personal impressions of the war. Many generals published war memoirs in the inter-war period, and more recently the diaries, letters and recollections of numerous subalterns have appeared. We are thus well-provided both with strategic and political interpretations of the war at Army and Corps levels and with the combat experiences of company and platoon commanders. However, the practical day-by-day running of the great war machine by battalion, brigade and divisional staff officers has seldom been so graphically and interestingly described as in Walter Guinness's diary and letters. Although Guinness personally experienced and described a great deal of frontline fighting in Gallipoli and, later, on the Western Front between mid-1916 and the end of the war, his recollections are probably more valuable to historians for the light they throw on the articulation of the fighting units through training, supply arrangements, the demarcation, repair and maintenance of the trench system, signal communications and liaison with flank units and with the supporting artillery. These aspects may be less dramatic than the great battles from Neuve Chapelle to Passchendaele, but they are essential to an understanding of how the war was actually conducted. Serious students of the war, as distinct from readers who merely wish to reinforce preconceptions of its frightfulness and futility, will profit from Guinness's informative but largely unemotional account. As a family man, politician and amateur soldier the diarist was eager to see an end to the war, but he never doubted that Germany had to be defeated.

Before providing a brief introduction to some of this volume's interesting aspects, a few words must be written about the nature of the documents and how they have been edited for publication. As the introductory note makes clear, these are not, in the strictest sense, diaries. Guinness records in 1919 that he had not had time to keep a diary and that his recollections were already becoming blurred. Unfortunately the top copy of his original memoir of 1919 has disappeared and with it the maps and appendices to which he occasionally refers. Fortunately, however, large batches of his daily letters to his wife and pencilled notes which he enclosed in them have recently come to light, and from these it is clear that Guinness wrote up his 'diaries' from the letters and notes. In some entries the diaries exactly reproduce the letters, while in many others there are only minor variations. Obviously in writing up the diaries (possibly for later publication), Guinness was inclined to omit purely personal matters, such as enquiries about his family's health and the career prospects of relatives and friends; he also omitted, toned down or summarized some bitter outbursts about the incompetence or unpleasantness of individuals. But after a careful comparison between the typed copy of the diaries and the surviving letters and notes the editors felt that the latter added significantly to the diaries at only a few points. Extracts from letters or notes have therefore been inserted in the appropriate places. The editors have also made minor amendments to the text in the way of spelling out abbreviations, clarifying ambiguous sentences, deleting repetitions and correcting obvious typing errors. We have kept explanatory notes to a minimum on the assumption that most readers will have a sound general knowledge of the First World War and access to the standard works of reference. Unfamiliar names are another matter, however, and we have included an appendix of biographical notes for virtually all identifiable individuals mentioned in the text, marking their inclusion by an asterisk at the first mention of their names. Sketch maps have been provided to enable the reader to follow the diarist's movements, particularly in the battles in which his unit was engaged.

* * *

Walter Edward Guinness was born in Dublin in 1880, the third son of Edward Cecil Guinness, later the first Earl of Iveagh. He was educated at Eton where, in addition to athletic prowess, he developed a deep and enduring interest in biology. He thought of pursuing this subject at Oxford, but instead in 1899 he volunteered for service in South Africa with the Suffolk Yeomanry. He was wounded, mentioned in dispatches and ended the war with the rank of captain in the Yeomanry and honorary captain in the Regular Army. He first stood for Parliament in the general election of 1906 but was defeated in the Stowmarket division of Suffolk where his father had purchased Elveden, the famous sporting estate. In 1907, however, he was returned at a by-election for Bury St Edmunds and continued to represent that division until 1931. He was also a member of the London County Council from 1907 to 1910. He remained in the Suffolk Yeomanry and on the outbreak of war in 1914 was second-in-command of a regiment with the rank of major.

Readers will probably conclude that Guinness did not attain rank or exercise responsibilities commensurate with his abilities, dedication to duty and experience. He was unlucky in that his Yeomanry regiment was not sent overseas until the autumn of 1915 and then, after the harsh experience of the final phase at Gallipoli, was left for several months in idleness in Egypt. At the Anzac bridgehead Guinness had taken command of a battalion (1/10th London) and was briefly in charge of another (1/5th Norfolk) at the same time, owing to the acute shortage of officers; but when he at last arrived in France in August, 1916, he again found himself in the rather humdrum appointment of second-in-command of a battalion and a poor one at that (11th Cheshire). Guinness craved a front-line command or, failing that, an active staff appointment with troops, as distinct from a comfortable headquarters assignment in the rear. But he was in competition with ambitious regular officers and, rather modestly in view of his sharp criticism of several individual regulars, felt that they deserved priority. Critics like Sir Philip Gibbs have indicted the High Command for its 'trade union' mentality in blocking the promotion of able young amateur officers, and indeed of regular officers without the Staff College qualification (p.s.c.) to staff appointments. But by 1916 there was such an acute shortage of competent officers that staff positions, especially at brigade and divisional level, were given to talented amateurs. In addition to Walter Guinness, these included E. M. W. Grigg (later 1st Baron Altrincham), W. A. Greene (later Baron Greene), Oliver Lyttelton (later Lord Chandos), J. H. Boraston (the lawyer who edited Haig's despatches) and Anthony Eden (later Earl of Avon).

As the diary shows, each grade of command and staff duties required a special expertise, and until he had taken a staff officers' course in France, Guinness did not feel himself qualified for the pivotal post of brigade major. As an MP and long-serving Yeomanry officer, he could have received a rearward staff position for the asking, but in several passages he expresses his contempt for these all-too-often arrogant and incompetent upstarts who tended to keep well clear of the front line. In 1917 Guinness became Brigade Major to 74th Brigade in 25th Division and on leaving this appointment he was briefly Brigade Major to 198th Brigade in 66th Division commanded by Alan Hunter. He was succeeded by Anthony Eden who was then only twenty years old. In the Spring of 1918 Guinness followed in the wake of his former commander, the dynamic Keppel

Bethell, to 66th Division as GSO 2 (General Staff Officer second grade). He ended the war in this appointment with the rank of lieutenant-colonel. His post-war political career will be summarized later.

It is only necessary here to mention the main phases of Guinness's military experience with a foretaste of the graphic descriptions and comments which give the diaries much of their appeal. First, however, it needs to be stressed that Walter Guinness was an exceptionally brave officer. Anthony Eden, who knew Guinness well in 1918, placed him in the rare category of men 'who could discipline themselves to be insensitive to danger and who lacked neither brains nor imagination'. Eden illustrated his point with the following anecdote:

> On one occasion, I would guess in the early autumn of 1918, we were walking down a road deep in discussion about some future plan Walter had brought to me when I noticed that about 200 yards ahead the Germans were shelling heavily a cross-roads we were approaching. We continued to walk, Walter to expound and I to listen. I began to look anxiously at the shelled cross-roads, for it was a frequent practice of the Germans at this late period of the war to mine important cross-roads as they retreated and then to shell them to prevent their being repaired. Walter made no sign, but I could bear it no longer and stopped in my tracks with the comment: 'I don't know, Walter, whether you intend walking into that barrage, but I am against it.' Walter surveyed the scene, as it were for the first time. 'Oh yes,' he said, 'they do seem to be shelling quite heavily. What do you suggest?' 'I suggest,' I replied, 'that we go round and rejoin the road beyond the shelling.' Walter agreed readily enough, but I wondered to myself what would he have done if he had been alone with his thoughts.†

Similarly, in a obituary tribute in *The Times* (7 November, 1944) Lord Cranborne wrote: 'Many men are brave; but Lord Moyne was more. He had, in the highest degree, that spirit of daring which delights in danger.'

He did not reach the Anzac bridgehead on the Gallipoli peninsula until mid-October, 1915, by which time the campaign had clearly failed in its original purpose and – unless the operation was abandoned altogether – a winter defensive in terrible conditions was in prospect. On 17 November torrential rain flooded the trenches and added greatly to the privations and misery. On 28 November it began to snow and freeze. Guinness's troops, lodged in the precipitous gullies above Anzac Cove, were without shelter and were not permitted to cut even green wood around the camps. The diarist protested about these conditions and predicted a disaster if the terrible weather continued. He found the New Zealanders who relieved

†Anthony Eden, *Another World, 1897–1917* (1976), pp. 132–133.

his regiment virtually impossible to deal with and he was even more critical of the Australians. On 2 December Guinness and his unit embarked for Mudros in the remarkably well-organized evacuation but left all their baggage behind. They had been shelled to the water's edge and suffered several casualties. Guinness mentions a magnificent ex-Guardsman standing bolt upright through the shelling and merely remarking, 'A bit of that there shell hit my boot.'

Much of the staff work in the Gallipoli operation was notoriously bad and made a permanently unfavourable impression on the diarist. On 26 April, 1916, he told his wife about the experience of his friend George Lloyd who had remonstrated with a senior officer at Gallipoli about staff officers 'who care nothing for the lives and comfort of the troops but only about their own decorations and promotion'. Lloyd now refused to wear the red tabs of the staff because he was so ashamed of what he had seen. In a diary note of 23 August, 1916, Guinness recorded the view that: 'Certainly many of our young staff officers seem quite unfit for their jobs and are hopelessly careless about details such as giving map references, places and times of rendezvous accurately.' Guinness reiterated that he would infinitely prefer a battalion command to a staff appointment, but eventually allowed himself to be nominated for a six-week staff course in October, 1916. In a diary note on 9 October he wrote: 'There's no doubt that a Brigade Major's job is the most attractive to my taste. One never sets eyes on the Staff of any bigger command anywhere near the trenches.' Anthony Eden clearly explains why this appointment was so important:

> To be a brigade major was a job I always coveted, whether seen from below as an adjutant or from the, to me, less congenial remoteness of divisional headquarters. The brigade and its staff seemed of exactly the right size and scope for individual efforts to be rewarding, while the contacts with units were close enough to have a human interest. This applied particularly to the last months of the war when the brigade could be expanded to include cavalry and artillery. The work was strenuous and, even by the standards of trench warfare, there was little chance of sleep; by day attack, by night preparing and issuing orders for the next advance.†

Between 18 December, 1915, and 8 May, 1916, Guinness was kicking his heels in Egypt and wondering if he would ever get to an active theatre. A few pages have been cut out from this section since the diarist himself admitted he was bored and had little of interest to record. He arrived in France in August, 1916, to join one of the original New Army battalions (11th Cheshires) which had suffered severely in the opening phase of the

†Eden, *Another World*, pp. 149–150.

Somme campaign (75% casualties, including 300 men from machine-gun fire in a few seconds in the attack on Thiepval) and was thoroughly disorganized. It belonged to a division (25th) which was in a similar state of disorganization and low morale.

From late August to the end of October Guinness, as second-in-command of 11th Cheshires, witnessed some of the hardest fighting on the Somme, culminating in the successful attack on Regina trench. Even in the support trenches the troops were pushed to the limits of endurance. Supplies had to be carried to the front line under cover of darkness along trenches ankle- or even knee-deep in mud. 'It is an odious business having to force men to do what you know to be impossible. The Staff Officer sits in a well-lit warm dug-out and works things out on paper, assuming good conditions and everything going right. The regimental officer has to get the impossible done somehow with the men dead beat and no guides able to take them to the map references in the trenches which in many cases are absolutely obliterated and consist of a waste of shell holes' (30 August). On 3 September he recorded that after days of agonized uncertainty his battalion's part in an over-ambitious attack was called off. The troops from other battalions which did attack reached their objective only to be blasted to pieces by our own artillery. This incident provoked one of the diarist's several scathing criticisms of the British gunners. He thought their inefficiency was partly due to the Forward Observation Officers (FOOs) not getting far enough forward and misdirecting fire onto parts of the line held by our troops under the mistaken assumption that they were still in German occupation. 'The artillery duels of which one reads too often mean that the infantry are being blown to bits' (4 September). At this stage of the war he recorded that 'our gunners aren't a patch on the French', but later he thought our Artillery tactics had improved – as indeed they had (see R.G.S Bidwell and D.Graham, *Fire-Power*, 1982).

The diary entries graphically describe deteriorating conditions in the forward areas in the Autumn of 1916 and how they affected the soldiers' lives. Thus on 2 October: 'Incessant downpours of rain. Managed to get remainder of men under some sort of cover (four-fifths had been sleeping out without any shelter), chiefly tarpaulins, bivouacs, etc, stretched over unroofed dugouts.' In some respects he felt it was better to be in the front trenches than to do this heavy carrying and digging work (3 October). Later in October torrential rain caused several postponements of the assault on Regina trench, to the misery of the densely-packed troops anxious to get the ordeal over with. On 20 October he recorded that field guns were hopelessly stuck in the mud two miles behind the line. 'I have just seen a man stuck in the mud up to his knees whom they took an hour to get out.' He was lucky because a man in the adjacent battalion went raving mad and died after a similar experience. Guinness raged at the incompetence of the medical arrangements in these abominable conditions. 'We simply couldn't get the wounded in and the outrageous failure of the Field Ambulances to carry out their duty to evacuate our advanced dressing station must mean death to many of the cases who would otherwise have been saved' (22 October).

On the Somme and later we are reminded that Guinness was a cultivated, fastidious gentleman who found the boorish company of many of his fellow officers scarcely tolerable: 'Out of the line one finds this life very narrowing as ... one has very few interests in common with those among whom one lives.... The Mess of the 10th London was less trying as there were several people who took an interest in books and politics' (8 September).

After the Somme campaign had ground to a halt Guinness's battalion spent the appalling winter of 1916–1917 on the inhospitable River Lys section near Ypres. On 30 January, 1917, he noted: 'Still freezing hard and some more snow. Living as I do in a dugout with plenty of clothes and blankets, I can realize how much the men are suffering in this weather with no blankets in the trenches and no dugouts owing to the wind being in a dangerous quarter for gas.' Shells exploding in water-filled craters left ice fragments at least six inches thick. Wire defences could not be improved because it was impossible to drive in the pegs. Despite these dreadful conditions he found the men 'wonderfully cheerful'. In the entry for 16 February he vividly describes a minenwerfer barrage followed up by a lightning trench raid on his battalion by a Bavarian unit.

In April and May, 1917, Guinness, now brigade major to the 74th Brigade, describes his unit's preparation for the brilliantly successful capture of Messines by Sir Herbert Plumer's Second Army. Since this operation is rightly cited as an unusual example of meticulous staff work, it is fascinating to discover how thoroughly the attack was prepared for at brigade level and below. In ten days of strenuous training out of the line the German trenches were marked out to scale with flags and each battalion practised its part in the attack separately before finally doing it all together. 'We had got the plan worked out in considerable detail and represented the barrage by a line of drummers moving back at the scheduled times and making the necessary wells just behind each trench line to enable the attacking troops to do their mopping up' (30 April).

It is interesting to note that Oliver Lyttelton and Anthony Eden both paid similar compliments to Second Army's preparations for Messines in their war memoirs. Thus Lyttelton, who was then staff captain of the 2nd Guards Brigade, recalled that 'We trained intensively ... for the battle: large-scale models of the ground were constructed and the most careful study of the terrain was carried out daily. We were confident that we should succeed'.† Eden, who was already Adjutant of his battalion (60th Rifles) at the remarkably early age of eighteen, wrote: 'We were now plunged into an intensive system of training such as we had never known.... This is characteristic of the way in which the Army Command missed nothing in detailed preparation for the battle, down to battalion and battery level, months before the event.'††

Guinness also provides an exciting, detailed account of the capture of Messines on 7 June, starting with the unprecedented explosion of enormous mines all along the German front line. He adds the interesting detail that, as his brigade advanced into a black fog, his incessantly active brigadier (Bethell) 'sat with a volume of Shakespeare open in front of him, shouting to me in the next room every minute or two demands for information which of course we couldn't get'. He also noted that the Australian Division did not reach its final objectives because men gave priority to souvenir hunting.

One character looms larger than life in this book, namely Guinness's brigade and later divisional commander, Keppel Bethell, a dynamic and irascible soldier of a type later made familiar by the novels of Anthony Powell and Evelyn Waugh. Bethell lurches like an angry bull through the later pages of this diary arousing in the diarist mixed feelings of mounting exasperation and grudging admiration. The most remarkable point about Bethell was his age: he commanded a brigade at 34 and a division (albeit a ramshackle, composite one) at 35.

Hugh Keppel Bethell was born in 1882, the son of Colonel E. H. Bethell, and educated at Charterhouse and Woolwich. He was commissioned into the Royal Garrison Artillery but later transferred to the 7th Hussars. He passed through the Staff College, Camberley, before the war and by 1915 had achieved command of a battalion in France. Bethell, known throughout the Army as 'the Beetle', was a thruster in a class of his own. He was distinguished, or notorious, for flouting regulations and higher authorities, 'poaching' officers and equipment from other units and driving his staff to distraction by a flood of contradictory or impossible orders. Guinness's first description of him was 'like quicksilver'. At 74th Brigade Headquarters he tolerated none of the usual hangers-on, and indeed hardly allowed his staff a moment to look at a newspaper (23 February, 1917).

Against his dynamic qualities, Guinness was soon (23 April) noting Bethell's defects. 'He becomes frightfully impatient and unreasonable when things don't go right.' He gave an impossible order for wire to be laid in no-man's-land in the dark and, when he discovered some of it in the wrong places, 'Vesuvius in eruption couldn't compete with Bethell'.

†Oliver Lyttelton, *The Memoirs of Lord Chandos*, (1962), pp. 75–6.
††Eden, *Another World*, p. 135.

Bethell's temper worsened through the summer of 1917 until, under the strain of the Ypres offensive, he became impossible to work with. Guinness describes an incident (5 and 6 August) when Bethell accused him of losing a paper which turned out to be in his own pocket all the time. Things reached such a pitch that none of his staff would eat with him, but this particular crisis eased when Bethell's voice gave out. In another incident (6 October) Bethell flew into a rage and 'poured torrents of abuse' over the phone to the Divisional staff for failing to produce transport for his troops. It transpired that he had left his headquarters before the buses were due and they had actually arrived on time. Eventually (letter to his wife dated 1 April, 1918) Guinness had to have a straight talk with Bethell, pointing out that his rages paralysed everyone around him and reduced their effectiveness by 75%. This plain speaking seems to have had some effect.

Bethell's infantile behaviour when out of action should not be allowed to obscure his outstanding record as a commander in battle. Guinness's diary entries for 21 March, 1918, and succeeding days testify to Bethell's admirable handling of 74th Brigade during the retreat and counter-attack.

Describing Bethell as 'a wonderful fighting soldier, but a terror to the administration of an Army,' Lieutenant-General Sir Gordon Macready recounted Bethell's idiosyncratic behaviour on taking over 66th Division in March, 1918.† On the night of 20–21 March the 66th Division was one of the units surprised and out-flanked in the Germans' brilliant, surprise attack. The next ten days were a nightmare of continual retreat and confusion until the division reached the outskirts of Amiens with only 800 officers and men left. Bethell arrived to take over the shattered 66th at Abbeville with a completely unauthorized staff. Rather like Rommel in the Second World War, Bethell abominated inaction. Only two days after arriving he informed Macready, his senior staff officer, that they were to resume fighting immediately as a machine-gun division. Few additional troops would be needed but Macready must procure several hundred machine-guns; no small order after a disastrous retreat and while the battle was still raging. Bethell personally would square this unorthodox arrangement with his polo-playing friend 'Duggie' (the Commander-in-Chief). By devious methods, such as approaching units from the direction of the fighting rather than the rear, Macready was able to fulfil Bethell's megalomaniac orders, in the process depriving the Machine-Gun School at Camiers of its weapons! Bethell, pleased as Punch that he now commanded a division with several times the fire-power of an ordinary infantry division, went off to tell Haig that his division was ready to

†Sir Gordon Macready, *In The Wake Of the Great*, (William Clowes, London, 1965), pp. 24–27.

plunge into battle. He returned crestfallen, having been reprimanded at GHQ for, in effect, stealing officers and weapons from other units. Instead of the coveted role in battle, 66th Division was given the unglamorous task of training American drafts.

This disappointment, as Guinness shows, did not ruin Bethell's career or diminish his enthusiasm. His division, assisted by two squadrons of the Royal Air Force, a brigade of cavalry and other attached units, played a distinguished role in the final months of the war, operating as the spearhead of the Fourth Army in the advance to the Rhine. Bethell was mentioned eight times in despatches.†

In the light of this meteoric rise to temporary general's rank by the age of 35, the reader may wonder why Bethell's name is not as well known as, say, Wavell's, Gort's or Ironside's for later military achievements. Bethell's career after 1918 was not undistinguished but he never had another opportunity to command in battle and received no further promotion beyond Major-General. After the war he held the prestigious appointment of Military Attaché in Washington until 1923, when he returned to command a brigade in the Rhine Army. In 1927 he was appointed Brigadier, General Staff, Northern India but not until 1930 was his temporary war-time rank of Major-General made substantive on his appointment to the military command of the Presidency and Assam District. On giving up this post in 1934 he retired from the Army. He died in Kenya at the age of sixty-four.

* * *

Guinness allowed himself to be recruited as GSO 2 of 66th Division with reluctance, Bethell having pressed high authorities for his transfer. He found little interest in the work of training, billeting, feeding and generally looking after green American troops with an inadequate staff. Inspections by visiting dignitaries were another source of complaint. As he wrote home on 30 May, 1918: 'Milner inspected our people the day before yesterday, Pershing yesterday, Haig this morning, Army Commander this afternoon, Corps Commander tomorrow. I hate all generals.' On 25 June he noted that Sir John Seely, a former War Minister, had recently left France for a job in England and reflected, 'I shall soon be almost the only MP out here, and I really feel that my present work is not good value. It was different when one was risking one's life as Brigade Major.'

However, the diaries end on a high note with the 66th Division's part in the attack on the Hindenburg Line (entries for 8 October and following days) and the steady advance into Belgium which continued until the Armistice on 11 November. Thereupon the 66th had the honour of being

†*The Times* obituary, 10 March, 1947.

one of the nine British and Imperial divisions selected for the post-hostilities advance into Germany. Guinness, however, did not stay on to witness this triumph but at once returned home on the announcement that there would be a general election.

After the war Guinness pursued an extremely full life, combining a promising political career with scientific travel, a share in his father's benefactions in England and Ireland and in the management of the Guinness breweries. In 1922 he was appointed Under-Secretary of State for War, followed by the financial secretaryship of the Treasury in 1923 and again in 1924–5 under Sir Winston Churchill as Chancellor of the Exchequer. He was sworn a Privy Councillor in 1924 and entered the Cabinet in 1925 as Minister of Agriculture. He retired from office when the Conservatives were defeated in 1929, and in 1932 was raised to the peerage as Baron Moyne.

Lord Moyne served as chairman of numerous committees in the 1930s including the Royal Commission on the University of Durham (1934) and the West India Royal Commission (1938–39). In these years Moyne also used his private yacht to travel to places as distant and remote as New Guinea, Honduras and Greenland in search of biological specimens and archaeological material. He published two travel books, Walkabout; *A Journey in Lands between the Pacific and Indian Oceans* (1936) and *Atlantic Circle* (1938).

In 1941 he succeeded his old friend Lord Lloyd as Secretary of State for the Colonies and Leader of the House of Lords. In August, 1942, at a moment of crisis in the North African war, Moyne was given an important assignment as Deputy Minister of State in Cairo. In January, 1944, he succeeded Richard Casey as Minister Resident in the Middle East, but on 6 November that year he was assassinated in Cairo by terrorists from the Stern gang based in Palestine.

Brian Bond.
Simon Robbins.

The Diary

I have so often regretted that I have no record of my movements in the South African War that I am putting together these rough notes of my experiences in the European War from letters, reports on operations, etc. I unfortunately did not keep a diary, and during most of the more interesting work there would in any case have been no time to write it. Already (1919) my recollections are getting rather blurred, and, owing to the gaps in material, my account must necessarily be an imperfect one.

1914: SUFFOLK

July, 1914

After a weekend of intense excitement, during which it was generally known that the Government were trying to find a way out of their obligation to stand by France and Russia, Sir Edward Grey* made a statement on the 3rd August, from which it was clear that we should certainly take part in the War.

I did not actually receive the order to mobilize until the early morning post of Wednesday, 5 August. It had been arranged before the War that each squadron of the Suffolk Yeomanry should be mobilised at their respective headquarters, and, prior to concentration at Ipswich, the pre-arranged War station. Evelyn and the children came down by motor to the Manor House, Bury St Edmunds. Charlie (Willoughby's)* Brigade marched down to Hertfordshire, and Muriel and her children came down with us. On arrival at Bury, the headquarters of the Suffolk Yeomanry, I found that the Regimental Headquarters and most of 'B' Squadron had already turned up. The regiment was commanded by Freddy Jarvis, with Ernest Northern of the 19th Hussars as Adjutant, and myself as Second-in-Command. 'B' Squadron, which I had commanded for about two years, had recently been taken over by Frank Goldsmith, who was Member of Parliament for the Stowmarket Division, and Edward Greene was his Second-in-Command.

6 August

We spent a very busy day valuing for purchase the horses which the men had brought up, and arranged to take over other horses locally. By the morning of the 7th (Friday) the Regimental Headquarters saw 'B' Squadron march off by road to Ipswich before ourselves going there by train. We got to Ipswich about 5 p.m. The Beccles Squadron had marched in by road and the Cambridge 'A' Squadron arrived by train. On mobilisation, the Peace establishment of four Squadrons was changed to the War establishment of three Squadrons, and this was effected by breaking

*Indicates biographical note in Appendix, pp. 244–50.

up the Ipswich 'C' Squadron and dividing the personnel among the other three. Billeting arrangements had been made prior to the outbreak of war, and the officers who had gone on before found no difficulty in accommodating the troops in Ipswich. Regimental Headquarters were at Colonel Flint's house, The Mote, Tuddenham Road. Regimental Headquarters had not been there more than a few minutes when orders came that the Regiment might be needed to leave Ipswich at once for some other destination. Orders were then sent for those troops who had already arrived to concentrate at a field just by Ipswich Railway Station and we sent out to divert those who had not already reached their billets. The Suffolk Yeomanry were part of the Eastern Mounted Brigade, whose headquarters were already established at the White Hart Hotel, Ipswich, and we went up there to see Brigadier-General H. W. Hodgson.* The Eastern Mounted Brigade consisted of the Norfolk Yeomanry, commanded by Colonel Morse, the Essex Yeomanry, commanded by Colonel Deakin, and ourselves, but the other two regiments had not yet reached the War Station. General Hodgson, late 15th Hussars, had commanded the Brigade for some years, and his Brigade Major was William Gibbs of the 7th Hussars. Under the Territorial Force organization, the Staff Captain never really functioned until mobilisation. This appointment had been given to Jack Agnew of the Suffolk Yeomanry. I found this staff assembled at the White Hart Hotel, much worried by the peremptory orders of the War Office that a train was to be kept with steam up at Ipswich Station and that any troops that had already arrived were to stand by ready to entrain in case of news of a German landing.[1]† As a large proportion of the Regiment had marched anything between fifteen and twenty-five miles, we all naturally wanted to let them get into billets to settle down, but the War Office messages left no discretion in the matter. The Regiment stayed on the field by Ipswich Station until about 4 a.m. on *Saturday, 8 August*, when the order to stand by was cancelled.

During the four days we spent at Ipswich there was a great amount of work to be done. We had as Quartermaster Captain Earle, who had formerly been Regimental Sergeant-Major. Although formerly an excellent Cavalry NCO and an efficient quartermaster for the annual camp, where he was sure of plenty of time beforehand to think out and make his arrangements, he proved absolutely hopeless in the hustle of mobilization. The system of the Territorial Force made the County Association responsible for equipping units. A large proportion of the 'Unit Equipment' was only drawable on mobilization from various contracting firms, who were supposed to keep a stock earmarked for military purposes. Owing, however, to the competition between various Territorial Associ-

†For notes see pp. 251–254.

ations and the insufficient supply of equipment available, we were not completely fitted out until long after this time. To add to the rush, at 2 a.m. about the second morning we were at Ipswich, a wire came from the War Office asking for the number of men who would volunteer for overseas service. This return had to be furnished in an absurdly short space of time, and caused a lot of trouble. Being called for in such an urgent hurry, the men not unnaturally thought that it meant that they were going to be sent over in a few days, and many of those who were otherwise ready enough to volunteer felt that, in view of the absurdly insufficient training done by the Territorial Force under peace conditions, they ought not to be asked to go overseas until they had had a much more thorough training. The men being in scattered billets, it was in any case a very difficult matter in the small hours of the morning for the Squadron Officers to get round and see the men individually so as to explain and get them to sign the necessary obligation.

On *Wednesday, 12 August*, the Regiment marched to Woodbridge, the Regimental Headquarters being established in Colonel Carthew's house at Woodbridge Abbey. The Eastern Mounted Brigade Headquarters were at the Bull Hotel, Woodbridge, the Norfolk Yeomanry at Wrendelsham, and the Essex Yeomanry at the village of Melton. In view of the excitement about volunteering for overseas, we little thought that we were doomed to sit in Woodbridge until 26 July, 1915.

The authorities were very nervous for the first part of the time as to the possibility of a German landing. For the first few days the Eastern Mounted Brigade and the local Infantry Territorials were the only troops in East Anglia. As soon as arrangements could be made, however, two other Mounted Brigades moved into Norfolk and Suffolk and, with the Eastern Mounted Brigade, constituted the first Mounted Division under Major-General Alderson.* With the exception of two men who had left the country for Canada, the whole of the Suffolk Yeomanry, without a single absentee, turned up on mobilization and very much inconvenience and loss were caused to many farmers and others who had to leave their businesses at a few hours' notice. We very shortly filled up the few vacancies which we had in the Regiment. There were, of course, far more applications to join than we could possibly accept, and in view of the expectation that we should shortly go abroad, we set a very high standard of riding for our recruits. I used to go down and see Frank Goldsmith putting them through the most brutal bareback tests, and we undoubtedly rejected lots of men who rode badly, but who would have been invaluable if we had realized the length of time in front of us for training.

Jarvis had for many years served in the South African Constabulary, and he brought in a certain number of men who had served with him in that Force. The strong local prejudice, however, made it very difficult to bring in non-commissioned officers from outside the County. We got as Quartermaster a wonderful old man of about seventy, Major O'Donnell, who had for many years been Quartermaster of the King's Dragoon Guards. He was never known in the Regiment by any other name than 'Click-Tooth' because of the remarkable noise made by his very ill-fitting set of teeth. However, in spite of this dilapidation, he had astounding energy. His great fault was that he was very talkative and increased the difficulty of getting Jarvis ever to come to any quick decision. During our time at Woodbridge we suffered from what I believe were almost universal troubles in the Territorial Force, namely the excess of local feeling, which very much interfered with efficiency.

'A' Squadron was commanded by Royce Tomkin, who, though formerly a regular soldier, was most difficult to deal with. He had in his Squadron Pym, who, formerly, when he was in the 5th Lancers, had been our Adjutant, and Sir Cuthbert Quilter, the Member for the Sudbury Division, who, after a good many years in the Regiment, had left a year or two before and rejoined from the Territorial Force Reserve. These three officers strongly objected to the Territorial Force serving abroad and actually discouraged their men from accepting that obligation. The figures in 'A' Squadron compared very badly with those in other Squadrons and we had a great deal of friction on this account. A Cavalry Regiment is necessarily much more widely distributed in billets than an Infantry Battalion, owing to the extra accommodation needed for horses. This made anything in the nature of a Regimental Mess out of the question, at all events during the early stages. Some months afterwards the authorities decided to build huts at Woodbridge and we then brought over our own huts from the Regimental store at Bury and set up our own Mess. By this time, however, a great deal of harm had been done by the three Squadrons and Regimental Headquarters each living as a separate community, and the trouble continued, owing to the fact that by that time many of the married officers had taken houses and lived with their families.

I hated the job of Second-in-Command and wanted to go back to the command of the Squadron. This, however, was not allowed. My chief function was to smooth over personal difficulties which were greatly added to by a most mischievous Chaplain, by name Ernest Powles, whom we had for many years had in the Regiment and who encouraged the disloyalty of 'A' Squadron to Jarvis. The friction was much increased owing to differences of opinion about the command of the second line. When this was formed in the autumn of 1914 we had great difficulty in finding a local man as a Commanding Officer. Raymond Greene, the former CO, was already serving in France with the 9th Lancers and could not come back. Various other ex-Cavalry officers in the County were tried, but all wanted more active employment. No Senior Officer in the

Regiment was willing to go and 'A' Squadron were very keen to get certain friends of their own appointed, although these had nothing to do with Suffolk. Jarvis very rightly resisted this and put in Colonel Spragg, who had commanded a Regiment of Imperial Yeomanry in the South African War and who was a local man. Sir Cuthbert Quilter went to the Reserve Regiment as a Squadron Leader, and he did all in his power to make things difficult for Spragg with whom we could work smoothly, although it must be admitted that he was not altogether a success.

About the end of *September* Evelyn moved over from Bury to a house at Sutton belonging to Mr Lomax and which was sub-let to us by a tenant. During this time I continued to live at the Abbey. On *27 October* we moved into Mr Lomax's house, Sutton Hoo. It was a most delightful place to live in and we were most comfortable there during the time at Woodbridge. During the Autumn of 1914 I went several times to London and pulled every string I could to get the Brigade sent overseas. Our discouragement reached its height when the Essex Yeomanry was picked out from the Brigade and sent to join the 8th Cavalry Brigade in France, being replaced in the Eastern Mounted Brigade by King Edward's Horse. The latter, being Colonials, were a most undisciplined Regiment and were so indignant at being kept in England that they deliberately said that they were going to make themselves such a nuisance that the authorities would send them abroad. They contributed to this object by breaking the heads of men in the Monmouthshire Infantry Territorials who had been brought down to the neighbourhood to dig a line of trenches. When they were in turn sent abroad they were replaced by the Welsh Horse, commanded by Lord Kensington. About the end of September, General Alderson was replaced in command of the First Cavalry Division by my old friend Lieut.-General R. G. Broadwood.* The doctors at this time told him that, as he had only one lung, he wouldn't stand the life in France for more than a few weeks. As it turned out, however, his health greatly improved from driving all over East Anglia in an open motor car, and when at last he was sent abroad in command of an Infantry Division at the beginning of 1916, he seemed extraordinarily fit.

Apart from the restlessness caused by being kept at home, life at Woodbridge was very pleasant. At first we had many light alarms, but gradually settled down to work out the details of various schemes for harassing any force which might be landed in Suffolk. The general idea of the various schemes which were in turn adopted was that, in case of a landing, the first Mounted Division should do everything in their power to hold up the invaders so as to give time for troops to be rushed up from the West of England to hold the trenches, which had been dug on a general line from Ipswich to the Wash. The country to the East of this was to be abandoned to our activities, and elaborate plans were made for the removal of the civilian population from this condemned area in case of a landing. Apart from training, we used to get exercise with a drag which was lent by the Suffolk Yeomanry for the Eastern Mounted Brigade and which used to hunt twice a week.

1915: Gallipoli and Egypt

At last, in *July, 1915* we left Woodbridge and marched up to Leiston, where we remained until our embarkation in *September* for Gallipoli. Though Leiston itself is a horrible little place, the surroundings and the sea bathing in August were delightful. Evelyn moved on 31 July to a little house called Haylings. At the end of August we got the first news that we were likely to go abroad. It came in the form of a wire from the War Office asking whether the Brigade was willing to proceed overseas dismounted. Without waiting even to consult the Regiments concerned, General Hodgson wired back that they were, and the War Office letter then arrived ordering us to get ready to reinforce the Mediterranean Expeditionary Force. The saddest part was having to dispose of our horses, which we passed on to a second-line Yeomanry Brigade which came up to take our place.

I have forgotten to mention that the King, as Hon Colonel of the Royal Suffolk Yeomanry, had inspected us one day on Martlesham Heath and we had several visits from Sir Ian Hamilton* and General Smith-Dorrien* during the time that they commanded the Central Force or the First Army.

'Click-Tooth' the Quartermaster, was of course too old for foreign service and, to his intense indignation, had to be left behind, being replaced by the RQMS, Tuttle, who owned the biggest shop in Lowestoft and who, though he became a good Quartermaster, did not add to the amenities of our HQ Mess, having no interest but Lowestoft, which he looked upon as the hub of the universe! We also lost our medical officer, Stalk, who, quite a short time before our departure, went off to join the Essex Yeomanry in France, being replaced by one Taylor from the Lowestoft neighbourhood. We should have lost a good many more of the old officers if one had not continually been appealing to their esprit de corps. The Regiment would naturally have gone to pieces during the long period of waiting if everyone had followed their own inclination to get more active employment. As soon as the news came that we were going abroad, great indignation was caused in the Regiment by the departure of Jack Crossley as a Staff Captain for Embarkation duties at Mudros. His father, Somerleyton, had fixed this up with Sir John Cowans.*

We left Leiston by train at 6.40 a.m. on *Thursday, 23 September*, arriving at Liverpool at the Gladstone Docks about 4 p.m. We embarked at once on the *Olympic*. She was the largest ship in the world at that time, and after the sinking of the *Titanic* a false keel had been put on to her, bringing her tonnage to well over 50,000. This was her first journey as a transport and, in spite of her size, her planning made her a most inconvenient ship for this purpose. Besides the Eastern Mounted Brigade, we had on board the South Western Mounted Brigade, commanded by Brig.-General Moare (OC Ship), and consisting of the 1st Devons, the North Devon and the West Somerset Yeomanries. The South-Eastern Mounted Brigade were also there, commanded by Brig.-General Clifton Brown and consisting of the East and West Kent and Sussex Yeomanries. Among them I found many old friends, among Members of Parliament, Peter Sanders, Gilbert Wills, Winterton, Sammy Scott; also Camden, Hambleden and several other peers. It was generally said that the authorities had collected all these legislators on the same ship in the hope of getting them all drowned together and thus making Parliament more popular. After the absurd secrecy which had been maintained as to our destination and ship, it was amusing on arrival on board to find about 500 telegrams waiting for different officers. Apparently, the information that we were all embarking on the *Olympic* was given by Sir John Cowans to some of his lady friends. It caused the postponement of our departure and some anxiety to the authorities, as it would have been a great score for a German submarine to sink so big a prize. We hung about the Mersey until 10 a.m. on Saturday the 25th, when at last we made a start. I happened to be Field Officer of the day and had a great deal of trouble in getting things straight. There were about 5000 troops on board and, as the ship had been so long laid up, neither the embarkation authorities nor the newly posted crew knew much about the accommodation and arrangements. I walked literally miles to find posts for magazines and other danger points, and several further miles in pursuit of the key of the armoury where the rifles had to be cleaned, etc. Every hour from 10 p.m. to 5 a.m. I had to receive reports from each of the nine Regimental Orderly Officers that they had visited their sentries who were posted to close the water-tight doors in case of need.

26 September (1915)

Out in the Bay of Biscay, and our destroyer escort leaves us, as we are now in such deep water that it would be difficult for a submarine to be lying up in waiting. It began to blow very hard and must have been very uncomfortable for the men in the stuffiness of the close-packed troop decks down below, the decks above being soaked with heavy rain.

27 September

We went very slowly by day and put on steam by night. We could have got through the Straits of Gibraltar if we had hurried and gone straight, but, as it was, we delayed, apparently hoping that the extra 24 hours added to the time spent in the Mersey would cause submarines lurking in the Straits to imagine we had passed and to give up waiting for us.

28 September

Went through the Straits of Gibraltar about 8.30 p.m. just as a glorious orange moon was rising straight ahead of us. Great precautions were taken to prevent any of our lights showing, and it was very impressive before the moon appeared to feel our huge ship throbbing through the blackness at full speed, nothing being visible except the lights of Ceuta, Algeciras and Gibraltar and the white track of foam breaking away from our sides.

On *1 October* at about 3 p.m. we picked up two boat-loads of men from a French collier which had been sunk that morning. It seemed a foolish risk to pull up for such a purpose, as there were several sails in sight, and smaller ships could have rescued them without danger. It was obvious game for the submarines which had sunk the collier by their gunfire to lurk in the neighbourhood and wait for a ship to pull up and offer an easy mark for a torpedo. As nothing happened for about an hour, we began to think we had escaped the danger, but suddenly a submarine was seen 4 points on the port bow, at which our 12-pounder gun mounted on the bow opened fire. A torpedo narrowly missed us, but, as we were nearly an end-on shot, the chances of hitting us were not very great. When the submarine was sighted all the men were paraded at regimental stations on the decks in lifebelts. We changed our course and went west.

2 October

Arrived in Mudros Bay about 10.30 a.m.[2] The *Terrible* steamed past with her decks packed with troops, also entering the harbour. The GOC troops on the ship went at once to the *Aragon*, a large liner anchored here as HQ of the Mediterranean Expeditionary Force. There were no orders as to our further movements. Nothing had been doing in Gallipoli for the last three weeks, but troops were pouring in here. There is already one Yeomanry Division in Gallipoli. As, however, they have had to leave men behind to look after their horses, they are even weaker than we. Several of their officers came out to see us from hospital, and we then learnt that our strenuous efforts to get down our baggage to 35lbs per officer according to the secret instructions which had been issued on the ship had been quite unnecessary, as it was most advisable to land at Gallipoli with all one's kit. There was so little possibility of movement once one did get ashore that the transport difficulty did not arise. The orders on this subject were only one instance of the lack of co-ordination between the authorities at home and in the Mediterranean Expeditionary Force. We had also issued drill clothing just before we sailed which had all to be collected and returned to store at Mudros. Mudros seemed a very unattractive spot with little water or food, but plenty of dysentery and smallpox.

3 October

General Altham inspected us. He had sent three telegrams to advance GHQ at Imbros to find out what was to be done with us. The wireless news about the possibility of Bulgaria entering the War[3] was so disquieting that it was generally thought we were being concentrated for another destination than Gallipoli. If we were to be used in Bulgaria or Greece we were likely to go on to Egypt to collect horses and saddlery. Lying in Mudros Harbour, one heard a good deal of artillery fire from Gallipoli every night.

4 October

Went ashore in the afternoon to the town of Mudros. It consists of garish Greek churches and hovels built of unmortared stones. The flies and smells were disgusting. We saw several transports full of French troops go out of the harbour and turn West, which looked as if they were going to Salonika[4] or some destination other than Gallipoli.

5 October

Still no orders. Went to the *Aragon* to try and find out my prospect of getting to Gallipoli. Found the Adjutant on the *Aragon* quite civil, but very ignorant. The conduct of this ship was a great cause of indignation in the Mediterranean Expeditionary Force. Countless Generals lived on board with little to do but to mismanage the transport arrangements.

The discipline on board appears to be atrocious, the ship being run on Republican lines. Idle sergeant-majors sniff when they see humble regimental officers without red collars [i.e. staff officers] and no one in a private boat is allowed at the sacred starboard companion. Kensington, in command of the Welsh Horse, had been treated with scant courtesy by some young Staff Captain on board. He carried him off to some officer in a more responsible position and did a little plain speaking. At 6.50 p.m. an MLO (Military Landing Officer) arrived on the *Olympic* to say that Duncannon was to go back with him at once, having been wired for by advance GHQ at Imbros to report there at once for some special employment. He packed up and was carried off so quickly that he only had time to say goodbye to General Hodgson, Jarvis and myself.

6 October

Order arrived that we were to go to Gallipoli, embarking on the smaller steamer a brigade at a time each afternoon. After lunch, William Gibbs, the Brigade Major, told me that all Seconds-in-Command, both of Regiments and Squadrons, were to be left behind. I tried to get General Hodgson to let me go as acting Adjutant, but this was not allowed. Edward Greene, although Second-in-Command of 'B' Squadron, managed to be included on the list to go on the ground that he was an expert in bombing. As a matter of fact, he knew little more about bombing than I did, and Eddy Cadogan was perfectly furious at being left behind in his place, as he had just done a bombing course before leaving England. He went off to Edward Greene and told him that with the new bombs he would inevitably get blown to pieces within the first 24 hours, as he did not possess up-to-date knowledge. My own prospects of getting to Gallipoli seemed very poor, as there was little chance of exchanging with Jarvis. Even in England, where he had his extremely tiresome wife down with the Regiment, he only went away for about one day in three months, and Mudros was considerably less attractive than London. I could not tell Hodgson this, but I did point out that if I remained at Mudros for any considerable time it would be very difficult to arrive green at Gallipoli and to take command of senior officers who had been through their apprenticeship. Hodgson, however, said that it was not in his power to do anything, but promised to ask General Birdwood on the first opportunity to make an exception in my case and to get me over to Gallipoli in one way or another.

8 October

The South-Eastern Mounted Brigade, having left yesterday for Cape Helles, it was now the turn of the Eastern Mounted Brigade to embark for Anzac and the South-Western Mounted Brigade for Suvla. We began serving out the landing and iron rations at 5.30 a.m., then extra ammunition and finally rifles and bayonets from the Armoury. The Brigade at 1 a.m. began going on board a Khedive Line Boat of about 3000 tons, which in peacetime used to run between Constantinople and Alexandria. She was speckled with bullet holes collected on her nightly visits to the Peninsula from the 'overs' which drop out to sea, having missed the trenches on the high ground. Lying beside the *Olympic*, she looked like a small boat that could have been swung from our davits and one had to go five decks down to get level with the gangway leading on to her deck. After they had all gone, I found myself left on board among 50 officers and 400 men left behind by the three Brigades as reinforcements. Colonel Moseley Leigh, the Second-in-Command of the East Kent Yeomanry, is in charge and there were fortunately a good many of my friends remaining, including Eddy Cadogan, Redmond Buxton, Slug Marsham and Camden; also three MPs, Pearson, Winterton and Wills.

9 October

Orders to leave the *Olympic* today. All our camp kettles and cooking pots having been sent on to Gallipoli, I went to the *Minnetonka* (supply ship) to draw them. I then went and saw Dudley and Acland at East Mudros and got a good deal of information. We began loading up the steamer which was to take us ashore at about 2.30 p.m., but there was so much baggage to get on board that we were not able to land at West Mudros until just after sunset. We naturally wanted to unload at once so as to be ready to march to camp early the next morning, but this was forbidden. It was pitch dark and the men lay down on some very dirty ground near the ramshackle pier. No sooner had they got to sleep than orders came for the ship to be cleared during the night, as she had to leave again at 5 a.m. We therefore spent most of the night unloading and packing everything on to trolleys and pushing them up a couple of hundred yards, where we stacked the baggage of the Brigades.

10 October

In the early morning we got some motor lorries and began shifting the baggage to camp. I went on with the first load across very rough tracks through hospitals and innumerable camps of details to a Bay, 'Port Kendia', facing west and separated by a narrow neck of land from Mudros Bay which lies to the east. Lemnos is provided with the most wonderful harbours. At Port Kendia the sandy beach shelves quickly down so that big ships can lie within a couple of hundred yards of the shore. Tents were very scarce in our camp. We could only get 50 for over 500 officers and men. I share one with Redmond Buxton and Eddy Cadogan. The Suffolk Yeomanry details arrived rather hot after nearly six miles' march. They had come very slowly, as Eddy Cadogan was rather like a Christmas Tree with equipment, including a heavy pack, and could only set a pace of about two miles an hour. We were very short of food and had no Mess equipment. I bought a few things at outrageous prices in a little village about half a mile from our camp and stewed two onions, some beef, bread and rice to make an excellent dinner which we ate out of our mess tins, as we had not a single plate between us. Fortunately, the weather was glorious and most of us slept outside our tents.

11 October

Ginn was very unhappy all the morning, having lost his false teeth. It really was very serious, as he would certainly starve before he could reach a dentist capable of producing a new set. However, soon after breakfast they were fortunately found in Eddy Cadogan's blanket none the worse for having been lain on all night. Went over to a repair ship lying in Port Kendia in a native boat to try and get some food and plates. The officer of one of the many mine sweepers lying alongside presented us with three very battered enamel ones which greatly improved our mess arrangement. Although the ground on which our camp is pitched is quite clean, if one leaves food uncovered for five seconds it is black with flies.

12 October

Went to the *Aragon* to try and get information as to how long our marooning was likely to last. We had a luxurious lunch on board with Arthur Acland Hood. We bicycled up hill over very rough ground and found to our delight that instructions had been received that we should be rejoining our units the following day, though no definite orders had as yet arrived.

13 October

Embarked at 11, getting on to the tender at 'Engineer's Pier' which took us out to the Khedive Line Boat on which we were to do the journey. We had a comfortable crossing to Walker's Pier at Anzac, there being very few people on board beyond the details for the Eastern Mounted

Brigade. It was surprising to find the beach show up clearly as a line of lights, but they show, of course, only towards the sea, owing to the high ground behind them and the Turkish positions. The Hospital Ships lie in the Bay and are ablaze with green lights and red crosses. As no lights were allowed on our boat, I had told off all our men before sunset, one half to carry rifles and kit bags and the other half to whom I allotted particular packages of equipment, kit, etc. A lighter came alongside our gangway and I got my lot on board at first. The lighter had been specially constructed for the Gallipoli landings and we were tightly packed below the armoured deck from which there ran a gangway and sloping companion way so that men could pour up six or eight abreast and jump ashore off the bows in case of a forced landing. We got ashore about midnight at Walker's Pier and stacked baggage under a guard. Major Chamberlain, the MLO, said that he had been asked by Edward Greene and Frank Goldsmith to try and get me something to do at the beach, but that he understood that this was now no longer necessary, as we were all rejoining our units.

14 October

At 12.45 a.m. we started on our four-mile march to join the Regiment, who were in a rest camp in 'Bedford Gully'. Two men, who had been sent down by the Brigade, acted as guides, but it was quickly evident that they did not know the way, as they soon admitted that the road twisted far more in the dark than it had appeared to do in daylight. The road was a communication trench about six to eight feet deep and wide enough to take loaded mules. After going for about 1½ miles through this passage from which many branches ran, one of our guides said he would go on and make sure of the way. After waiting about 20 minutes, Eddy Cadogan and I explored another sap and finally found a camp occupied by the Australian Light Horse, who, none of them, had any idea of the way to Bedford Gully. As it was evident that the guide, having first lost the way had then lost us, we returned to the beach and lay down for a couple of hours until daylight. It was abominably cold and, as there was nowhere to lie but on the road, there was not much sleep to be got. At 5 a.m. I rang up the 54th Division on the telephone from the MLO's office, a little cubbyhole cut in the side of the road. Eventually they sent down a guide and we got up to the Regiment by 8 a.m. Bedford Gully, so called because it had formerly been occupied by a Battalion of the Bedfordshire Regiment, is a little valley about 30 feet deep on the lower end running east and west down to the Aghyl Dere, up which ran the main sap. Our gully had sides covered with scrub, the southern slopes honeycombed with dugouts, but the north-western side was forbidden territory, being in view of the Turkish trenches. Bullets which missed the trenches came

ANZAC AND SUVLA BAY October – December 1915

Ghazi Baba
oint
'A' Beach
Hill 10
Azmak Dere
IX CORPS
11 Div
SUVLA BAY
SALT LAKE (dry in summer)
88 Bde (29 Div)
SUVLA PLAIN
South Pier
Lala Baba
13 Div
Chocolate Hill
Scimitar Hill
W. Hills
Ismail Oglu Tepe
'C' Beach
Azmak Dere
2 Mounted Div
Azma Dere
'B' Beach
29 Ind Bde
Kaiajik Dere
East'n Mtd Bde
Hill 60
Azmak Dere
ANZAC CORPS
Hill 100
N.Z. & Aust. Div
Aghyl Dere
AEGEAN SEA
Taylor's Gully
Walker's Pier
Ocean Beach
Bauchop's Hill
Koja Chemen Tepe
Hill Q
Chailak Dere
SARI BAIR RIDGE
Apex
Chunuk Bair
Table Top
Fisherman's Hut
Nek
Battleship Hill
North Beach Piers
Baby 700
Sphinx
Anzac Cove
2 Aust. Div
Lone Pine
Hell Spit
1 Aust. Div
Brighton Beach
Gun Ridge
Cape Helles

Allied trenches
Turkish trenches
High ground
11 Div Allied formation
Corps boundary

TURKEY
nothrace
Gallipoli
approx. area of map above
EAN SEA
Dardanelles
Imbros
C. Helles
20 miles
30 km

0 1 mile
1 km

down our valley, especially at night, which, with the Turkish fire, is very wild. So far the Turkish Artillery had not apparently located a camp in this valley, although they had knocked out half-a-dozen men of the Suffolk Yeomanry and the Welsh Horse on the previous day in the gullies on each side. Eastern Mounted Brigade Headquarters were on high ground at the bottom of the gully, and, having reported there to General Hodgson, I went off to find Jarvis. There is no accommodation in the valley except little holes scratched in the ground, timber being absolutely unattainable and sandbags very scarce. The weather, however, for a few weeks was glorious, though cold at night and one really suffered little inconvenience from the lack of roof. We had brought half-a-dozen boxes of provisions out from the Army and Navy Stores and these were very useful and enabled us to supplement the rations.

Soon after arriving I walked round the trenches with General Hodgson and Jarvis. Our 'A' and 'B' Squadrons were learning their business, attached as understudies to the 11th London Regiment and 6th Norfolks in the line. 'D' Squadron was attached to the 6th Bedfordshires, but were in reserve trenches. Although our Mounted Brigade, consisting of three Regiments of 480 apiece instead of four Battalions of nearly 1000, should by its establishment be only about one-third the strength of an Infantry Brigade, we found we were considerably stronger than the remainder of the 162nd Brigade which we were now understudying and were in a few days to relieve. We have been put into the 54th (East Anglian) Division as an extra Brigade. General Inglefield,* who had been known all his life as 'Tangle-foot' from his extreme incompetence, is fortunately away sick, so General Hodgson is for the moment in command of the Division. On our way round the trenches we met General Mudge* commanding the 162nd Brigade. Also Colonel Dacosta, GSOI of the 54th Division.

The trenches run up hill and down dale, separated at the north end of our sector by about 200 yards from the Turkish line, but at the south end by a very much greater distance. In many places our trenches were very precipitous and one had to clamber along by means of steps cut in the sun-baked earth, which, in wet weather, became a muddy slide. These precipitous places were very difficult to screen from Turkish observation and several times when we passed such exposed spots bullets came close enough to convince us that there were Turkish snipers in the thickets between the trenches. The line seemed to be very thinly held and the fact that Turkish deserters frequently crept in by night to our trenches and gave themselves up showed that they could probably rush our line if they chose to face the necessary casualties. It was said that we did not hold the lines by the infantry in the trenches so much as by the heavy Naval guns behind. As a matter of fact, I found our artillery arrangements astoundingly primitive. On this first morning I was struck by the accuracy of the Turkish shelling. I only saw them land two shrapnel in the valley containing our reserve trenches and found they had knocked out Private Smith of 'D' Squadron. Jarvis was living with 'B' Squadron in the valley occupied by the 11th London Regiment and just behind their lines. I was kept there longer than I intended, as, just after my arrival, the Turks began putting over light shrapnel which knocked a lot of stones into the shelter where we were sitting. I found afterwards that the habit of the Turks was to fire a burst of about ten shells at intervals. As soon as one heard the shells coming over one naturally got under cover and they apparently realized that it was no use going on after the first surprise effect, which enabled them from time to time to catch people in the open. I returned to Bedford Gully Camp with Regimental Headquarters and a few details looking after the improvement of the primitive dugouts there. It was very hard digging, especially as the caked clay was full of tree roots which were very tough and difficult to cut.

15 October

Regiments here are, of course, without any transport which is all run centrally. Rations come up every night by packed mules under the charge of Indians and when one needs transport for baggage, etc. one puts in an indent through Division. Owing to the stupidity of the Sergeant that I sent down to bring up our baggage, etc. he came away without bringing it up, and, without a blanket, I found the climate much colder than it looked.

Spent a good deal of time in 'B' Squadron trenches. Their posts on the left are within 200 yards of Sandbag Ridge, Saddleback, running down from the high ground of Sari Bair.[5] Snipers there are very active and as soon as one puts a periscope over the parapet bullets are scattered in all directions. Our snipers so far seem quite unable to keep down their fire. We got a good many periscopes broken and a certain number of casualties from sniping on the left of our line, largely due, no doubt, to the men exposing themselves in their inexperience.

16 October

Went up to the trenches at 3 a.m. for an idiotic demonstration which must have caused great amusement to the Turks. At 4 a.m. the fire balloons were sent up and the whole way along the British line each man fired one round at the Turkish trenches. Bayonets were then fixed and all the troops shouted. This was followed by a burst of fire from the Naval guns. The object was to obtain information of the number of rifles in the Turkish reserves and the volume of fire which they could develop. Naturally, the

Turks took no notice and, as far as one could see, hardly replied to our fire. It was pitch dark and they could not possibly see our bayonets; besides which, if we had really been attacking, we should obviously have begun with artillery fire.

Eddy Cadogan and I went off afterwards to see the trenches of the 1st Australian Division, who held the extreme right of our line to the south of Anzac. We had a five-mile walk and Colonel D. J. Glasford, GSOI of the Australian Division took us into his dugout at White Valley and gave us a most interesting account of the methods by which the Australian line had been won. He then took us up to see the tunnels which had been driven through very hard ground and must have involved much labour. The smell in certain places was very unpleasant, a lot of corpses being packed away behind only about one layer of sandbags. This was especially so in a kind of labyrinth of communication trenches which had been won by fierce hand-to-hand fighting and which led back from the captured Turkish fire trenches. We found certain places here where our trenches ran perpendicular to those of the Turks and where our sentries, armed with revolvers, waited to stop any attempted rush in the communication trench within a few yards of the Turkish sentry. Although in several places here the British and Turks were only 20 yards apart, I noticed that one could hold up a periscope much more freely than at our part of the line, as the Turks dared not put their heads opposite a loophole to aim at such short range. At our end, where the sniping is so much more troublesome, I am sure it takes place, not from the Turkish trenches, but from the tangle of scrub oaks and shrubs. We had rather an unpleasant time walking back along Anzac beach, as a burst of half-a-dozen shells came all around us, the shells dropping in the sea just beyond; a shrapnel case narrowly missed William Gibbs, who was just behind me.

At last, having got my kit up from the beach, I moved up to join the Regiment in the gully just west of the Brighton Road trenches. Jarvis and Grissell (who had succeeded Duncannon as Adjutant) had been sharing a little shelter built of reserve ration boxes, and we spent the afternoon in extending it to accommodate our larger Mess, which now consisted of Blincowe, the new Chaplain, Musker (Signal Officer) and our three selves.

The ordinary dugout accommodation in this gully was still occupied by the London Regiment, whom we are understudying, so we are very much cramped for accommodation. Every Battalion HQ is fortunately supplied with a large dump consisting of about six weeks' or two months' emergency rations, and these boxes are invaluable as materials for a sheltering wall. We are also all of us burrowing into the bank to make our own dugouts. Tuttle of 'B' Squadron was hit this afternoon when drawing stores by a stray bullet and which has impressed on us the utility of having some kind of cover. Some rain fell during the night, but fortunately not anything to matter. We dine at 5.30 p.m., stand to from 6.15 to 7 and, soon after, go to bed, having neither light nor shelter in which to use it. We stand to again just before dawn from 5 to 5.30 a.m. and breakfast as soon as we can get our rations up, which is generally several hours afterwards. One can get a little dirty water for washing out of improvised pools, but we are very short of drinking water. The maximum is five pints a head, but it is often only four. It all has to be brought up at night on mules and is issued to us in petrol tins. It is very muddy and not safe to drink until it has been boiled. As it is, a lot of the men have dysentery. It is not surprising, as everything is black with flies. On the western slopes of our gully, less than 50 yards from our dugouts, there are lots of corpses among the brushwood which, no doubt, increases the danger of the plague of flies. Bullets are constantly falling on this exposed side of the gully so that in daylight one cannot search for the corpses. We shall, however, try to get some of them buried after dark.

17 October

It rained again during the night, but cleared up before the morning. Jarvis and Grissell dug hard all day at the side of the valley to make slits over which to fasten their waterproof sheets. I fixed mine up under some boxes across the corner of the shelter.

18 October

Rain began again about 11 p.m., but cleared up again in the morning about 7 a.m., all of us getting pretty wet during the night, and the mud in the morning made movement very difficult. Went round trenches held by the 10th London Regiment, whom our 'A' Squadron are understudying. There saw well contrived machine-gun emplacements at the end of a tunnel leading from the fire trench and with another branch tunnel for observation. The officer had prepared duplicate maps of the Turkish positions with the paths leading across the valley therefrom. For night work he had arranged wooden stops so that he could open fire on certain points for sighting, whereas a beam below the muzzle of the gun prevented these being displaced sufficiently to endanger our advanced listening posts. Walked down with Jarvis to see General Hodgson in the afternoon. We were still being administered by the Eastern Mounted Brigade, although attached to Mudge's Brigade (the 162nd) for trench work. Edward Greene went to hospital and thence to a hospital ship with a bad attack of dysentery. A lot of the regiment are down with it.

19 October

The 5th Bedfordshires relieved the 11th London in our section of the trenches. 'A' and 'B' Squadrons went down with the 10th London and the 5th Norfolks to their rest camps. We shall begin our regular roster of duties on the 21st, with five days' rest in Bedford gully after which we shall take over the trenches for five days. Went round the trenches with Lord Southwell (Eastern Mounted Brigade machine-gun officer). Heard that General Monro* is about to relieve Sir Ian Hamilton in command.

20 October

Went round the trenches in the morning with Colonel E. W. Brighten, a solicitor, but a very efficient soldier from Luton, of the 5th Bedfordshires, who are taking over our section. He knows every detail of the line and was very instructive as to the improvements which ought to be carried out. We moved out to Bedford gully rest camp in the afternoon and again dug feverishly until sunset in our new home to get a waterproof sheet over our heads in case of rain. At 9 p.m. I rejoined Colonel Brighten and had a really good look at the ground by moonlight. We hold an irregular line north-east and south-west along a spur of ground from which gullies run down westward towards the sea. In front of us there is an irregular valley, very steep in places, separating us from the Turkish trenches on a flat crest of the Sari Bair (Koja Chemen Tepe) nearly 1000 feet high. On the left of our sector the Turks are only about 80 yards from us on Sandbag Ridge, but downwards from our trenches and up again to their position there is a steep ascent of crumbling clay which would be almost impossible to climb under any circumstances, and is enfiladed from the trenches on both sides of the valley. All this ground, right up to the Sari Bair, was fought over by the Gurkhas some weeks ago. They reached the crest and looked down on the Dardanelles, but being ahead of time were destroyed by the shells of our own naval guns and also by a fierce counterattack. In the moonlight we walked about in the scrub to decide on a line for a new sap. One could see the record of the Gurkhas' fighting written on the ground. The high ground just behind our fire trench was scraped into little holes where the Gurkhas had tried to flatten themselves to avoid the invisible fire which poured on them from the thick bushes and stunted trees. Then a little beyond one saw a line of corpses where the fire had caught them in a forward rush. Near the little holes in the ground lay entrenching tools, almost in a line as on a practice parade, and one could reconstruct what happened. The Gurkhas must have risen and rushed forward with their fixed bayonets and kukris, feeling that if they lay where they were they would die like rabbits scraping at the ground, whereas if they went forward they could get their steel into the throats of some of their enemies. The ground was littered with equipment and cotton bandoliers full of cartridges thrown away before their final rush. A little further on the dead Gurkhas were lying face downwards, their fixed bayonets pointing in the direction of the Turks they could not reach.

21 October

Moved into the rest camp in Bedford gully.

22 October

A very cold day with a strong north-westerly wind. Went to Division Engineers to try and get sandbags. Managed with difficulty to get 500 with which we set to work to improve the dugouts. Rain came on in the afternoon and lasted all the evening. We are very cramped in the gully and had a good deal of trouble in redistributing the ground between Squadrons. We took turn and turn about in the valley with the Norfolk Yeomanry and there is not much room for reserve Headquarters and Stores which have been left in the valley by both Regiments in turn, one being in the trenches. Hear that Paton's Division is going to Mudros to rest. Wastage from disease is appalling. Our Division loses about 500 per week. One Infantry Brigade which should number about 4000 is down to less than 1000. This expedition seems to be a dangerous gamble on the alleged unwillingness of the Turks to take the offensive.

23 October

Went to Divisional Headquarters and got letter from the AAQMG (Colonel Evans) to the ADOS (Colonel Austin) at Corps Headquarters asking him to issue any further waterproof sheets that might be available. Found Colonel Austin very reasonable, but unable to give us any more waterproof sheets, as there were none available. I pointed out that in ten days we had lost about sixty men out of 460 from sickness and that it was cheaper to misapply any material he might have rather than allow the epidemic to spread by leaving men exposed to the weather. He then agreed to let me have some old blankets which had been collected from casualties, etc. and with which we could roof our dugouts. Sent down 50 men to draw 500 blankets, also sailmaker's needle and twine. Evans told me that the 54th Division had arrived four weeks before, 12,000 strong, and were now only 5000. Probably our men are handicapped by the starvation diet provided for them by the White Star Line on the *Olympic*. It is certainly curious that, in spite of the high proportion of sickness among men, only one officer is down out of twenty-four.

24 October

Another bleak, wet morning, but not so much wind. Our Regimental Headquarters Mess of eight is too big to get under cover and we have so far been feeding out in the open. Have now arranged for Musker and Flint (Machine-Gun Officer) to mess with 'B' Squadron, as, under present conditions, it is impossible to run larger messes than six. The rations are very good; excellent bacon every day and bully beef and fresh meat (1 lb. per head) generally on alternate days; 4 ozs. of jam; 1 lb. bread or biscuits; and condensed milk, 2 ozs. The supply of bread and fresh meat depends on what is landed from Mudros daily and as the weather gets worse we shall probably get a larger proportion of biscuit and bully beef.

24 October

Walked over with Freddy Jarvis to lunch with his brother Weston, who commanded the 2nd Company of London Yeomanry in Paton's Division. Very cold wind and good deal of rain. On the way we went through trenches held by the Scottish Horse and Lovat's Scouts. It is a curious chance which has thrown Tullibardine's and Lovat's Brigades together, as they are said to dislike each other more than the Turks. Tullibardine's absurdities cause much amusement. On one of the first nights that they were there the Scotch Horse began cheering at about 11 p.m. and the Turks became so excited that they blazed away about 100,000 rounds of ammunition. The cause of the cheering was said to have been that a Scotsman found 6d in the pocket of a pair of trousers which had been thrown into the refuse destructor. However this may have been, Tullibardine was so pleased at the waste of Turkish ammunition that he made his men cheer again the next night and also ordered his pipers to play. The whole Division stood to arms, but the Turks were naturally not to be caught twice and, though they had been sniping freely, immediately ceased when the hubbub began. Went over the ground where Paton's Division lost so heavily west of Chocolate Hill. The whole manoeuvre seemed to have been quite unnecessary. Paton's Division had been put under cover of Lala Baba and were ordered to go on to Chocolate Hill (which we already held) in broad daylight. If they had been sent across the plain and Dry (or Salt) Lake under cover of darkness they need not have lost a man.

I don't envy the waterlogged trenches of the 2nd Mounted Division. They will be canals when it rains and we at least have mountain scenery in front of us and can look on the other side on an ever-changing seascape and glorious sunsets behind Imbros.

25 October

Message received last night from Lord Kitchener that we should dig ourselves in deeper, as Bulgaria's participation in the war would mean more high explosive shells. Very difficult, however, to improve our dugouts owing to the impossibility of getting any timber. There certainly are more high explosive shells than when we first arrived. The trenches are the safest place and we have had many more men hit cooking, drawing water or going to hospital in the valleys behind the line. Went round the trenches in the morning which we are to take over tomorrow. They are at least 900 yards long and we succeed the 5th Bedfordshires and the 11th London. As we are down to about 330 effectives, our line will be very thin. General Mudge, however, says that these two Infantry Brigades together were no stronger than our present numbers. While writing letters, the Turks began shelling us with shrapnel and a bullet dropped on the table through our waterproof roof. It is curious how little damage is done by these shrapnel bombardments. Everybody every day seems to have a narrow escape and yet there are very few casualties.

26 October

Took over the trenches at 6.30 a.m., being succeeded in Bedford gully by the Norfolk Yeomanry.

27 October

Last night and again this morning went round the trenches with General Mudge to discuss improvements. There was a heavy bombardment enfilading our trenches from the north, but it only lasted about ten minutes. On returning found another hole through the roof of our dugout. If we could get more timber and galvanizing sheets we could make it sufficient even against shrapnel, but we have only waterproof sheets and they, of course, will not support any sandbags or earth. The weather has changed and it is again very hot.

28 October

At 4.30 a.m. I went out to the observation post south-east of our barricade across the North Aghyl Dere which has to be relieved every morning before dawn. This gave me a good opportunity to see our line by a bright moonlight from some distance in front of it. Spent most of the day surveying the ground in preparation to going out on patrol in the evening. It is not easy to learn geography from a periscope, especially when, as in our left-hand trench, as soon as one puts one up the Turks begin sniping at it. I have got a very convenient little periscope with a Zeiss attachment, but it is far too valuable to risk in this corner, besides which it is so short that it brings one's head uncomfortably near the top of the sandbags. At 7.30 p.m. went out to search Bulgar Bluff for any Turks who might be holding their detached post and, in view of a report that a Turk was seen to have been knocked over there during the bombardment the previous morning, to search for his body. We walked down the slope from our lines diagonally on a bearing of 154°; before reaching the dry watercourse at the bottom we heard digging and Turkish conversation just to our left. These sounds, however, ceased as if our arrival was either seen or heard. We found that Bulgar Bluff was thickly wooded on the north side and we walked down the Aghyl Dere and climbed it from the west. It was rather exciting going up to the Turkish observation trench, as if they had been in it they would have had all the advantage of the ground and, if they had the nerve to hold their fire until one is pretty close up, should have been able to make sure of their aim. Fortunately there were no Turks in the trench, but the earth on the parapet and newly cut trenches showed that they had been working there within the last couple of days. Found no fresh corpses near the post, but several decomposed Turks and Gurkhas. Came to the conclusion that patrolling in this way is not a sound method. The 11th London had some men killed last week during the same game at Bulgar Bluff. Think one should go out a much larger party and try and get up to the higher ground behind and rush down on them.

29 October

At 6.15 p.m. had another expedition with a view to catching any Turks who might be patrolling down the dry water course between Sandbag Ridge and Woodhouse Cliff. Took out Eversden and Crisp with me with nine other ranks of 'D' Squadron. On reaching the main Dere, turned north-east until the watercourses divided. I there detached Eversden to prevent us being cut off from the north-west and with the remainder of the party lay up in the scrub overlooking the watercourse against a light background, by which one ought to get a good view of any men moving down. I had arranged with Eversden that he was to lay out until just before the rising of the moon, when he was to go back independently to our trenches. He, however, found himself blocked by a sandy precipice and therefore came back to us after being away 2½ hours. Half an hour before, we thought we had heard them shooting and believed them to have been in connection with the Turkish patrol. When, therefore, lying at the bottom of the valley, we saw figures coming down against the sky, we thought they were probably Turks. Crisp, who was next to me, whispered that it could not be Eversden because, whereas his party were only six, he professed to count nine figures approaching. We all had them covered with fingers on our triggers and I had arranged previously that in such an event I should fire a flare to light up the enemy and as a signal for our party simultaneously to shoot. Crisp begged me to fire this flare, but thank goodness I did not, and when I called out, 'Is that Eversden?', he fortunately heard us and answered. If any of our party had lost his nerve and fired without my order, no doubt everybody would have followed suit, and if Eversden's party had not all been knocked out, they would naturally have shot back, believing us to be Turks.

30 October

Spent the morning spying for snipers, etc. Owing to the amount of sickness, there is great difficulty in finding enough men for our posts. In 'A' Squadron especially, owing probably to the foulness of the ground where they are living (just behind our barricade on the Northern Aghyl Dere), there are so few sound men that they are practically all on trench duty, two hours of sentry and four hours off every night. General Hodgson sent word that I was not to go out patrolling, but I suppose I shall be able to do so when there is some definite object. The 5th Norfolks last night on our right managed to ambush a Turkish patrol and to knock out two of them.

31 October

We were relieved at 6 a.m. by the 11th London and 5th Norfolks. Spent much of the day digging to increase my dugout. Very inconvenient living in a home not suitable in size for a large rabbit. Whenever I turn round avalanches of clay come out from the wall, and even if one keeps still, chunks of clay roll down underneath one's waterproof sheet and cover everything with dust. My sandbag wall supporting my roof of waterproof sheeting was apparently only held up by that sheet, and when I unhooked the waterproof sheet to readjust it the whole sandbag wall collapsed, squashing me against precious belongings. My talc lantern was completely destroyed and I was reduced to writing by a flickering candle which poured its grease into the bristles of my hair brush and caused a lot of damage.

1 November

A strong wind arose suddenly last night, picked up glowing embers, sparks and dust and came like a brown wall into my dugout, putting out my candle. It was followed by heavy rain. The rest camp brings little repose to the men. Besides making dugouts, there are many fatigues for such objects as road-making. We have also to send three times a day for our water ration, as there are not enough petrol tins to draw it all at once, even if the filters when it is chlorinated were capable of dealing with the whole of it together. A good many casualties took place on these fatigues, as, in addition to pretty well the whole area being liable to shell fire, the Turks kept most of the exposed parts of the saps leading back from the trenches and to the beach under occasional fire. Harry Day (my motor driver in civil life and now our cook) got a bullet through the top of his sleeve, and a few moments afterwards in the same place a bullet struck between me and the Colonel as we were walking back to the camp in single file.

2 November

Weather still bright and warm, but very blustering.

3 November

Went with Grissell to see the trenches held by the 161st Brigade on our left, which are for the most part much better than ours, being on more level ground. These trenches were held by battalions of the Essex Regiment. The men seemed fearfully weak from dysentery. Physically, far the finest men I have seen are the Australians. They are of medium height, but with deep chests and necks like bulls. They seem to stand the climate very much better than the British. Noticed on the way back in several places booted feet sticking out of the ground along the watercourses. This no doubt is a fertile cause of disease. Everywhere our dead seem buried in the bottoms of the valley with the result that all the water which we get from there for washing and drinking is full of undesirable ingredients which even chlorinating would not entirely remove.

4 November

Rained in the afternoon. Jarvis has been laid up for the last day or two and will not be able to go up with us to the trenches when we relieve tomorrow. Went up to see Brighten and to fix up details.

4–5 November. Night

Took over trenches. The weather has cleared up again, a delightful spell of still warm autumn weather. My recollections of cold and wet weather in Constantinople at the beginning of October were no doubt of quite a short spell of bad weather which is said to come on regularly at that season every year. It is said that we shall now probably have fine weather until the beginning of January.

5 November

At 3 p.m., as I was going into the Mess next door to my dugout, a shell burst right over me. I was fortunately just behind the barricade of boxes on which the bullets rattled. Goddard, who was posted by the signal box on the other side of my dugout, got a bullet in the groin. The next shell burst about five seconds afterwards and the iron plate in the base of the shrapnel case went through the shoulder of my servant Murray's coat which was hung up on a bush just outside the Mess. One man in 'D' Squadron was sleeping in his hole. He was suddenly wakened, as he thought by someone touching him, and came out and asked what it was. They looked at his cap and found two holes through it and three through his blankets.

6 November

Eddy Cadogan was looking through a periscope this morning when a sniper hit it and his nose and chin were cut with splinters. It must have been a very narrow escape for his eyes. We have got a new catapult for throwing bombs and we used it after dark this evening. It is rather a jimcrack affair made by Harrods. We sent a couple of bombs into the Turkish wire which stopped them working at it for several hours.

7 November

Frank Goldsmith and Musker are still down at Anzac in hospital. Frank writes that they are sleeping on the ground and the great disadvantage of the place is the number of rats which run over them all night.

8 November

We heard this morning that Lord Kitchener is on his way out.[6] It is difficult to see how we could withdraw from here without great losses. Never can a campaign have been worse managed. Although 17 Divisions have been sent out here, it has always been by driblets which have not even sufficed to replace the wastage. If all the men who had been out here could have been available simultaneously something might have been done. As it is, however, the line has merely been lengthened piecemeal and is now dangerously weak in view of the small number of men to hold it. Jarvis is now all right again. I have been rather seedy for some days, but, by means of dieting, have now recovered. Hear that Musker is leaving for England, but that Frank Goldsmith is coming back in a day or two. The hospital where they are on the beach is a very uncomfortable place and continually being hit by bullets. There is no cover there, merely marquee tents pitched close to the sea.

9 November

Yesterday afternoon watched our guns registering on Sandbag Ridge trench in the afternoon. Very poor shooting. Yesterday evening we tried to stop the Turks who were on a wire entanglement. We sent up a couple of flares and hoped with their help to do something with bombs and machine-gun fire. As a matter of fact, our eyes were so dazzled by the flash and so confused by the moving shadows as the flare shot across the valley that one certainly could not have got sights on to the Turks even if they had been there. Eddy Cadogan was convinced this evening that a Turk had jumped across our fire trench. There is a general belief that there are Turkish snipers lying up on the high ground within our lines. If well dug-in, a Turk might certainly live in the thick scrub and take pot shots at our communication trenches almost indefinitely. As a matter of fact I do not think in this case there was anything in Cadogan's story. We were relieved at dawn this morning and returned to our rest camp. For the last five days we had had a party under Tuttle (the QM) putting up some corrugated iron, which we had managed to draw. I have now got a splendid dugout in which I can stand up. I took a good deal of exercise digging a shelf, putting the earth as I picked it from the wall into sandbags and filling up between them and the side wall so as to make a bed to sit and sleep on. We have also got a dugout where we mess, so life in the rest camp is now quite comfortable. Frank Goldsmith returned from hospital and has taken over 'B' Squadron again from Eddy Cadogan.

10 November

Some rain and wind during the night. Dust storms all day. The dust, however, is probably very poisonous as there is no grass or weed to cover the bare earth and to loosen it with roots. The water cannot thus get down into the stiff clay and carry oxydation to the organic matter. The Turks have been putting a good many high explosive shells on to Anzac beach, but almost entirely by day. I cannot imagine why they don't do it at night, as they must know the exact position of the pier on which our supplies are disembarked and could make things almost impossible by well-directed fire. We are warned that the Turks intend to use gas in their next attack, and have now all got good gas helmets which cover the whole head and have talc slits for the eyes. Personally I cannot imagine how in such precipitous country gas could be used in an attack, as, whatever may be the case at Suvla, here at least all our positions would be uphill to the attackers.

11 November

Bramwell Jackson arrived from Imbros bringing back stores from the canteen and the Greek villages. We were able thus to get some condensed milk and coffee which are a great addition to our diet.

12 November

Rain again last night. I was able to collect enough water almost to fill a canvas bucket. This was invaluable for washing up plates, etc., and also for scrubbing a new table which we have made for our mess out of a disgusting old packing case which I found in an old Turkish bivouac. In the afternoon walked up to the right of the 161st Brigade and looked from there at the back of Sandbag Ridge and the left of our own trenches. Found that the Essex Regiment, who had been there last week under Major Jameson, had been relieved by the 8th Hampshires commanded by Major Marsh. On their right they have no trenches, but inhabit dugouts in a precipitous rock, quite bare on its western slope, but running down eastwards towards 100 Metre Hill and the end of Sandbag Ridge in a steep scrub-covered face. Although we cannot communicate directly with them owing to the precipitous descent between us and east of Hampshire Lane, our left is pretty safe as the 161st Brigade have posts across the watercourse opposite the end of their rocky escarpment, and others again tunnelled right through the rock near its southern shoulder and running in a deep sap diagonally across the valley towards our left. Without ladders I don't think the Turks could get up towards us as the crumbling clay face rises nearly sheer 80–100 feet. I shall therefore feel less anxious about that flank when we return to our dugouts in King's Own Avenue.

13 November

Walked down to Anzac with Frank Goldsmith and Tommy Grissell to get money for paying the men. The Field Cashier has nothing except 10/- notes. It is most inconvenient in view of the men's purchases of stores brought back from Imbros and which of course do not come exactly to 10/- apiece. Met General Hodgson coming back from seeing Lord Kitchener who had landed and had a look at the ground from the Australian line. We saw Lord Kitchener's launch on its way back to a torpedo boat. Frank, Grissell and I all felt very limp. It is curious how the climate and living here takes away one's strength. Those who have long been ashore seem incapable of walking except with a distinct slouch and become physically unable to run uphill or to do anything with vigour. Probably for this reason troops have generally been used for an attack as soon as possible after landing.

I received today interesting statements by Turkish deserters. The most intelligent man came in from a regiment on Sandbag Ridge. He said that the Turks no longer have moving patrols from that sector out in our valley but merely rely on a couple of stationary parties to lie out in front of their line. One of the bombs from our catapults fell on the head of one of these men the last night we were in the trenches. I am sure that the Turkish system is right, as moving patrols, although dear to the heart of General Inglefield, are at a hopeless disadvantage on this kind of ground where men on the move are obliged to keep at the bottom of the valleys and thus offer an easy mark to a party lying still and waiting for them in the scrub. The deserters say there is no present intention of a Turkish attack but that they are looking forward to annihilating us when Germany sends the promised guns and shells. Certainly the haste with which the Turks are putting up wire and improving their trenches at the back of Smythe's Spur looks as if they feared an attack from us rather than contemplating one themselves.

16 November

After posting letters, I returned to my dugout and just as I was sitting down heard the thud of a heavy projectile close by. Hearing no explosion, I thought it was shrapnel which had failed to burst and went to my door to warn any men who might be standing about to take cover in case more should (as usual) follow. Greene, the Colonel's servant, who was by the kitchen dugout of our mess called out to me that Harry Day was hit. I ran up and found him lying on his side with his head upon the step leading up from the dugout. Though not 15 seconds could have elapsed since he was struck, he was quite dead, the case of a .75 shrapnel shell having struck him between the shoulders and passed right through him. The shell had been fired at one of our aeroplanes and had burst no doubt high in the air so that I had not noticed it from among the continual explosions which take place. It came down almost vertically and went through the waterproof sheet with which the kitchen dugout is protected from the rain. His death was absolutely instantaneous. Murray was with him at the time and said that he had only at that moment crossed the kitchen from the corner to where he was struck.

Poor Harry's death was a great shock. He has been invariably willing and cheerful and turned out an excellent cook. I attribute the freedom of our Regimental HQ Mess from any serious cases of diarrhoea to the care with which he always cleaned our cooking pots and boiled all our water. To me personally his death is a great grief as he had been with me for many years and I feel responsible for his having enlisted. I tried to telegraph to his father and to Evelyn, but, although Redmond Buxton called to see General Hodgson about it and the latter sent up to Divisional HQ, nothing could be done in view of the censorship regulations forbidding 'reference in postal matter to casualties previous to the publication of the official lists'. Though I cannot therefore telegraph I am none the less writing in spite of Monro's order of 4 November saying that 'serious action will be taken if censors allow such statements to pass through the post'. The regulation appears to me outrageously harsh. It is no doubt convenient to the authorities to conceal the true numbers of casualties here, but in effect it means that one could not write details of his wounds or death. The official lists do not appear until long after the casualty, and they do not reach us here perhaps until a month after that.

We could not bury poor Harry by daylight owing to the continuous shelling of our gully, so the service was held in the olive grove just below our camp at 6.30 p.m. by the light of a brilliant moon. Few men could get away from the trenches to attend and Murray helped to fill in the grave. It is a curious coincidence that poor Harry was killed within a yard of the spot where last week the disc from the base of a shrapnel went through the shoulder of Murray's coat. It is no more than a coincidence in that one shell was fired at an aeroplane and fell by chance, whereas the other was directed low and had as usual burst to rake our dugouts with bullets. After the first shot of the latter kind one is duly warned and can usually take good cover under the wall of one's dugout. From shells fired at aeroplanes and dropping by chance there is, of course, no such protection.

17 November

General Hodgson was up in the morning and said that the Eastern Mounted Brigade were to be brought together again now Inglefield had returned. Our section of trenches would be immediately on the left of those which we now held. His machine-gun officer (Lieut Southwell) came up also and insisted that a dead mule with an abandoned pack saddle nearby was a Turkish observation post. The mule is our side of the valley only about 200 yards away from our trenches. We have often seen it and know it well to be a mule. Southwell, however, was so delighted with his discovery that he fired with a machine gun half a belt of ammunition into it and, as the skin was then flapping about and showing the white ribs beneath, he was satisfied that he had cut the sacking with which the Turkish loophole was covered. He also could see with his glasses that the old telephone (Turkish) wire over which our patrols trip nightly was connected up to this observation post. He later saw General Mudge, who ordered a patrol of 15 men to creep out at dusk, surround the post and capture the occupants. The patrol went out accordingly at about 6 p.m. At 7 o'clock it began to rain and by about 7.30 there was such a downpour that the valleys were full of water and one could hardly stand on the shiny clay. Suddenly the usual desultory sniping burst out into a crackle of fire. Flares were sent up and the pandemonium spread far along the line with a good many bomb explosions to our left and right. We saw a red flare go up from a post on our left about 300 yards away and the Colonel called the few servants, etc., who were not in the trenches to stand to. He waded into the Signaller's dugout, then ankle deep in water, and telephoned for a company of the 11th Londons, who are in support of us, to come up. I then went up to the trenches on our left, not an easy matter, as it is 300 yards uphill and the water was pouring down, making the hard clay so greasy that one kept slipping back. I found that on the left our men were not shooting. The fire was coming from the Turkish trench and ours was being held until some target offered. Frank Goldsmith had sent up the red flare by mistake for a white one to try and get a view of the ground in front. Further to the right, posts in 'D' Squadron said they had been fired on at close range and had seen figures about 40 yards off. I think most likely they were shrubs swaying in the storm. The patrol returned about 9 p.m., having found nothing but the dead mule, though they searched carefully for anything in the nature of an observation post or trench. The fusillade was no doubt caused by the Turks having seen our patrol crouching down in the light of a flash of lightning. They thought they were being attacked and began firing wildly at them and at our trenches. Southwell is an excellent fellow and very keen on his job, but I wish he wouldn't come up and discover imaginary trenches when these are only hummocks of clay and dead mules, thoroughly familiar to the sentries who gaze at them for hours every day. We all got very wet and our feet brought large lumps of wet clay into our blankets when we returned to our dugouts.

18 November

On going round trenches in the early morning before stand to, found the men were very wet and cold, but wonderfully cheerful. Some were consoled by thinking that, whereas the wind was at our backs, the icy blast was blowing straight into the faces of the Turks. Others were consoled by my telling them of the Turkish deserter who said that a few wet nights would cause the whole of his battalion to follow his example. 'A' Squadron dugouts in the Aghyl Dere are quite flooded out. The water there is at least a foot deep in the communication trench and, being at the bottom of the watercourse, there is no possibility of draining it.

I am glad we are moving to new trenches. I went to look at them yesterday afternoon. They are now held by the 8th Hants and run along the edge of an escarpment, sloping pretty steeply towards the Turks, but quite precipitous on the back side where our dugouts are placed. Though, like our left-hand posts, they are only on the 100-metre contour line, they are far better drained and are on sandy soil in parts. Owing to the wind, there was very much dust and the dugouts are fearfully exposed. Several of the posts have no trenches, as the knife-edge escarpment is too narrow at the top. They merely hold the edge as a breastwork standing on a path or in niches cut into the rock. When the move takes place there will be a General Post in the Division and General Mudge's Brigade will be further to the left again, opposite to Hill 60.

19 November

The Turks, judging by the numbers of shells they expend upon us daily, now certainly seem to be better supported with artillery ammunition. At least two or three times a day we get a dose, and they are able to enfilade our trenches according to the set of the fuse from only 2000 yards away, somewhere probably behind Sandbag Ridge.

The .75 shrapnel which we had hitherto received have had brass fuses with the scales marked in Turkish numerals. Yesterday, however, a fuse dropped just below our dugouts, with the nose and rings of aluminium round a brass core and the figures in the numerals of Western Europe. This may perhaps mean that they are now supplied with German or Bulgarian ammunition. As I write this an Engineer Officer who has seen the fuse states that it is undoubtedly German, as he saw others of just the same kind earlier in the War when in France. Since the rain of the night before last, the weather has quite settled down again and it is calm and sunny though much colder. I am now wearing all my available clothes – warm coat, thick jacket, leather waistcoat and woolly and find it none too hot.

Went down to 'A' Squadron dugouts which are still flooded out in Stafford Gully. Tomkin last night had a very narrow escape. He was sitting on the edge of his dugout intending in two minutes to lie down in his blankets when the top fell in, hitting him in the middle of his back and sending him head first off the edge into a foot of water and mud which stood in the sap. If he had been lying down he would have been buried under a ton at least of wet clay and no one would have heard the fall take place, and none might have passed along the sap until too late. As it was, he was standing soaked through in the sap, above his ankles in water for an hour before it was possible to dig away the loose earth and recover his buried kit and dry clothes.

20 November

Returned from trenches in the early morning. In the afternoon orders to 'detail Major Guinness to report to HQ 162nd Brigade at 10 a.m. tomorrow with reference to his taking over temporary command of the 1/10th London Regiment'. Went to see General Hodgson who said that weeks ago he and all Brigadiers had been told to recommend Battalion Commanders for emergencies and had sent my name in for that or employment on the General Staff. He said no doubt in the long run almost all senior officers would be wanted for other units, as the sickness had been so high. I said I should hate to be left here if the Yeomanry were ever mounted and sent elsewhere, and he answered that of course in that case he would apply for me to come back. There was no question as to whether I wanted to go, either from him or Mudge. I shall remain on the strength of the Suffolk Yeomanry and be, so to speak, seconded. All appointments since mobilization are temporary and the only substantive rank is that which existed previously.

The proposed redistribution of the line has been postponed until Hill 60 is rendered more satisfactory. The mines dug and exploded by the Welsh Horse last week were completely successful, and there would have been no difficulty about occupying the craters. General Inglefield, however, wouldn't allow it, some say because General Hodgson, whom he had superseded as Divisional Commander two days before, was in favour of pushing our line forward. The net result of a month's hard work by the Welsh Horse and a ton and a half of explosives has been, therefore, to improve the Turkish position and to make Hill 70 (metres) instead of Hill 60.

21 November

Reported to General Mudge. Jarvis came too and said it was abominable to take me away from the Regiment. Mudge said it really had nothing to do with him. He reported the sickness of Colonel Lambert to the Division, and yesterday a telegram came detailing me to succeed him. He then took me up to the camp of the 1/10th London, where he left me with Clutterbuck, the Adjutant. He is the only soul in the Regiment that I had ever set eyes upon, and then only to say Good Morning and to direct him to the orderly room when two days previously he had arrived to take over part of the trench line from the Suffolk Yeomanry. (This was afterwards cancelled.) He is a very good-looking, curly-headed boy of 21, a regular, attached from the Royal Scots. He caused enormous amusement because Jarvis said, 'Are you the Adjutant?', and he answered, 'No, the Commanding Officer.' He was asked by Frank when he would send up his officers to take over and said, 'Very early, as they are so extraordinarily stupid,' or words to that effect. He said officers nearly old enough to be his father, but all of them (except one Captain) subalterns of only a few months' experience, were following him like dogs. Frank said he was quite nice about them and did not speak in any objectionable way. We were so much interested in this curly-headed, blue-eyed youth with a Scotch cap that we asked Colonel Brighten about him. It appears that he won the Military Cross in France, was wounded twice at Ypres and Neuve Chapelle and was referred to by 'eye-witnesses' as the curly-headed boy, who looked as if he ought to have been at school, leading an officerless Battalion 'at the end of some bloody fight'. Mudge told me he was a capital boy, full of energy and dash, and that he had been in two minds as to whether to recommend him to command the Battalion. He felt, however, that at the age of 21 he needed someone less impetuous to restrain him.

I spent an hour with Clutterbuck, returned to camp, settled things up and, having said goodbye to the Suffolk Yeomanry, went up in the afternoon. The 1/10th London are in the trenches on the right of where the Suffolk Yeomanry hold in the alternative five day period. On the other side they adjoin the 2nd Australian Division. It is a delightfully safe bit of trench and only one 'double company' in which these weak Battalions are now organized is in the fire trench at a time. The other Company is in the rest camp 150 yards back, in local reserve. We play box and cox with the 1/5th Norfolk Regiment who are organized on the same basis and have a rest camp adjoining our fire trench Headquarters on the other side. They are in Brigade Reserve for these five days.

The Regimental Headquarters of the 10th London when in the trenches feed back in the rest camp and sleep in the fire trench Headquarters. My only companions are the Adjutant and the Canadian doctor, Ball by name. The machine-gun officer, signalling officer and quartermaster have all disappeared, sick or wounded. There was a Chaplain attached, an awful man with a voice which would have driven me mad. Fortunately the provisional arrangement, now cancelled, that Mudge's Brigade was to go to Hill 60 was too much for him, and he has inflicted himself on the Brigade Mess instead.

The Welsh Horse are having a bad time at Hill 60. The new Turkish trench on top of the exploded earth is so silted that bombs roll off themselves down the slope into our trenches. They have also lately heard the Turks mining and though they dug hard to sink a shaft and intercept them they were not quick enough to prevent the Turks exploding a mine and killing several. Others were buried in a tunnel and they are now digging frantically to try to get them out alive.

22 November

Our trenches are delightfully quiet and safe. To our right there is a new Australian post thrown forward which protects us from the only dangerous side. To the left there are such steep slopes that I cannot imagine the Turks choosing to attack us rather than the two left sectors of which I fully realize the weakness from the experience of the Suffolk Yeomanry. If, however, they did attack the latter, we run forward at such an angle to the main watercourse which runs parallel to the front of the centre and left sectors that we would bring very effectual enfilade fire to bear. Here one can study the country directly over the parapet, as there is hardly any sniping from the Turks. A delightful change from our left-hand posts last week where they had at least one periscope broken every day and the top layer of sandbags daily cut to rags by ceaseless sniping. Spent most of the day trying to get the hang of things. There are only 10 officers and 254 men left, and this is the strongest Battalion in the Brigade.

In the late afternoon General Mudge sent for me to say that the Colonel of the 5th Norfolks had gone that day to hospital sick, and that I was to take over his Battalion as well. They are very weak, only 12 officers and 165 other ranks. Their reputation is none too good. Almost all the senior officers were wiped out in the first landing, as they went on and the men didn't follow. They then had a very slack Colonel. The Brigadier had actually twice to speak to him about shaving himself and when he was asked why the men were so dirty and had not shaved, the answer of the Colonel was 'because we've never been ordered to'. Mudge says the men would be all right if properly handled. Their most senior remaining officers joined since mobilization. I am a little uneasy about the job of running the two Battalions together. Mudge says the whole question is to go to GHQ for sanction, but Clutterbuck tells me the same thing was tried in France and it was found that only the Army Council could authorize it. They didn't do so, but on the contrary sat on the General who sent it up. Apparently there must be a complete Regimental organization for each separate unit, and there must not only be an Adjutant but also someone drawing command pay for each. Telegram reads, 'On departure of Colonel Kinsman (a regular who succeeded the slack Colonel) 5th Norfolk Regiment will be attached to 10th London Regiment and be commanded by W.G. Interior organization of each Battalion will otherwise remain as at present.'

Clutterbuck says the officers of the Norfolks are a very nice lot and that, although there was friction between the two units originally, it has now quite died down. Cubitt the Adjutant and Birkbeck (a brother of Birkbeck in the Norfolk Yeomanry) came up to report to me. We received today official intelligence report with maps of where the various Turkish Divisions are located. This shows four Divisions in the Southern (Cape Helles) Zone and eleven in our zone from Anzac to Suvla. The Turkish Division consists of 9 Battalions besides artillery and cavalry, 12,000 to 13,000 all told. Even assuming them to be 6,000 strong each (most improbable in view of our experience of war wastage) 15 divisions would only amount to 90,000 men. Probably there are really far fewer, and in any case it is absurd for Asquith to state that the Dardanelles Expedition is holding up 200,000 Turkish troops.

23 November

Spent most of the morning at Norfolk camp. Cubitt and the other officers appear to be a very nice lot. As in the case of Norfolk Yeomanry they appear to have come out a kind of family party. Cubitt told me that when they first landed at Suvla he lost two brothers and two first cousins. Altogether his Battalion lost 450 men and 23 officers in that fight. Most of them were returned as 'missing' but must almost certainly have died as neither side could possibly pick up the wounded in the thick bush where it took place, and it was all burnt that night so that those who were still alive no doubt died in the flames.

I was agreeably surprised at his grip of details as to internal economy in his Battalion and he seems very energetic and capable. Clutterbuck told me afterwards that he had been very much 'fed up' previously and that everything had got very slovenly, no doubt as a result of having so many officers killed. Lately he said Cubitt had bucked up and he had seen a great difference in the Battalion. The men seem a much better class than the

Londoners, but there is certainly much less smartness and chic about them.

Visited camp pretty thoroughly and discussed details. Internal management, cooking, sanitation, cleanliness seem good. Very few men verminous whereas practically all the Londoners were. Found corrugated iron shelters had been erected on a terrace which happened to be cut at just the right depth and height for dugouts on the principle of those of the Howitzer Battery by our Divisional Headquarters. Explained the principle and got a large party at once to work on the face.

To start with, in order to avoid waste of space by deep terracing, the tunnels are only 4½ feet high. When we get in I hope to raise them to steep arches with rounded corners below, to decrease danger of earth caving in. The lateral communications are a safeguard to enable men to get out if part of the entrance is blocked by a high explosive shell.

Temperature after lunch 100.5. Took quinine and aspirin. Arranged to take Orderly Room every morning at each Unit Headquarters and to meet the two Adjutants at 4.45 p.m. at each unit on alternate afternoons to settle joint orders. Organizing joint machine-gun and signalling courses to enable men to be divided into classes according to the amount they know. I shall continue to sleep every night at fire trench headquarters and to mess at the Londons and wash, etc. in the better dugout there with the corrugated roof. My sleeping dugout gave way last night and three sandbags at the end fell in, one giving a considerable wrench to my hair and missing my face by about ½ an inch. Although the dugout was so shallow that it only fell about 4 feet, it would have been unpleasant on my head. Had dugout reconstructed by cutting trench along one side so that I could put mattresses on other side and have enough head room to sit up. Covered it with 3 Government waterproof sheets.

24 November

Very busy on details of organization.

25 November

At 7.15 p.m. I carried out a plan which I had long meditated of tackling Bulgar Bluff with a strong patrol of thirty. On the last occasion I went there it was of course from the north; this time we approached it from the south and went out somewhere near Warwick Castle. Just as we got out of our trenches one man got a bullet through his foot and shortly afterwards two shots were fired at close range from some thick bushes where we rushed in with bayonets, but could find nothing. As there was a good deal of machine-gun fire on the line which I originally intended to follow, I went north on to the Aghyl Dere and climbed Bulgar Bluff from the West end. The men proved to be quite untrained in night work and made a most unfortunate noise. A figure was seen in a Turkish observation trench on the top of the Bluff but did not wait for the patrol to arrive. As we reached the trench the moon rose. I posted Corporal Jacobs and four men fifty yards east of the post to command the path leading eastward, along a kind of saddle-back to the higher spur, Chamchik Punar. I instructed him to remain out himself with one other man until the following night and to send in the remainder on seeing a Verey pistol fired from the barricade. As the moon rose figures were seen slinking away along the Deres on the north and south of Bulgar Bluff. They had no doubt heard the beaters getting up behind them. My plan needed far more silence than was possible with these Londoners, untrained in stalking. Having made a thorough search round the Turkish post which only produced a Turkish jampot bomb with a fuse attached and a quantity of ammunition, I ordered the patrol to go in a north-easterly direction, keeping to the left. The Turkish inhabitants of the bushes had, however, cleared out and corpses were all we could find. We came in to the barricade on the North Aghyl Dere held by the Suffolk Yeomanry and I waited there until the three men of the rearguard rejoined. They stated that after we left a shot had been fired at them from the bushes at quite close range and a man shouted at them in Turkish. They did not reply and shortly afterwards, on seeing my signal, left to rejoin us.

Shortly after 1 a.m. Corporal Jacobs, who had remained out on Bulgar Bluff, reported to me that, directly the three men of the rearguard had left him, five or six Turks advanced to reoccupy the post. They shot one Turk at very close range. Private Beasley then had his hip shattered by a bullet. In spite of the Turk following him up, Jacobs managed to get him down to the Aghyl Dere, where he left him while he went in to the Suffolk Yeomanry at the barricade to get stretcher-bearers who carried him in. It was thus very unfortunate that Jacobs came into collision with the Turks, as otherwise we ought to have obtained very useful information of their habits and probably would have been enabled to discover the post some other night. After seeing Jacobs I went up to one of our machine-gun posts and turned them on the Turkish observation trench on Bulgar Bluff.

26 November

Orders this afternoon for East Anglian Division, but not EMB, to go and rest at Mudros. Downpours of rain which is very unlucky as men had extra blankets withdrawn ready to be packed on transport.

Sent all baggage down to Beach last night. It was a great labour to get it down to the bottom of our camp, torrents of rain having made the ground so slippery that one couldn't stand.

5th Norfolks were relieved in trenches by New Zealand 'Mounted' Rifles. Bitterly cold day and unfortunately in the rush of yesterday I forgot to keep my warm clothes.

The Australians and New Zealanders were an infernal nuisance and I had to put on a guard to prevent everything being stolen. I found four men had actually demolished a large dugout on which we had been engaged for several days, capable of accommodating thirty men, and were in the act of removing timber and corrugated iron from the terrace. When I caught them they said they were New Zealanders, but when I sent a hot letter to the OC New Zealand Mounted Rifles to complain, they proved to be Australians. They say here that the Australian would steal your toe nail and attribute it to the convict origin. It is among them a case of every man for himself and there is no thought or consideration for anyone else. They all seem to address their officers as Bill or Dick and though wonderfully brave have absolutely no discipline. At 2 p.m. it began to rain and I got wet up to the knees going along the saps to the Suffolk Yeomanry rest camp to say goodbye to them. I found them in the depths of depression as they had got soaked in the early morning and had then heard that they were to move off to another bit of the line where it is apparently impossible to make proper dugouts as the Northamptonshire Regiment have just dug pits which are of course full of water and at the same time prevent the ground being properly terraced. It certainly is rather bad luck when by their own efforts they had made such a good rest camp they are now to be turned out. I could find no sympathy in my grumbles at being sent to Mudros, and everyone said they'd give anything to be able to do the same.

I got a lot of rain down my neck through the roof of 'B' Squadron Mess dugout while arguing the point, and began to think they were right. I had little time to see anyone and had to be content to leave my farewells as the Colonel insisted on telling me at great length how he had met a New Zealander yesterday and had met the same man's cousin in South Africa before. Shortly after my return orders came about starting this evening, but these were immediately afterwards cancelled, and from the foam on the sea it was quite obvious that we should not be able to start. We have only got with us what we carry and I was horribly cold last night, having kept no blanket, only a waterproof sheet. Tonight I have also two waterproof sheets which were part of our wall but for which we have substituted the wet blankets under which we used to dine, and which, having been picked up from dead men, are not desirable to sleep in. The men expecting to go have for the most part given up, or rather been squeezed out of, their dugouts by the newly arrived Australians and have no shelter at all.

28 November

It began to snow in the night and the ground is all white. The men are half dead and I have not often felt so cold. We got some rum to warm the men up but what is most urgent is something hot to drink. The ordinary miserable wood ration of 1 lb per man of wet log was not drawn yesterday as we were supposed to be going. We had to send a man to hospital in a state of collapse from cold. I went to see Mudge and told him the men were wet through and without shelter for 36 hours and needed most of all fires and that it was impossible to kindle the wet green wood, which further it is forbidden to cut round the camps. Mudge not only gave me a letter to the AAG of the 52nd Division which I sent up with a fatigue party to bring the wood, but further he went up to the Division himself to see what could be done, which was very good of him as it involved wading through 1½ miles of flooded sap. If this weather continues I think there will be a disaster to the Expedition. As Clutterbuck says, in France the men were properly dressed and fed, and after a few days in the trenches could get to a house to be restored to warmth. Here, however, there is no shelter to be had. The New Zealanders were mad with excitement this morning, never before having seen snow. It is now past four and has been snowing almost incessantly with a bitter wind.

Soon after four, got orders to stay here tonight owing to the weather but to send the left-hand Battalion of the Londons and the whole of the Norfolks down to Anzac so that room might be found for the New Zealanders. Last night, as we expected to move, these New Zealanders occupied our corrugated iron terrace shelters, and our men had to stay out, not liking to disturb them when it was cancelled. Our second blankets all went down to the beach with the baggage and the men, having in most cases no shelter, had to stand about all night.

As soon as our move today was postponed I had to try and make arrangements for the night. The New Zealand CO, however, was quite impossible and refused to do anything to help us. He said that we had no right here at all as his lot had taken over the whole area. Finally I had to go to Mudge who immediately came round and tackled not only the CO of the Auckland Regiment but also his Brigadier who happened to be with him at the time. Mudge explained that he had vacated the lines occupied by the 11th London and the 5th Norfolks so as to make room for the New Zealanders and that they would find them more convenient to the fire trench. The New Zealand Brigadier, however, said he would support his officer in any action he thought fit to recommend, and was about as unobliging as possible. Finally they agreed to give up one of the three dugouts which was the least they could do seeing that they had only seven men in each of the three Norfolk dugouts each built for twenty.

The night was so awful, a bitter wind and driving snow, that Clutterbuck and I vacated our own dugout and the Doctor cleared out of his, and we all three doubled up with Taylor, who commands the right half-battalion. The New Zealand CO, seeing us moving, immediately tried to get in himself but we got our own men in and, by being so grasping, he has just succeeded in getting the two best officers' dugouts, to which he would naturally have succeeded when we left, thoroughly infected with lice. We four in Taylor's dugout slept so close that we were touching each other, but it was a comfort to feel that all the men were under cover. It froze hard during the night and in the morning my canvas bucket was covered with 1½ inches of ice.

29 November

Very cold but bright morning. Heard from Mudge that the Suffolk Yeomanry had been moved up to Hill 60 in the morning. Went in the afternoon to try and collect a few boxes of firewood which I found in my old dugout. On returning found that the Quartermaster of the New Zealanders was calmly reconstructing our reserve ration dump having refused to acknowledge the authority of our Quartermaster Sergeant who was in charge. This same Quartermaster had been most offensive the previous day, asking when we were going to turn out of the one or two NCO's dugouts near the dump, and adding that we had no right to anything in the area which they had taken over. On coming down and asking by whose authority the boxes were being moved he was most impertinent. I told him they were in our charge and belonged to the Brigade as reserve rations. Being for 5600 men they were of some value and could not be handed over until I had written authority from his or my Brigadier. He said, 'All right, there will be no difficulty about that, and meanwhile my men will go on rebuilding the wall so that I can get them under cover before it is dark.' I told him that, on the contrary, he would remove his men until he produced his authority as my men were in need of the place for shelter. He was in a great rage but cleared out. An hour later a telegram came from Division to hand over Brigade reserve rations at once. I sent for the list of stores and took it in to the New Zealander whom I told that they could have the dump as soon as they signed my receipt. This of course they refused to do, until they had checked the things, the result being that we keep the dump until tomorrow morning at 9 and the men will be under cover tonight.

30 November

Lovely day, hard frost and bright sun. We shall doubtless start tonight. Hitherto the wind had been off the shore here and blowing right into Imbros so that the lighters could not get out to fetch us. In any case it would probably have been too rough to get the lighters alongside the piers, or thence alongside the boats which go to Mudros. It is remarkable how little firing there is in the trenches during the cold weather. It is as if both sides were too miserable to touch the cold metal of the rifles.

Although yesterday was quite calm, we got no orders to move. Rumour said that the lighters had not arrived from Imbros. I walked round to the EMB after lunch but only found Hugh Buxton and Southwell, the General being at Hill 60.

We have now been five nights without our kits, cramped up in a dugout so small that one cannot stand upright, and sleep touching each other. Since the order to go we have had nothing to eat but bully beef and biscuits, all our extra food being on the sea shore. We have made a fireplace out of a biscuit tin and are gradually burning all our furniture. We cannot do much cooking, however, even of tea as the water ration is now down to a pint a head, probably because everything is frozen up.

At 8 p.m. received wire: 'Brigade will not move off Peninsula at present. You will move tomorrow to Waterfall Gully. The move will not take place till after dinner.'

1 December

Beautiful frosty morning. General Mudge knows nothing as to the explanation of last night's wire and has sent Staff Captain down to Division to find out.

The hospitals are, of course, congested, as we know by their having sent us back a wounded man who was hit yesterday in his dugout, and whom we are quite unable to treat properly. It may be that they cannot get us off until they are cleared. On the other hand I hear that the Suffolk Yeomanry had two men killed and several wounded yesterday and are now so weak that they said they could not hold their line with safety, with the result that Norfolk Yeomanry and Welsh Horse had to come up in support. It may be that they are going to keep us here to strengthen the line. If so it is outrageous to have kept the men in such grave discomfort for the last five days. The men have been suffering much from rheumatism and jaundice and we have had two cases of collapse from cold, and this morning one of frostbitten feet.

Things still seem very quiet. Whereas a week ago we used to see half a dozen aeroplanes overhead daily, we lately have seen none. It used to be annoying to see German aeroplanes sailing overhead, greeted only by our machine guns, whereas ours were always met with puffs of bursting shrapnel. I saw two of our aeroplanes so hit that they had to plane down into the sea where they were picked up.

Walked down to Post Office in the morning to enquire about mails. Met General Hodgson who said he hoped I would not mind but that he had wired yesterday asking for me back as the Division was leaving. Of course it may not be allowed and, there being very few Suffolk Yeomanry left, the job of 2nd-in-Command is even less attractive than before. On returning saw General Mudge who said we were to go to Taylor's Gully, not Waterfall Gully; that there was no cover there and we'd better take any corrugated iron that we could. Accordingly got fatigue party to work with result that OC New Zealand Regiment rushed round to ask me to stop while he communicated with his Brigadier. I said I would demolish nothing if he had no objection to our having a couple of dozen loose sheets. While he was referring this to his Brigade and Division I had the sheets sent off and quickly followed. Of course the Division forbade it but by that time they were two miles away and Russell (our Brigade Major) could only express his regrets.

On arrival at Taylor's Gully found it perfectly filthy. The whole place littered with empty tins, jam, food and rubbish. Turned on every available man to clean it up, and to scrape the floors of the dugouts which looked very doubtful. Our predecessors were a battalion of the Essex Regiment who had been here for a day. When we told them they were dirty brutes they said it was the fault of the New Zealanders. We found five New Zealand rifles covered with rust in the dugouts, and also masses of mark VI ammunition which they had left behind.

Hear today that delay in starting due to necessity for clearing hospitals first. It is said that thousands of troops have been frostbitten at Suvla and that the saps yesterday morning were full of poor devils on all fours with bleeding feet crawling down to the beach as there was no one to carry them. The Australians one night were badly shelled at Lone Pine with high explosives, and there are about 300 of them badly wounded waiting to get off. Five Australian sentries are said to have died of exposure at their posts.

General Inglefield came up and looked at our camp about 10 a.m. and shortly afterwards returned with General Birdwood who now commands the Army Corps, and General Godley* who commands one of the Australian Divisions. Birdwood is a little man with a keen face and bubbles with energy. Godley is a long, limp man. Birdwood must be a man of extraordinary tact to have succeeded so well with the Australians who are a most difficult and undisciplined though very brave rabble. Some say he is popular with them because he lets them do as they like and take whatever there is at the expense of the Territorials. Birdwood told me we had done well to have had only half a dozen cases of frostbite as the Army Corps at Suvla had 150 deaths from exposure and drowning. A whole Turkish Battalion was also said to have been destroyed and many Turkish corpses and mules had been washed down by the flood into our trenches.

Mudge says the Division have as yet no orders to give me back to the EMB and he thinks it will not be allowed. He told me that there was little notice taken of Regiments and Brigades out here and that when GHQ attached officers to units they generally left them there in spite of protests. On the whole I think I'd rather stick where I am as the Suffolk Yeomanry is no stronger now than the 10th London and it is more interesting to run one's own show. It is, however, an absolute gamble as, if sufficient drafts are not forthcoming, we may be sent to some such backwater as the Suez Canal.

Had physical drill to warm the men up and went down to see our left half battalion who were moved 5 nights ago into the 1st Australian Hospital by Walker's Pier. They had been shelled a good deal and really one cannot blame the Turks for shelling hospitals when they are used for accommodating troops. This hospital is close to guns and a large depot of their ammunition. It was just the same down towards Suvla. There were two guns on the beach quite close to the East Anglian Hospital where I went to see our men a fortnight ago.

2 December

Began raining in the night and there was a warmer temperature. Sandbags got wet and two fell in on the end of Clutterbuck's bed, missing his legs but smashing framework. He had only yesterday afternoon sent for it from Anzac and will now have to sleep on the ground.

The cheek of the Australians is wonderful. General Mudge supports his waterproof sheet roof with about 12 sandbags which he brought down with him. Yesterday on returning he found an Australian had calmly emptied them and was about to carry them off. We've had no bread or fresh meat for over a week now. Some was landed two days ago but has no doubt been kept for the Australians.

Went down to No. 1 Australian Hospital at Anzac to see left half of Battalion. Inspected their arms and tents which were dirty. While there got shelled. Mostly burst on sea or water's edge 100 yards away, but one shrapnel burst on to a tent killing two orderlies and wounding 5 men. Horrible mess – one man carried past me with his legs so badly mangled that both had at once to be amputated. Clutterbuck meanwhile was nearly hit by water's edge. One Regimental Sergeant-Major (Higgins), an excellent fellow who looks as if he'd got a poker in each trouser leg and sleeve and who was in the Coldstream Guards, stood bolt upright being far too dignified to allow a mere 6-inch shell to disturb him, while Clutterbuck and everyone else had flopped down into the dust and squeezed themselves into the smallest possible space. Higgins merely remarked that 'a bit of that there shell hit my boot'.

There were expectations of the Division starting today but the whole thing was definitely cancelled about 3 p.m. and orders issued for drawing their usual rations. We had previously seen a couple of lighters making tracks for Imbros and were told that the Naval Authorities foretold a storm. It was a drizzling day with a SW wind, which is of course a bad quarter for Anzac. Just as we were going to dine at 6.15 Mudge sent for Clutterbuck, having just got orders that we were to embark at Walker's Pier, Anzac at 7.30. This gave little time as for heavily laden men in such pitch darkness it was a ¾-hour march. However, we got off as soon as possible and were down in plenty of time. There was only one lighter available as the Naval Authorities had taken the others away. We got on board the Khedivial Boat *El Kahiora* about 11 p.m. after long delays due to conflicting orders by the Military Landing Officers, the rudder chain coming adrift and general mismanagement. Boat packed – quite impossible to extricate units who had been mixed up by the MLO. All our baggage left behind and I suppose we shall never see it again.

3 December

Arrived at Mudros about 8 a.m. Landed West Mudros (North Pier) about 9, and marched 3 miles up to camp. We got there first and General Mudge allotted us what seemed to be about the best quarters. Tents very scarce, no orderly room or stores, 12 men per tent and 3 officers. As CO I get one to myself. Foraging in villages round produced some really fresh eggs which we had for tea, the first for two months.

4 December

The quiet here seems extraordinary after the ceaseless musketry fire at Anzac.

6 December

We made friends yesterday with Major van der Golt, commanding Indian Mule transport camp, and Clutterbuck and Ball (the Doctor) went over this morning to draw three ponies as arranged. They are Indian country breds, mine a confiding sure-footed bay, and Clutterbuck's a dun which often rears over on being mounted. We had rather a job with our grooms who seemed frightened of the ponies, and three times let Clutterbuck's loose. We built a shelter of stones and managed to peg them down pretty securely in spite of the rotten worn-out ropes and saddlery which arrived with them.

In the afternoon we rode to Thermos by a rough and precipitous mountain track. We had to lead our ponies over much of the steepest and stoniest parts. At Thermos are hot springs and after an enormous and excellent tea from an omelette of eggs bought at a farm by the way, of bread and lard and honey, we had deep baths in white marble let into the deep floor. Never have I enjoyed a hot bath so much. It is the first really useful one I have had since leaving Woodbridge. It was nearly dark when we left and we came back by tracks down the valleys, fearing the precipitous mountain path by night. As we did not know the way and only had a rough idea as to the direction of our camp, we were not back until about 8 p.m.

7 December

Moved our lines, so that instead of Brigades and Regiments being jumbled together they are now laid out in regular streets. We are still without our luggage which was left on lighters at Anzac. I fear very much we shall never see it again as no one was allowed to stay to look after it. I have practically no clothes with me, not even a spare shirt.

Re-laying the camp took all the morning as ground is most awkward for a large number of tents. Rode afterwards to West Mudros where Clutterbuck took me to see Colonel Agnew, the Commandant, his former Commanding Officer. Got passes to ride tomorrow to Kastro from Ennismore who is APM here.

Went to see our draft of 160 men at detail camp. The officers seemed pretty good as far as one could judge in a few minutes' conversation. General Mudge told me there is another large draft waiting for us at Alexandria.

8 December

Rode over and bathed at Thermos, then on to Kastro, the capital of the island. Found Acland Hood there, who has been appointed Camp Commandant for General Monro's new HQ's which are to be moved there. He took us all over interesting old castle, originally Genoese, fortifying the rock which divides two bays on which the town is built. Very interesting old cannons (Spanish one with arms of Philip V) chain shot and kinds of ancient cannon balls lying about in heaps. Clutterbuck carried off fragment of grenade which in shape and size was indistinguishable from the cricket-ball bombs which we are now using in Gallipoli. Delightful spot, but should have thought Mudros, with its huge bay covered with shipping more suitable for Headquarters. Had tea at Kastro and rode back in pitch darkness 8 miles to camp. We struck the road after about 4 miles and did last part straight over mountainous country, only guessing direction by dark peaks on either side across sky. Finally saw lights of camp below us, and I nearly had a bad fall as I did not realize how steep it was and rode straight down. When I threw myself off, found it difficult to keep my feet and almost fell on a smooth and quite perpendicular rock.

9 December

My sack of underclothes not having yet turned up and only possessing the shirt on my back, I rode down to North Pier to look for it. On my way back called at Ordnance but found they had no khaki shirts.

10 December

Inspected draft of 160 men and two officers who joined us yesterday. They look promising, many of them men from 30–35 who should have more stamina than the undersized youths of whom we have so many.

Brigade Conference of COs in evening. General Mudge had just been to the *Aragon* and hinted that we might be off at very short notice. Orders came later from Division that no one is to leave immediate precincts of camp without leave, and that COs are only to grant leave in cases where people can be recalled at very short notice. It sounds like early move, probably to Egypt. After 13 days, my sack of (dirty) clothing turned up. Immense relief. Mess box still missing. As it is marked Suffolk Yeomanry I suppose it will not come. Arrangements about baggage are perfectly disgraceful. We were not allowed to have a guard over it and the least the MLOs might be expected to do is to prevent it being looted. As it is, almost everyone has lost some of their kit, and even where they have received the packages, their contents have been stolen. Anything valuable such as glasses, money, revolvers, etc., have generally been taken away. If they want to send us away it seems absurd not to say so, as it is most inconvenient and irritating being kept hanging about without even the chance of getting any exercise.

11 December

No one allowed to leave camp owing to probability of moving.

12 December

President of Field General Court Martial to try three men of Northampton Regiment who had shot themselves on Hill 60. Captain Cronin of Bedfords, and Stanbrook (10th London) members. All charged under 2 sections of Army Act 18 (2) and 40, first with wilfully maiming themselves and second with negligently discharging rifle and thus shooting themselves. Acquitted one of both charges as it was his first night in the trenches and he had only joined two days previously with a draft, and the Sergeant's evidence of having warned men to unload after standing to was unsatisfactory. Found second man guilty of second charge and condemned to a week's field imprisonment No. 2. Third man had loaded his rifle with only one round and said it had tumbled down and shot him in his dugout without anyone touching trigger. Being dusk he had not even seen it on the floor, but remembering that he had left it loaded he had hopped off and told a corporal that he was shot in the foot by his own rifle. We found him guilty of first and second charges and condemned to 3 months' imprisonment with hard labour. This will almost certainly be remitted as no sentences seem to be carried out at the time. Men are usually given 3 months' trial and if well reported on by their COs are let off altogether.

Dined with General Mudge who had the most delicious tinned chicken and plum pudding!! Gallipoli has made me frightfully greedy. We are definitely to embark tomorrow.

It is annoying not to know more of what is going on. A typical sample of the official news circulated out here is: 'Reports persist that Russian Armies have entered Bulgaria'. The authorities must know whether such reports are true or false. If false it is outrageous to publish them in an official telegram. Orders about 9 p.m. that Northampton Regiment and Bedfords and half 10th Londons are to embark tomorrow on *Alaunia* with all baggage. Other half Londons and Bedfords to follow later.

13 December

Went over to camp of details of 29th Division owing to telegram saying that officers who had lost their kit might find it there. Drew a blank but heard good deal of news from Suvla end. One of their regular Battalions is only 50 strong, so 10th London with 400 is not so weak for these parts as I had thought. Perhaps we shall soon get another show after all.

Australians to a man seem to break into everything they can find. It is a case of every man for himself, probably a reversion to the ancestral type of the burglars who were transported to become the fathers of the Australian race. Certainly they are fine fighters, but the damage they have done to discipline out here is untold. The Authorities are afraid of them and they know it.

Saw first half of Battalion off on return to camp and General Mudge told me that the remainder could not embark until tomorrow. Owing to the idiocy of Divisional Staff we had to send off our baggage at 6.30 this morning so we shall have another blanketless night to knock out more men with rheumatism and jaundice. The cases of frostbite which my Battalion had in Gallipoli are nothing to the scores we have had as a result of the night on deck coming from Anzac to Mudros, when the men were so tight packed that they could not move about to keep warm.

14 December

Orders at 7.45 a.m. to be down at Engineer's Pier by 10 a.m. Marched at 8.45 and in spite of thick fog arrived in good time. Men much fitter and did not fall out on our way up, partly perhaps because they'd got their heads towards home. On arriving at pierhead, no lighter to take us off and did not get away for 3 hours. Even then had to leave 50 men behind for second journey. The *Alaunia* is a Cunarder of 14,000 tons. Under normal conditions she takes emigrants across the Atlantic, and the 2200 troops which we have on board are far better accommodated than on the *Olympic*. The 1st class cabins are rather scarce. Only Generals Inglefield and Mudge have single cabins. Clutterbuck shares mine which is quite comfortable. Unfortunately, as the 10th London came on board in three batches, they are scattered about the ship owing to the stupid way messes were allotted, and this of course increases the difficulty of looking after them.

We started about 5 p.m. and at 5.15 all the Battalions were paraded at their boat station. The rule is that whenever at sea everyone must wear or carry a lifebelt.

I sit next to the Purser who told me extraordinary instances of the incompetence of the Embarkation Authorities. Lately a ship arrived full of stores for the Director of Works at Mudros. It happened that two locomotive engines were loaded on top of certain stores which were wanted, so the ship was made to go out to sea and drop the two engines overboard. A steamer recently waited for weeks at Malta with nothing to do. One day they were told to go alongside the wharf, load up with 100 firebricks and sent to Mudros without anything else on board. Troopships almost always come out with no other cargo, inconveniently light and high in the water while other vessels are sent out laden with the cargo they might have brought. In certain cases ships arriving laden at Mudros have been sent back without being unloaded! This ship had just come from Alexandria with 1200 sheep on board and the decks are of course in a filthy mess. It took four days to sling the unfortunate sheep on one by one, and the same morning that they started the work a ship left Alexandria for Mudros quite empty, which had been specially built for carrying sheep and cattle, and had wide doors on to a lower deck so that sheep could walk straight on board. One of the ships which go daily to and from Cape Helles went alongside one of the storeships to get one case of eggs which was needed for a hospital there where the consumption was about 3 dozen daily. The authorities, however, proceeded to pack 160,000 eggs on her, and these are now lying at Helles going bad. This ship had been used for taking convalescents home and the purser once got up a concert to amuse them. One of the men asked whether one of the ship's officers who was performing could sing an awful sentimental song called 'Thora' as an encore. 'Yes,' said the purser, 'but why do you want it?' 'Because our Lieutenant Smith was singing it to us one night in our rest camp, and just as he got to the chorus, a shell came and took his head off.'

Dinner was the first civilized meal and I didn't know how greedy I could be. The Purser says there ought to be a special rate for the feeding of troops returning from Gallipoli.

15 December

Lovely weather and a calm sea. At about 8 a.m. we arrived at Milo and anchored in the harbour until 1 p.m. so as to pass the channel to the NW of Crete in the darkness. Milo is protected from submarines by bombs and nets and is crowded with French warships and other allied shipping. I wonder how the allies have excused themselves for appropriating it. They argued that Lemnos was still Turkish, as, although it was in Greek occupation, the Treaty by which it was to have been handed over after the Balkan War had not been formally ratified. No such plea can be advanced in the case of Milo which has long been Greek. It was curious to see the MLO come alongside in a British Man-of-War boat flying the Greek flag. The harbour is a fine land-locked bay with deep water close inshore. Just before coming in we passed close to Antimilo, which I at once recognized from its shape. When we passed it 9 years ago in the *Lady Evelyn* on our way to Alexandria I cast longing eyes upon it, as it is the only one of the Cyclades where the wild goat is still to be found.

Left Milo at 1 p.m. and passed west end of Crete just after sunset and before rising of the moon. Sea rather rougher to south of island.

16 December

About 2 p.m. wireless message was received from vessel in front of us that she was being pursued by a submarine. Our course was therefore altered and during much of afternoon and evening we zigzagged in a westerly direction.

17 December

If we had steered a straight course we should have arrived last night. We are now going east and should arrive early tomorrow.

18 December

Arrived Alexandria 7.30. Orders at 11.20 were to disembark in two half-battalions at 11 and 11.15 after issuing two days rations! Got off by 12, marched 2 miles to Ramleh Tram terminus and after a 6-mile train journey another mile from Sidi Bishr station across deep sand to camp. Hardly any tents available until evening, then only just enough to get men under cover, so officers slept out, baggage and blankets having fortunately arrived about 8 p.m. Got quite civilized dinner at Beau Rivage Hotel about 9 p.m.

19 December

Struck tents and rearranged camp. Herbert Musker and Leslie came to see me and told me Jack Agnew was also in hospital here, having left the Peninsula on December 10th. There was then no information as to EMB leaving. Musker and Clutterbuck dined with me at Majestic Hotel Alexandria.

20 December

We are still MEF not Egyptian garrison which means we may be sent anywhere at short notice. Hear that Senussi showed considerable training at recent fight at Matruh (west of here). They had machine guns and came on like civilized troops in open order. A Yeomanry Squadron which charged were unaware of a deep watercourse just in front of Senussi position and suffered rather badly.

In spite of our still getting orders from GHQ, MEF, it is generally thought we might be sent west to the Senussi, or east to the Canal if Maxwell is short of troops. They have found that the Yeomanry Brigade who were at the Matruh fight have used up all the water in the wells for their horses, and more mounted men are not likely to be sent. A good many infantry are along the lines of communications running west.

Very busy day. COs meeting in morning when Mudge said we were for the moment to worry more about organization than about training so as to be ready for men when they arrive. Went to Alexandria in evening. Called at 3rd Echelon and saw Sergt Fenn (Orderly Room Sergt, Suffolk Yeo.) who showed me list of casualties etc. to date. Several men killed since I left but no officer casualties. I was gazetted Temporary Lieut.-Col. to command 10th London in GHQ list 60 of 9 December to date from 21 November.

22 December

Herbert Musker sent over to say that he could not lunch as arranged with me in camp as he had just been ordered to prepare for the arrival of the EMB.

23 December

Went over to Yeomanry detail camp on seashore, 300 yards north of ours and found Eddie Cadogan, Grissell, Tuttle (the Quartermaster) and about 50 men of the Suffolk Yeomanry had arrived as an advance party. They had left in two different ships on (I think) the 13th and 14th and after, in the case of one party, two horrible days of semi-starvation on a 'Dump' ship at Mudros, had been sent on to prepare camp here. Until 11 December it had not generally been realized on the Peninsula that the complete evacuation of Suvla and Anzac was taking place, and people were taken in by being told that they were to go and rest at Mudros. When, however, the advance party came away the intention was pretty clear as they were ordered to leave practically all their kits behind. The Turks did not show any signs of increased activity and appeared to have evacuated their trenches on Hill 60 as sniping had ceased and when our men fired at the Turkish trenches they seemed only to disturb birds. I hope therefore, in view of statement in last night's official telegram, that evacuation has been completed with hardly any casualties and that the Suffolk Yeomanry may have got off without much trouble. Eddie Cadogan is bright yellow and very thin as he has jaundice.

24 December

General Mudge sent for COs at 7.30 p.m. and showed us orders to be in readiness to move at short notice. Probably the 162nd Brigade will be sent to impress the nation and to look out for Senussi raids on the Cairo–Alexandria line. Three Battalions would go to Hosh Isa on the Eastern edge of the Sahara, the fourth remaining 15 miles further east at Damanhur, a considerable town on the Cairo–Alexandria railway 40 miles SE of here. Damanhur is on all the maps but we cannot find Hosh Isa. No maps, however, are issued and we have only maps in a pocket atlas and a local guide book.

25 December

There is a hitch about the move as Mudge is senior to the GOC, Alexandria, in whose area we should be. It will probably be got over by putting us still nominally under Inglefield. Yesterday I received a letter from Evelyn that all was well, the first news from home since 3 November.

Heavy rain in the morning which prevented Church Parade. Men were provided with Christmas dinner out of messing allowance of 8½d per head which is allowed over here above bread and meat ration. They had local plum pudding and turkeys, fruit, etc. I tried to give them beer but could not get a barrel anywhere. Finally, too late for dinner, got 3 cases of Guinness's stout and 3 of Bass which allowed a bottle per man which they had in the evening. Probably somewhere there is a mountain of plum puddings sent out by some fund with no one to eat them.

Ford Moore, a senior Major of the 10th London who was wounded in the landing, is now to rejoin us, and as he is quite fit to command I asked the General if I had better apply to go back to the EMB. He told me there had been considerable correspondence about me, and that he was trying to keep me. I am quite glad to stay as it is better to have something to do instead of kicking one's heels as 2nd-in-Command of a Yeomanry Regiment who will probably never see any fighting except as infantry. At the same time Ford Moore is probably 20 years older than I and, being a retired Major of Volunteers who joined the 10th London as a Captain on its formation, may well look on me as an interloper.

26 December

Remainder of Eastern Mounted Brigade turned up last night. Jarvis came over and dined and gave me much interesting information about withdrawal. His first knowledge was about the 10th when an order came that troops were to eat the 7 days' reserve dumps of rations. Everything was thought out very carefully, and from the 14th onwards parties were detailed from the Regiment and embarked each night. The last of them left on the 19th, Jarvis, Frank Goldsmith, etc., from Anzac and the final party of 21 'sprinters' in parties of 7, each under an officer, from a little jetty at the mouth of the Kaiajik Dere in small boats. Previously they had buried and destroyed ammunition, stores, surplus equipment, etc. On the last morning there was an unusually severe bombardment of Hill 60 in which we lost several killed and wounded, and for a moment it was feared that the Turks had discovered what was going on. Their intelligence service must have been very bad as for days previously they could see from Hill 60 the conflagrations of stores being burnt at Suvla.

To give the impression we were still there, Jarvis put rifles in the trenches with tins attached to the triggers into which it was arranged for other tins to allow a trickle of water so that when the tins became heavy enough the rifles were fired. The dumps of rations which were not destroyed were filled with explosives so as to blow up if the cases were moved. The Turks had apparently no suspicion of the evacuation having taken place, as they were bombarding the empty trenches again the next (last Monday) morning.

27 December

Went to see Paymaster, etc., and met Frank Goldsmith who was trying to get some clothes, having left everything behind on the Peninsula. We lunched together and I returned before the arrival of our reinforcement of 5 officers and 83 men who had been collected from hospitals, etc at the base detail camp.

28 December

General Mudge went to see General Boyle, GOC Alexandria. I intended to go in to post letters, etc. but it was too late when he returned. At 6 p.m. meeting of COs. Bedfords are to go to Damanhur and we to Hosh Isa with the 4th Northamptons and 11th London. At latter place is large Arab encampment about seven thousand strong of Aulad Ali tribe who are apparently wavering in their loyalty. Three-quarters of the tribe are by religion followers of the Senussi.

We shall probably have pretty hard work getting the place in a state of defence at first, but after that I expect life at Hosh Isa will be rather tedious, as no one will be allowed out of camp in smaller parties than 10 men or 4 officers, and always armed. We had to send all luggage off at 8 a.m. as it had to go 5 miles to be loaded on to trains and there is a great shortage of wagons. We also struck half our tents to supplement the local supply at Hosh Isa, so I shall sleep out tonight which is rather pleasant provided that it doesn't rain. We start early tomorrow morning and as we are to go by the first train, I hope we may get through by the evening. The last part of the journey from Damanhur is by a light rail or tramway on which very little rolling stock is available, so we shall probably have a good deal of hanging about.

29 December

General Mudge told me that General Inglefield who came over to see him this morning wished me to go back to the Suffolk Yeomanry so that Ford Moore, a middle-aged Major, 19 years in some volunteers before he joined the 10th London Regiment at the formation about 3 years ago, might take command. Mudge, however, told Inglefield he preferred to keep me, giving the reason that Ford Moore had not yet completely recovered from his wounds and was being massaged every second day. Inglefield said he ought in that case to stop at Alexandria and Mudge told me he was going to press him to do so, and that on his return to the town I was to send him up. Ford Moore on his return saw General Mudge and told me he had urged him to stay until completely cured, but that he refused unless positively ordered to do so. Ford Moore seems quite harmless. Clutterbuck tells me that a few of the old officers who have rejoined us since the Peninsula are anxious to get him back in command as he is very slack and a typical old Volunteer officer. I don't mind one way or the other as I expect life at Hosh Isa will be pretty dull and the Suffolk Yeomanry might possibly get horses and be sent somewhere more interesting.

30 December

Started at 7 to march 1½ miles to trains; all sent off by 8 a.m. Got off trains at Sidi Gaber where we entrained for Damanhur in open trucks, a journey of 1½ hours. Our rations and other baggage, cooking pots, etc., kept until last moment, were to have left camp at 6 a.m. but transport did not arrive owing to heavy sand and we did not get them today. At Damanhur we marched across to the light railway and reached Hosh Isa at 1 p.m. It is a small town on rising ground surrounded by a flat plain where the cultivated land struggles with the edge of the desert.

No officers or men are allowed into the town, but fortunately we've brought a native cook who can make purchases for us of local produce.

31 December

Spent most of day repitching tents which had been occupied by half a provisional Battalion (whom we relieved) and adding to them enough to fit in the 1/4th Northamptons and the 11th Londons. The remaining Battalion of the Brigade, 1/5th Bedfordshire, has been left to garrison Damanhur. All the officers of the Brigade live in a barbed-wire enclosure surrounding the house inhabited now by General Mudge and formerly by irrigation officials and office. The three Battalions and Newfoundland Transport Corps are on parallel lines across one end of the enclosure, packed pretty close so that the perimeter of our trenches may not be too much extended. Mudge asked me this afternoon whether it would suit me to become his Brigade Major. Russell, who belonged to the 10th London, and who since the departure of his former regular Brigade Major, has been acting in his place, having been given a regular commission as Captain in the Cameronians, has been recalled to their depot. This leaves him with only his Staff Captain whom he cannot make Brigade Major because he is really 2nd-in-Command of the 1/5th Bedfordshires and in the event of anything happening to Mudge he would find it difficult to carry on the Brigade until a successor were appointed as it would involve giving orders to his own CO. Mudge says it is most inconvenient having no Brigade Major as there is a good deal of extra work thrown on him here and he cannot possibly reconnoitre the country around as he would like to. For instance, he had just heard that a canal about 4 miles away, on which he had relied as an obstacle, was dry and easy to cross. I told him that I knew nothing of Staff work and that he ought to get a regular. He agreed but said they assured him a regular would not be forthcoming and he would prefer to have me than some possibly unsuitable Territorial who might be sent. I told him I was quite happy in my present job and he asked whether I preferred it to being Brigade Major. I answered that I really didn't mind one way or the other and would gladly do whatever he wished. He said it was of course rather delicate to ask for me as BM as the answer might be, 'You said this officer was necessary for the 10th London and now you propose to remove him. As he is therefore not indispensable he is to return to the Yeomanry and we will give you someone else.' I do genuinely feel rather diffident about taking on such a job, though it would of course be interesting if one had the necessary qualifications. I haven't the same contempt for Brigade Staff Officers as for those of higher units, for whereas the latter never go near bullets, the former are continually in the firing line under such conditions as Gallipoli. Mudge strongly advised me to apply to go back to the Suffolk Yeomanry, as the authorities would not understand the circumstances and think it was due to lack of zeal. I left myself at his disposal, so that if circumstances make it advisable he can take me without any feeling that I should dislike going. The more I see of Mudge the more I like him. He is full of decision and energy. He was continually in the trenches at every hour of the day and night and even going out in the front of them alone. He is absolutely clear and to the point in all his orders, and it is extraordinary to see, as I did the evening we got orders to embark from Anzac, how quickly he crystallizes Inglefield into a shape which everyone can understand. He is only a Major in his own Regiment (the Queen's) and would I suppose never have been heard of if he had not happened to go to Helles on the staff of another Territorial Division in the original landing.

1916: Egypt and the Western Front

1 January, 1916

Mudge took round COs in the morning to see line of trenches to be constructed round camp. We are responsible for the east side (towards village of Hosh Isa). Pegged them out during afternoon. In addition to fire trench along edge we are to make screen trenches in front of the openings of the 4 roads which run into the camp on our side. This cuts up the line so much that it took some time to get the fire trench symmetrically planned. We shall not be able to start digging until tomorrow (Sunday).

2 January

COs, 2nds-in-command and Adjutants received horses, which will be a great resource when we get more settled. I chose a chestnut which was brought out by the 162nd Brigade from England 5 months ago. The grooms who had been left in charge said he was dangerous to ride and continually standing on his hind legs. I expect it was due to their heavy hands, as when Clutterbuck and I tried our mounts this evening he seemed quite well-mannered. Although it was Sunday we spent the afternoon digging in two reliefs. The 10th London are responsible for the East side of the camp, towards the village, and in a couple of hours we practically finished roughing them out and will finish parapets and parados tomorrow. To have dug trenches a couple of hundred yards long in the Peninsula would have taken many days owing to the hardness of the ground, but here it is sand and very easy to dig. After the first 6 inches the soil becomes a bit stiffer and holds up pretty well. I fear, however, it will cave in before long unless we can fit material for revetting. The east side is believed to be the most threatened as attack would almost certainly come from Hosh Isa in collusion with the inhabitants.

3 January

I saw Intelligence summaries which had been delayed owing to evacuation. The total number of Turkish troops on the Peninsula (including reserve at Bulair, etc.) is given as 14 or 15 Divisions, 107–114,000 rifles of which 90,000 were in firing line. Only 3 Divisions were said to be at Helles. I fear the latter positions will have a very bad time now that the distraction of Suvla and Anzac no longer exists, and all the new Austrian and German guns are available for the southern zone. An estimate is given from Constantinople, dated 22 November, of the strength of the Turkish Army. Total troops under arms 650,000 called up since the beginning of War, 1,250,000 estimated liable and available (in addition to above) 250,000. Casualties to 30th September 520,000. Information is given from various Turkish sources that a serious attack is to be made on Egypt. A reliable German report of 10 November is quoted that a new Saxon Army Corps has been constituted, entirely of young men who were being trained for operations in Suez Canal region. They had tropical helmets, khaki clothing, and an unusually large train and special arrangements for the transport of water. I should imagine that all these rumours of an attack on Egypt might be bluff, as in the case of the invasion of England. Having gained control of Eastern Europe and secured the blocking of Russia's communications through the Dardanelles, it would be unnecessary to offer hostages to fortune, as it would be, if without Sea Power to ensure its supplies, Germany should launch an expedition on any scale along the very bad and long communications of the Anatolian and Syrian systems.

Hosh Isa. 3 January

Downpour of rain and trenches dug yesterday washed in. Even where water was prevented from running in over the top by dams, drains, etc., it often burst out 2 or 3 feet down as the sandy loam seems full of underground crevices into which the water trickles down from the surface. My tent quite flooded across the middle.

4 January

Dug drains. More rain in afternoon. OCs met General Mudge in afternoon, who explained situation. A scrap between police and friendly Arabs on one hand and hostile Arabs on the other took place two days ago, our side of Numaria Canal 12 or 15 miles from here. The leader was captured and came through here yesterday.

5 January

Went for route march in the morning. In the afternoon Clutterbuck, Farmer and I rode to the edge of the sandy country beyond Hager Canal, SW of here. We were allowed out mounted in parties of three, or dismounted 4 officers or 10 men, always armed. Saw lots of duck, snipe, plover, etc.

6 January

Torrents of rain during last night. Fortunately yesterday we only filled up old trenches and dug drains past ends, so no further harm done. Many heavy showers of rain during the day.

7 January

The camp is still very wet though hardly any rain fell today. We could not therefore go on with trench digging this afternoon and made drains instead.

8 January

Brigade marched through streets of Hosh Isa with fixed bayonets to overawe the natives. It is a filthy little town with indescribable smells. We zigzagged about the narrow alleys and finally reached a kind of market place where most of the population seemed to be collected. They were apparently much interested and some looked very surly.

General Mudge said he saw General Inglefield yesterday at Damanhur and that the latter told him Col. Lambert (my predecessor) was back from hospital and wished to rejoin. For the moment this had been staved off by sending him to the detail camp, but as Lambert was sent out from England specially to take the Battalion, I gathered that it was only a matter of time. Inglefield then asked Mudge what he proposed to do with me. He said he would like me as Brigade Major. Inglefield said he had already written to Cairo to ask for someone else but did not know yet if he would be available; besides, he might quite possibly want me for another Battalion. Subject to these uncertainties he would not object to me becoming Brigade Major. The whole position is rather perplexing. I don't a bit want to be Brigade Major, still less do I wish to become a kind of Flying Dutchman, condemned to wander about without end from one job to another, as, if I went to another Battalion, no doubt someone would turn up again with another prior claim. Besides, Mudge is the only Brigadier worth anything in the Division, and some of the Battalions are appalling. One of the Brigades is made up of three Battalions of Essex and one of Hampshire Territorials and it is difficult to say which are the dirtiest, worst disciplined or most slovenly. I am in two minds to ask Mudge to get me sent back to the Yeomanry.

9 January

Finally decided not to say any more to Mudge but to let things take their course, as with an old fool like Inglefield nothing can be arranged, as he forgets from one day to another what he has decided. For instance he told Lambert (whom Clutterbuck saw at Alexandria last Thursday) that he could not have this Battalion again because he had promised it to someone else! He, however, said nothing of this to Mudge and talked of Lambert returning.

Went for a long ride to Nubaria Canal which by the map seems to divide us from the Sahara. It is practically dry and one can easily walk across. The scrap with the Arabs a week ago was on our side of this canal. The desert there is not bare sand as near Cairo, but is covered with a kind of low-growing prickly scrub. Where the waters do not reach at high Nile, it is yellow sand, but where the ground is a yard or so lower and subject to the yearly flood, the soil is almost black from the deposit of fertilizing mud.

10 January

Did a few Brigade movements on the open space near the local fair to impress the natives and then did a route march. On the way back General Mudge took us by the road past the fair. The people refused to get out of the way but sat obstinately on the ground so that he had to call out to us (who were leading the Battalion) to clear a road which we did by pushing the donkeys etc. which cumbered the road on top of their owners who looked much astonished and quite furious. The young men are the most unfriendly but the old men who remember Turkish rule do not wish for its return. When it was announced in the town that the Provisional Battalion who preceded us were leaving there was great and public rejoicing. When, however, three Battalions marched in the same day to take their place we were told by an old Frenchman who lives near here that hundreds of people were literally weeping in the streets. In the afternoon I was President of a Court Martial on a man in the North Hants Regiment who had used bad language to an NCO. He pleaded guilty but this did not relieve me of the trying task of reading out the summary evidence in which three witnesses testified that when ordered to fall in to his left by the Sergt he remarked, '..... or words to that effect'! I kept my eyes fixed on the evidence and everyone else looked over each others' heads and tried to appear as solemn as the gravity of the offence warranted. Having committed five previous crimes, he will now have two months Field Punishment No. 2 in which to realize the necessity of doing what he is told. Since I came to this Brigade I have sat on Courts for 4 men of the North Hants, and there have been other cases as well. During that time I have not had to apply for a single Court Martial on any 10th London man.

11 January

Heard today that Helles has been evacuated. No one here had any idea that such an operation was going on.

Hill (the Staff Captain) came back from Alexandria having heard from the DAQMG that we should not remain here but should be withdrawn to Damanhur or Alexandria as soon as either the Eastern Mounted Brigade or SW Mounted Brigade receives horses and can replace us. It is said to be necessary to have mounted troops here instead of infantry. We are going on steadily with training the men back to the smartness which they lost at Gallipoli. The 10th London are certainly in this respect the best in the Brigade or even Division. This is due to their having been formed only a couple of years before the War, and not being cumbered with a lot of slack old Volunteer officers. Prittie (a son of Lord Dunalley) was Adjutant from the start until he was wounded at Suvla and ran the Battalion as regards discipline on lines more nearly approaching the regulars than is usual in the Territorial Force. The men are of rather a low class but are said always to do what they are told. The trouble is that they have very little initiative or dash, and almost all their officers and experienced NCOs were shot in supplying this deficiency, as they had to show themselves when moving about to tell men exactly where to go.

12 January

Telegram arrived from 54th Division to Brigade to say that Colonel Lambert was returning to take over 10th London. Nothing was said about me, but Mudge said I had better move up to Brigade HQs and act as Brigade Major until some decision is arrived at. Clutterbuck told me that the officers were like a hive of bees. Apparently they hated Lambert and on hearing of his reappointment they sent Cowley to Hill, the Staff Captain, to ask whether it could not be stopped as things were going on very smoothly and the friction which would be caused by the change would be so bad for the Battalion! Hill told me of this with some amusement this evening, adding that if only they had said so sooner Mudge might have been able to prevent the change, but that the officers who rejoined at Alexandria had at that time been not at all pleased at finding me in command. Inglefield apparently took the bit between his teeth and wouldn't listen to anyone. Hill told me that Mudge had had a terrible struggle to prevent either Lambert or my being transferred to command the other (11th) London Battalion. The present Colonel (Windsor) has commanded them since August and is quite efficient, so that his supersession would have been absolutely unjust and is a good example of the dotage of Inglefield. Mudge did not of course tell me about this but I suppose he agreed to the present solution rather than upset two Battalions. It is just possible that instead of becoming Brigade Major I may be sent back to the Suffolk Yeomanry. The arrival of Lambert is really very unfair to Ford Moore who by the Army list is junior to me but three weeks senior to Lambert. Undoubtedly Ford Moore would have succeeded to the Battalion without anyone being brought in from outside if he had not been hit by three bullets last August and thus been absent when the original vacancy for which Lambert was brought in took place.

13 January

Lambert arrived last night in time for dinner, and I am moving this morning up to Brigade Headquarters pending an answer as to whether my appointment as Brigade Major is sanctioned. Ford Moore came this morning at an early hour saying that he did not mind serving under me as there was no question of seniority, but that Lambert became a Major three weeks after he did and that he strongly objects to being passed over. I told him there was nothing to be done but he said he would this morning lay his case before Mudge.

Moved up to Brigade Headquarters. Rode with General Mudge in the morning. In the afternoon there was a strong SSW wind and dust storm.

14 January

We went for a route march of about 10 miles. At the village of Kone El Akhdar the General was invited to partake of lunch with the Mayor and the Manager of the Belgian company which farms the land. The Battalions were therefore sent on while we ate native bread and pastry, marmalade, honey, butter, cheese, etc. I have plenty of work to do, probably as there has been no Brigade Major since Russell left us at Alexandria and arrears have accumulated.

15 January

We rode, a cavalcade of 14 officers, some mounted police and 15 cyclists, to Abu Matamir, a market near the edge of the cultivated land where the only road eastward across the desert between Cairo and Alexandria comes in. There must have been quite 4000 to 5000 Arabs and the local police led us round through the crowd so that they might see that the British still hold Egypt. It is said that no British troops have ever before been to Abu Matamir. We then rode along the Nubaria Canal, now dry, which divides the desert from the town. We visited two police outposts on the way. The native police and 'Coastguards' patrol along the Nubaria Canal to warn us of any trouble and to prevent smuggling. Clutterbuck tells me that Ford Moore wrote a letter objecting to being passed over for the command of 10th London and that Lambert had to take it in to the General to forward to the Division. We got back to Hosh Isa at 5.15 p.m. after a 30-mile ride. A telegram had arrived to say we are to be relieved here next Wednesday by Mounted Troops and to return to Alexandria. I am sorry, as the conditions here are rather interesting, and the deep sand of Sidi Bishr is unsuitable for training the men.

17 January

Hill went on to Alexandria to lay out camp and to arrange for our arrival on Wednesday. Crawford (the Transport Officer) went to see Railway authorities at Damanhur. On his return got orders for the move on Wednesday.

18 January

Brigade sports in the afternoon. The most important natives of Hosh Isa came to tea and we fed them on cake and chocolate. On the Peninsula one would have given anything for cake. Now, however, Hill, the General and I are so overwhelmed with arrears of parcels that there is great competition to get them eaten, for which purpose the natives were very useful.

Baggage went off by train at 6.20 on the morning of the 19th.

19 January

11th and part of 10th Londons went at 10 a.m. and the rest of the 10th with Northamptons were to go by special at 12.30. The special, however, didn't turn up until past 3 as the Colonel of the incoming Battalion refused to go on from Damanhur until he had all his baggage trans-shipped to the light railway. I had therefore to pack off 250 by the ordinary train at

1 and wire to Damanhur for the Bedfords to fill up the special later train. The General waited until the new Battalion arrived to hand over, and we and the remainder of the Northants got off in the train which brought them.

The 21st Battalion of Rifle Brigade who relieved us are one of five Battalions who have been created from the National Reserve and attached to the Rifle Brigade for administration. They are old men, three out of four wearing medals. The CO looks about 70 but said he was 65. He is a nice old boy, formerly in the Indian Army. We got to Alexandria at 7.15. Inglefield refused to let us have trams to shorten the march of 6 miles through heavy sand to Sidi Bishr from Sidi Gabes Station, so the men had to march up with their heavy packs.

20 January

General Inglefield rode over to see General Mudge. There is as yet no decision about a Brigade Major for the Brigade, but Inglefield thought the man for whom he had applied would not be sent. On the other hand there are all the Headquarters Staff from Imbros to be fitted with new jobs, and pending this reorganization no new staff appointments will be made. Mudge, however, said that he thought it quite likely that I should be appointed. This afternoon saw Frank Goldsmith. Tomkin in hospital with jaundice and Jackson is ADC to Sir Alexander Godley so the Regiment is now at peace but very dull. General Hodgson told Frank two days ago that Inglefield had asked whether he had any objection to my doing Brigade Major, and Hodgson had said that he wanted me back, but did not mind my remaining with Mudge temporarily. I told Mudge this and he said for some reason Inglefield is very much afraid of Hodgson. I told Mudge that I hated the idleness of 2nd-in-command, that in England one had a few odd jobs such as running the canteen but that now there was absolutely nothing to do.

21 January

Saw General Hodgson. He said he hoped to get me back when they received horses. I told him I was quite happy as Mudge's Brigade Major and that under existing conditions there was really nothing for a 2nd-in-command to do. Inglefield had told him that Hay, the original Brigade Major (who went home soon after Mudge took over on de Winton being wounded), was returning. Mudge this afternoon was astonished when I told him this, and said Inglefield had never mentioned such a possibility. As far as he knows Hay is still in England.

Hodgson further said that Inglefield had talked of giving me an Essex

Battalion. I told him that that was a job which I should hate, as they are a very bad lot in that (161st) Brigade, and the Brigadier is not to be compared with Mudge from all accounts, though I have not personally come across him. As a matter of fact I don't feel very anxious about this, as Inglefield first talked of the same thing to Mudge, when first Lambert was heard of as out of hospital and nothing happened, so by now someone else must have been got for the battalion in question.

22 January

Inglefield came over to see Mudge. He had not even sent my name on as Acting Brigade Major and told Mudge that no pay attached to the job until after a fortnight. When Mudge told him this rule only applied to Generals, Inglefield promised to send Mudge's recommendation forward which he had kept for over a week. Mudge says that now I shall at least be considered for the job before an outsider is put in, but that there are of course many Staff Officers from Imbros now to be provided with jobs. Inglefield is much worried over the Lambert/Ford Moore controversy and of course tries to put the blame on Mudge.

24 January

Colonel da Costa (GSO 54th Division) returned from Cairo and told General Mudge he had on Saturday seen papers going through for the approval for the appointment of a Major Schuster, Liverpool Regiment, as Brigade Major for this Brigade. He is now GSO 3 to some division at Salonika and Mudge thinks he may refuse or rather get his General to say he cannot spare him. Although Brigade Majors get more pay than 3rd grade General Staff Officers, and it is therefore technically promotion, many soldiers are said to prefer Divisional to Brigade work. If he were to refuse, Inglefield might put forward my name, as Hodgson and the EMB are leaving for Tel El Kebir on Thursday and he won't be any longer, as now, staying at the same hotel as Tanglefoot and able to tell him he wants me back. I suppose we shall hear nothing definite for several days.

25 January

During the night it began to blow. At 1.30 my tent was flapping so violently that I went out and hammered in the tent pegs until they were buried in the sand. The wind was full of blinding dust and although the floor of my tent was shut everything inside was covered with a layer of dust. The gale became so violent that I got very little sleep, but finally dropped off just before daylight. Murray called me at 7 and said that many tents were down, including the General's. I went out and found him sitting in the cook's little shelter wrapped up in a blanket and looking pretty bad as he has a touch of malaria. The mess tent having blown down, we got a cold breakfast in my tent but swallowed as much sand as food. We went for a route march of about 9 miles in the morning. There were several very cold rain and hail storms. On the way back we met Inglefield.

In. 'Why didn't you go the way you said you would in your programme of work?'

Mudge. 'I never put down where I was going then because I didn't know, but I told da Costa yesterday we should be on this road.

In. 'You're wrong. I looked particularly and you said you were going along the beach.'

Mudge. 'That must have been General Ward's programme as I know he intended to take his Brigade there.'

In. 'Not at all. You both wrote you were going on the beach and I remarked that you would meet.'

No doubt the infernal old fool had looked at General Ward's programme twice over. It must be an odious position for Mudge to be under such an incompetent and offensive old beast. Inglefield is hardly on speaking terms with either of his other two Brigadiers and is only friendly with Mudge. In the early days after the Anzac landing when they were all suffering frightfully from thirst having only a pint per head, Inglefield used to have a bath of fresh water every day. He came up to one of the Battalions who had the previous day lost most of their officers, and swore at them because they hadn't leapt to their feet and saluted him. He had them all woken up from the first sleep they'd had for about three days, so that they should all salute him. I hear that he is not at all in his dotage as I imagined. Kensington told me that he was always proverbial for dunderheaded incompetence, and when he knew him 15 years ago was always known as Tanglefoot.

Many trees, lamp-posts, etc., have been uprooted by the gale. Hill, Harding (the Machine-Gun Officer), Hood (the Captain), and I went down to photograph the waves on the rocks. They were a most glorious sight, but our cameras got so wet that I fear the photos will be a failure. There is one place where there is a kind of entrance cut in the rocks on one side about 20 feet wide, through which the waves break into a rock pool beyond. I foolishly went on to the rocks on one side not realizing that the squeezing of the water to get through the narrow opening would make it rise higher on each side. A great wave struck me on the chest and carried me off my feet, very nearly over the wall of rock into the pool behind. As it was I got off with a black eye, a square inch of skin off my cheek, most of the skin off my knuckles and knees, and a thorough soaking. Never have I seen such magnificent waves. The other three all got wet up to their waists but, being 20 yards behind, were warned by my experience and didn't get knocked down.

26 January

Weather better. We have all been much interested in Sir Ian Hamilton's last dispatch. All the nonsense he puts in about collecting petrol tins for carrying water in no way excuses the precipitation and lack of preparation with which he started the Suvla enterprise. It was the business of his Staff to think about water for the troops, and they couldn't fail to remember it owing to the corresponding difficulty at Helles and Anzac of which they had known for months. There was no urgent hurry to make the attack. He admits that it was a defect that almost all the officers landing at Suvla were new to trench warfare. Why, then, were they not taken to see how things were done at Anzac or Helles? The troops meanwhile could have been landed somewhere nearby and got fit instead of coming straight off the long, overcrowded voyage from England. By waiting another month he would have avoided the sweltering heat and thus decreased the water difficulty.

If the British had succeeded in getting through and cutting the Turkish communications, the surrender of the Turkish Force and the opening of the Dardanelles would probably have been only a matter of days. September would have done quite as well as August, especially as there would by then have been time for proper preparations and an enormously increased chance of success. The whole conception, however, stands condemned in the dispatch. He talks of troops being within a couple of hundred yards of the top of Chunuk Bair and 'Victory'. (I forget the exact words as our only copy of the dispatch blew away in the gale.) If Chunuk Bair was really his goal as commanding Maidos and the Turkish communications, why did he bother about Suvla at all? He had actually been sent more troops than he asked for, and, if he had concentrated his efforts on getting through from Anzac, might have succeeded. As it was he attempted an impossible task at Suvla. The ground was unknown and the maps quite unreliable. The advances elsewhere on the Peninsula, owing to the same difficulty, were made by gradual stages, troops making good one position and getting in touch all along the line before they pushed on. In the early days at Suvla Divisional Staffs did not know the whereabouts of their Brigades, and Brigades often did not know where their Battalions had got to. Normal means of communication didn't exist. There were no roads and the thickets which covered the hillsides made it impossible to see troops moving perhaps 100 yards away in the same valley. Everybody got lost and could find neither each other nor their supplies and necessary transport. No doubt Stopford, Hammersley, etc., muddled things badly, but Hamilton should have realized that he'd got dugout Generals and inexperienced troops to deal with and not have attempted what might well have proved impossible to any troops.

They probably would have done all right if they had been used for attacking Chunuk Bair over ground already pretty well known from the Anzac trenches. There is not a word of explanation of the massacre of the Yeomanry. If the 2nd Mounted Division was wanted in reserve behind Chocolate Hill they should have been taken there under cover of darkness when they need not have lost a man. Peyton is said to have realized this and to have asked to be allowed to move before dawn but this was refused, and his Division were shot down for no military purpose of any kind.

28 January

Less wind but still enough to be unpleasant and smother everything with dust. The EMB were to have gone to Tel el Kebir tomorrow, but it has been put off, probably for at least a week or ten days. They have got four new officers and a draft of 50 men are on the way. This will bring up their strength to about 22 officers and 350 men. Now that the EMB are remaining, I am pretty sure to go back to the Suffolk Yeomanry as Hodgson is staying in the same hotel as Tanglefoot.

29 January

Orders arrived in the afternoon for our Brigade to send an officer and five men to Mena House Camp as an advance party. The Staff Captain, whose job it would nominally be, having much work in connection with reclothing the Brigade, etc., it was arranged for me to start tomorrow morning with Trew, DAAQMG, 54th Division.

30 January

Reached Cairo in time for lunch and, after going to Headquarters, went out to Mena House by a taxi and marked out with Trew the outlines of our area.

31 January

Spent most of the day laying out our camp with prismatic compass and tape measure. After settling territory and general lines of tents with officers from the 163rd Brigade, I pegged out positions for over 200 tents of our own Brigade.

1 February

Spent the day with an advance party which had arrived last night, pitching tents. About 11 p.m. General Mudge arrived. The new Brigade Major (Major Schuster, of the King's Regiment) arrived at Sidi Bishr after my departure.

2 February

Handed over everything this morning to Schuster and with many regrets said goodbye to Mudge and his Brigade. Slept the night in Cairo.

3 February

Guided Jarvis on a 12-mile route march. The Regiment must be horrified at my return with these new-fangled Infantry notions as to what is a reasonable distance to go on foot.

5 February

Very bored as 2nd-in-Command. No canteen or other means of interior economy to be seen to, no horses to look after and 20 officers in charge of 260 men. The only occupation I can think of is to refresh my German. Went in accordingly to Alexandria to try and find someone who knows the language. After being told in various places that German lessons were forbidden by *la Censure* I have at last extracted the name of a teacher from the Berlitz School and have fixed up to go and read with him.

6 February

Saw Sammy Scott, Sackville and Winterton for the first time since the evacuation of Helles. They had just spent a tedious month at Mudros and seemed delighted with Alexandria.

8 February

Went to Cairo where I saw Army Order constituting three new dismounted Brigades from the Yeomanry Brigades which landed in Gallipoli last August and September. The first two Brigades are made up of the Scottish Yeomanries and the old SW Mounted Brigade. We (the Eastern Mounted Brigade) are grafted with the SE Mounted Brigade to form the 3rd Dismounted Brigade.

The SE Mounted Brigade consists of the East and West Kent and the Sussex Yeomanries, a very nice lot. The Brigade is to be commanded by

Hodgson but we shall have a great surplus of officers even if they made us up to strength, as six Yeomanry Regiments would only then have the same number of men as an Infantry Brigade and double the number of officers.

9 February

Lunched with Clutterbuck and three of the 10th London Company Commanders. Inglefield appears to be more half-witted than ever. Clutterbuck had been in his Division and met him time after time for the last six months. Yet he came up to him yesterday and asked him to what Regiment he belonged. Clutterbuck told him '10th London'. 'What Brigade is that?' 'The 162nd.' 'What are the 163rd Brigade doing this morning?' 'I don't know.' 'Why not?' 'Because I am in the 162nd Brigade.' Inglefield then went to see Mudge and after a long talk said, 'Well now, I must be going as I want to see General Mudge.' He has only two Brigades and eight Battalions at Mena, but it is too much for his addled brain to remember them. Those who were at Helles, however, state that General Douglas* who commands the 42nd Division is even more imbecile than General Inglefield. Got word to go and see Mudge who wanted to know details as to age etc., as he was recommending me for Staff employment. Personally, I doubt if anything will come of it. Am bored stiff in Egypt and made enquiries about getting to the Persian Gulf, but this appears almost impossible from here as the expedition was organized and is being run from India. [On 10 February Guinness returned to the Suffolk Yeomanry. He had very little to do and filled his diary with speculations about his own future employment and whether his battalion would be posted to Mesopotamia or India. Eds.]

16 February (Extract from Diary written in pencil).

I go in every afternoon to Alexandria and talk German for an hour at the Berlitz School. Often I dine at one of the Clubs. The seven MPs† who came out on the *Titanic* (Sanders, Winterton, Goldsmith, Gilbert Wills, Sammy Scott and Pearson) are all here, and also Eyres Monsell who, after commanding a Monitor at the Dardanelles, became liaison officer between the Army and Navy. We dine with each other every two or three days and pass on the latest Parliamentary news which has been received.

I am apparently not at all exceptional in the ill fortune of having lost the command of the Battalion which I had at Anzac. Sanders had two of his squadron leaders taken at Helles to command Battalions, and both

†Presumably Guinness included himself in the seven.

have then come back to his Regiment since arriving here owing to the reappearance of their predecessors from Hospital.

14 March (Extract from letter to his wife, Lady Evelyn Guinness).

We go to Suez next Thursday night, to the Ninth Corps. The Corps General (Davies) is said to be good, but the General of the 42nd Division to which we are attached is said to run a close race with Tanglefoot for inefficiency and to be an objectionable bounder into the bargain. He had himself photographed in a tree in Gallipoli, and it was published in the papers broadcast for his advertisement 'How Sir William Douglas observes the doings of his brave troops.' The tree of course was down in a valley, and gave no view of either trenches, troops or Turks. I hope that we may only be attached to his Division for administration and not as a permanency. It seems criminal to leave such people in control of the lives of tens of thousands of troops. It is the English idea of compromise and never making scandals or being unpleasant to people. It's all very well for the people in control who sit at home no doubt but a very wasteful way of making war.

4 April (Extract from letter to his wife).

Winterton, Sammy Scott, Sackville, etc., etc. who were with them on the Peninsula, crab the 42nd (Lancashire) Division. They, however, covered themselves with glory at the 'Lancashire Landing' and it was not their fault that all their best officers were killed off. I cannot believe that Douglas can be as inefficient as Tanglefoot, and am not sure that those who crab him are very good judges as they seem obsessed with the snobbish idea that Infantry are not as good as Cavalry; this may be true under the false standards of peacetime but certainly the despised 'foot-slogger' is more than ever 'Queen of the Battle' in comparison with mounted troops in modern warfare.

16 April (Extract from a letter to his wife).

(On hearing that Jarvis had been passed over for command of a brigade and was returning to the Suffolk Yeomanry):

It means of course that in all probability I shall remain for ever second-in-command of this Regiment. If one's Colonel is considered unfit for promotion, and has the extraordinary health of the Jarvis family there is no opportunity ever to do anything but look on, an extremely unenviable position when things are done so sloppily as they are by Freddy.

It is annoying, too, to feel that one is wasting this period of such intense opportunity for so many, in the prime of one's life doing absolutely nothing, with not even the responsibility of a Second Lieutenant who at least has his troop to look after. I have now been a Major since 1903, and it is rather hopeless to feel that through bad luck one is stranded in a position where one cannot conceivably have the chance even of failing. Page Croft, a bounder of the most appalling description who is one of the stupidest men in the House of Commons, only became a Major in 1914 in the Hertfordshire Territorials and, though never a professional soldier or even in the South African War, is now a Brigadier-General!

27 April

Frank Goldsmith and I went down to Port Tewfik for dinner, it being very hot and dusty in camp. We there met George Lloyd* who happened to be passing through to take ship tomorrow to Bombay and Basra where he has been sent as Intelligence Officer. He dined with us. His knowledge of Turkish, Arabic and the Near East has given him an extraordinarily interesting time. First he was sent to Egypt and, according to his account, practically created Maxwell's Intelligence organization. Hundreds of refugees from Syria were told that they could only land in Egypt on condition that they first went back to Damascus, Jerusalem, etc., and gleaned information. They were called for at the same places as they were landed on certain nights and so perfect was their system that Maxwell knew the name and commander of every Turkish Regiment which was brought against him. The Turks, out of several hundreds of such agents, only caught about 16. After the attack on the Canal he went as Birdwood's Intelligence Officer and remained from the original landing until the very end with one interruption of very great interest. He was sent to Russia to work out plans of cooperation. From Gallipoli to Archangel took him only 12 days including one spent in London at the War Office. The cruiser which took him from Scotland to Archangel was blown up by a mine two hours after he was landed. He spent five days staying with the Czar and then went to the Army Headquarters in Galicia. He came back via Sweden and Norway and there met a Danish Member of Parliament who was friendly to England and who was on his way with permission to visit the British trenches in France and to act as counterblast to the pro-Germans of a party who had visited their trenches. He said that he saw little sign of real want in Germany though the richest people have only black bread and no butter. The people were extraordinarily confident and thought they were winning. The Government, however, knew they couldn't win a decisive success and were already probably convinced that they were beaten. He told us details of Stanley Wilson's capture with letters. Though specially ordered not to do so, he and one of our military attachés embarked on a Greek ship and actually entered their military rank on the passenger list. Being on a Greek ship they were never searched by the submarine. It merely ordered by signal the captain to come on board. There was plenty of time to hide or burn the papers while the Captain went off in a rowing boat, but Wilson just threw an unweighted dispatch box overboard. Seeing the names of the British officers, the submarine commander sent the boat back to fetch them. After going on board they again returned to the Greek ship to fetch their baggage. It was a dead calm sea, and by the time they returned, the dispatch box floated up to the submarine and was fished out. Unfortunately, it contained a letter from Whittal, the best-known British merchant in Smryna, mentioning by name two of his employees who at the risk of their lives had remained in Constantinople to help us. Poor Whittal is nearly mad to think that by relying on a King's Messenger he has probably caused these two men to be hanged. In carrying dispatches, they should be left in the engine room to be put on the furnace immediately a submarine comes along.

[Lloyd also told us of his days before the outbreak of the War. He happened to see Paul Cambon [French Ambassador in London 1898–1920], who is apparently a great friend, and Cambon could hardly speak to him. *'Vous nous avez lachés. Je n'ose dire à mon Gouvernement ce que Grey m'a dit aujourd'hui. C'est l'anéantissement pour la France. Ça se pourrait bien que le Gouvernement se trouverait forcé à céder aux demandes allemandes.'* 'But, M. Cambon, exactly what are our obligations?' 'Nothing on paper.' (Grey had said that anything written would embarrass him in the House of Commons.) 'But for ten years every plan of the French General Staff has been laid before your War Office and on your definite guarantee of our Northern Coast our fleet left the North Sea and is now based on Toulon. We can bring the ships back, perhaps, but how are we to bring back their stores and munitions?' Grey told me that England cannot stand by her obligations, as your party would not support the Government. 'That, M. Cambon, is untrue. The Unionists to a man are in favour of supporting you in resistance to Germany.' Cambon merely shrugged his shoulders; 'What do I know of your parties and their entanglements?' Lloyd went off to Charlie Beresford* and told him what Cambon had said, begging him to see Benckendorff. Beresford heard the same story from him and Lloyd was told by Sir Henry Wilson,* Director of Military Operations at the War Ofice, that Asquith refused even to delay the usual August dispersal of troops. No one of influence in London was on our side. He tried everyone he could think of on the telephone, Lord Lansdowne* was at Bowood, Austen Chamberlain* at Manchester, A.J.B.* and Curzon* at the seaside, and Bonar Law* down playing tennis at Wargrave with Goulding* and F. E. Smith.* Lloyd wired to Austen and went off by motor to Wargrave with Beresford. He waited an age for Bonar Law to finish his set, then at last explained what had happened. Bonar Law was for doing nothing, saying he had told Asquith the Unionists would give him every support. Finally he consented to go to London chiefly because it looked bad for no one to be on the spot representing the Unionist party. Lloyd met Austen just before midnight at the station and went with him to the 'Shadow Cabinet' at Lansdowne House. Sir Henry Wilson there corroborated the inference drawn by Lloyd from his talk with Cambon. A letter was then drafted not merely promising support, as in the letter afterwards published, but saying that they would hold the Government responsible if they failed to carry out their obligations towards France. This letter was immediately taken round to Asquith, whose Secretary, however, said that he was in bed and could not be wakened. The letter was therefore (I think) only delivered the next morning.

Towards the end of April I made up my mind to go home on leave and to look out for some more useful form of employment. Jarvis, having returned to the Regiment after a fortnight's command of the Brigade, showed that he was considered unfit for promotion, which meant that my own prospects were to continue indefinitely as his understudy and to look on at the Regiment being rather sloppily run without any power to improve matters. When Jarvis was away from the Regiment I found them capable of drilling extraordinarily well. No one, however, could drill smartly when every second word of command was wrong and when the CO never by any chance corrected mistakes. There was obviously no opening for a Senior Major in Egypt as no casualties were taking place in that Force and in the rare cases where vacancies might occur to bring in an outsider would be an unlikely course, as every Battalion or Regiment out in Egypt had plenty of Senior Officers who during 20 months of war had developed strong claims.

8 May

Left Suez by a ship of the Bibby Line which reached Marseilles on *15 May*. On reaching London I went to the War Office and saw General Sir Edward Bethune,* Director General of the Territorial Force. I explained that I was keen on getting to the Western Front and he told me that there should be little difficulty in being transferred unattached to the BEF. He said that that very morning the Adjutant General (Sir Nevil Macready*) had told him to wire out to Egypt with a view to collecting a few Senior Officers who were not required with the Dismounted Yeomanry Regiments, and to send them out as Seconds-in-Command to France to understudy for vacancies in the commands of Battalions which were of course taking place there in large numbers.

About this time, however, a complication arose in politics. After the Easter week rebellion Ireland as a whole had shown every evidence of disgust with Sinn Fein methods. Asquith, however, went over and so pandered to the rebels that the country suddenly realized that the rebellion had done more for the cause of Irish independence in a fortnight than had been achieved by fifty years of constitutional agitation. Asquith on his return appointed Lloyd George* to find a settlement of the Irish difficulty and with his usual adroitness Lloyd George began to offer bribes and baits all round, and to exploit the state of feeling in America for the purpose of compelling all parties in Great Britain to surrender their convictions on the union. I find that all opposition to the immediate grant of Home Rule had been entirely silenced in the House of Commons and, feeling that in view of the Irish character it would be disastrous to grant Home Rule apparently as a reward for armed rebellion, gave notice that I wished to raise this question at the Unionist War Committee. Carson* was then Chairman of this Committee, having left the Government the previous autumn. A special meeting was called on *20 June* for discussion of my Resolution. Before the business began, however, Carson got up and stated that he considered it most inopportune to discuss the Irish question at all and made it quite clear that he was not in favour of a settlement. He said further that he did not think the question was within the scope of the Committee's business. This appeared to me pretty hot in view of the fact that, through Terrell, the Secretary of the Committee, he had invited me to bring the matter up there rather than to call a special meeting of members interested, as I had thought of doing. Obviously the idea was to suppress my opposition by his authority backed up by the Unionist War Committee which had so far followed him implicitly in everything that he proposed. In view of his ruling that the matter was out of order, I had no alternative but to say that I would not of course bring it forward at that meeting but would hold another meeting an hour afterwards at which I hoped as many members of the Unionist War Committee as possible would be present. We accordingly held the meeting to which 42 members came, and it was decided that we would send out a letter summoning other Unionist members to a larger meeting to be held two days later. At this meeting we also passed a Resolution calling on Bonar Law to consult the Unionist Party before committing them to Home Rule, and pointing out that there appeared to be a considerable danger that we were to be presented with a *fait accompli* as the result of negotiations in which the Unionist Party had not in any way been consulted. At the second meeting held on *22 June* we got Sir Robert Finlay to take the chair and Bridgeman* (one of the Whips) conveyed an undertaking from Bonar Law that he would consult the party before committing it to any alteration in the Act of Union. I wrote Bonar Law a letter conveying the sense of the meeting which he answered on the 24th, saying that he had read it 'with great care' and 'I thoroughly appreciate your views. You may rest assured that the party will not be definitely committed until it has had an opportunity of expressing its wishes.'

About this time I was notified by the War Office that I had been selected as one of a batch of officers to be sent to France unattached and there to be posted as Second-in-Command of an Infantry Battalion, but, owing to the developments of the Irish question, I was obliged to ask them to postpone my departure.

I got in touch with Midleton* and Salisbury* and we formed the Imperial Unionist Association with a view to fighting the Government on their proposed surrender to Sinn Fein. Rupert Gwynne* became Joint Secretary with me in the Commons, and by the end of June we had enrolled more than 100 Members of Parliament.

Walter Long* was wobbling about this time and received us at the Local Government Board on *4 July* when he made a long statement of his position and consulted us as to whether he should leave the Government or not.

On *Friday, 7 June* Bonar Law held the party meeting which we had demanded at 11 a.m. at the Carlton Club, when some very plain speaking took place. We found a good deal of satisfaction in speeches by Walter Long and Lord Lansdowne, but Austen Chamberlain, Bonar Law and Carson were all for settlement, apparently on any terms. After adjourning for lunch, we re-assembled and our party leaders must have left the meeting with a realization that there was no chance of their carrying out any Irish settlement under present conditions except after a hot Parliamentary fight and probably at the cost of completely breaking up the Unionist party. I need not go at any further length into the fate of the Irish settlement for which Lloyd George was working. In view of the opposition which we developed, we caused sufficient delay to the production of the concrete proposals to enable Irish opinion to develop, and finally Redmond, at the *end of July*, repudiated the settlement on the grounds that the proposals did not carry out what the Irish Nationalists insisted on as an irreducible minimum.

On *7 August* I left Southampton for France, landing at le Havre at 7 a.m. on the morning of *8 August*. They could tell me nothing at Havre as to my destination, and sent me on for orders to the Base at Rouen. I remained there until *12 August*, attending lectures and getting the latest instruction as to gas, etc., which was of course entirely new to me after my Egyptian experience.

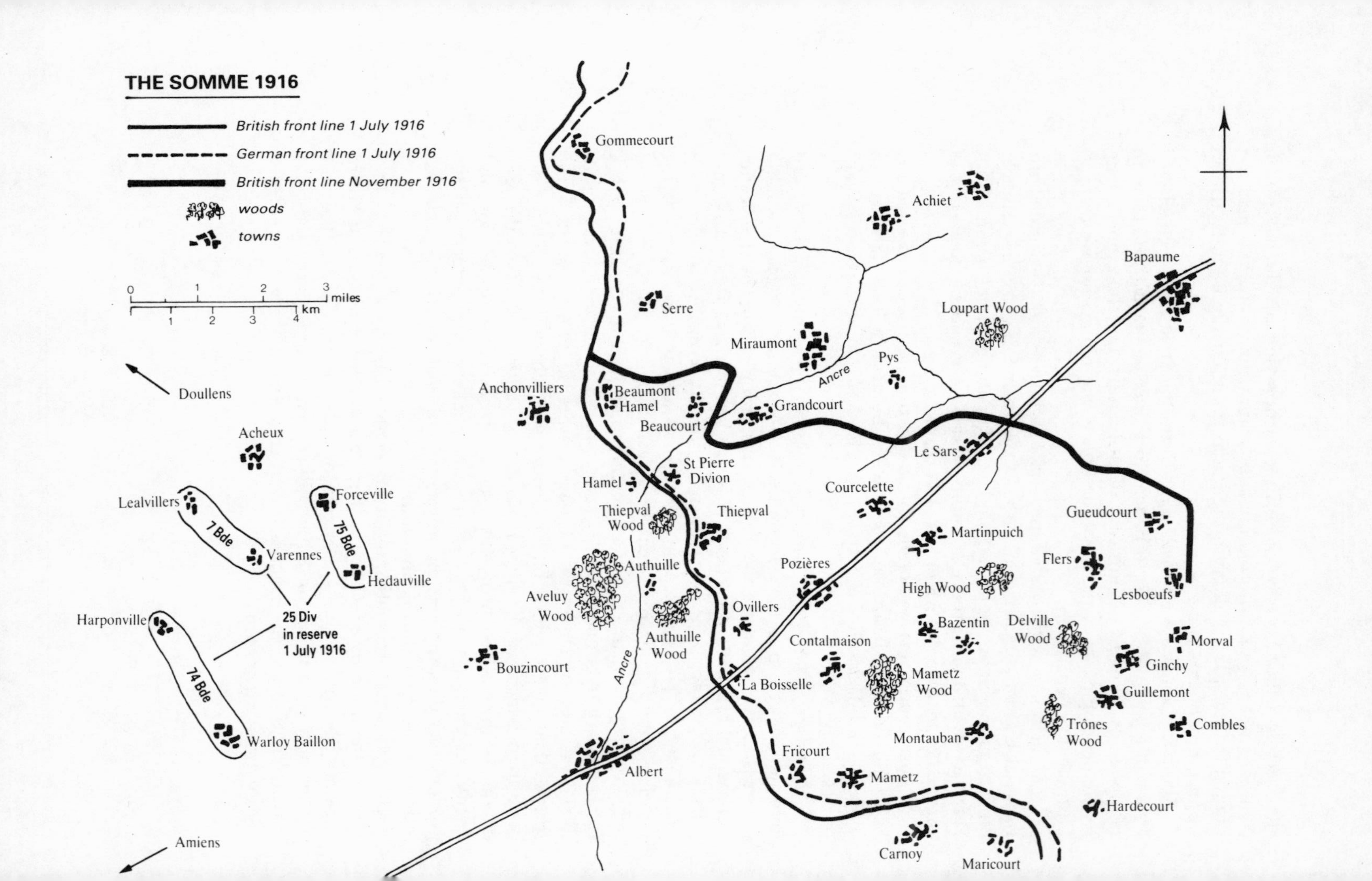
THE SOMME 1916
British front line 1 July 1916
German front line 1 July 1916
British front line November 1916
woods
towns
0
1
2
3
miles
1
2
3
4
km
Doullens
Amiens
Acheux
Lealvillers
7 Bde
Varennes
Forceville
75 Bde
Hedauville
Harponville
74 Bde
Warloy Baillon
25 Div
in reserve
1 July 1916
Bouzincourt
Anchonvilliers
Gommecourt
Serre
Miraumont
Achiet
Loupart Wood
Bapaume
Beaumont
Hamel
Beaucourt
Grandcourt
Ancre
Pys
Le Sars
Hamel
St Pierre
Divion
Thiepval
Wood
Thiepval
Courcelette
Martinpuich
Gueudcourt
Flers
Lesboeufs
Aveluy
Wood
Authuille
Authuille
Wood
Pozières
High Wood
Ovillers
Contalmaison
Bazentin
Delville
Wood
Morval
Ginchy
Guillemont
Combles
Mametz
Wood
La Boisselle
Trônes
Wood
Montauban
Fricourt
Mametz
Albert
Hardecourt
Carnoy
Maricourt

9 August (Extract from Diary note made at Rouen)

I am staying at the Poste Hotel but went out early to the camp to see the OC and Adjutant who were out when I called yesterday. I found that the only thing which I had to do before going to the front was to be gassed. I therefore drew a couple of helmets and went up to the School of Instruction where after a lecture we put them on and walked through a covered trench full of Phosgene. Although I got none of the gas, I nearly suffocated myself inside my helmet as I found it very difficult to breathe as one should, in through the nose and out through the valve which one holds between one's teeth. I suppose since my operation my nose has become so clear that it is exceptionally difficult for me to breathe through my mouth. Afterwards we took off our helmets and walked through the gas given off by tear shells which made one's eyes water for about five minutes but had no further ill effects.

I found that there are various courses of lectures going on at the school, and though Field Officers are not supposed to attend them I arranged with the Commandant to do so while I am here as a good many things such as bombs have been considerably improved since my experience at Anzac.

Everybody here seems very optimistic about the war. They say the Germans are at the end of their reserves and will either have to shorten their line or before long get it pierced.

13 August

Reached railhead at Belle Eglise soon after dawn, with instructions to join the 11th Cheshires, but no further information beyond that they were in the 25th Division. I fortunately found in the train at Rouen Kincaid Smith who used to be with me in the House of Commons. We telephoned up to the 25th Division for transport to be sent for our kits, and then walked over from the station to Louvencourt, a little town nearby, to get an omelette for breakfast at the little inn there. Finally I got so impatient waiting at the station that I walked up to my destination, leaving my kit to be picked up when the cart should arrive. It was a scorching hot day and I had a very thirsty six-mile walk along a dusty road to Authies, where I found the Headquarters of the 75th Brigade. I there saw the Staff Captain, Urwick, who told me that no information had been sent of my being posted to the 11th Cheshires. Their CO having been killed a short time before, they had just been taken over by Colonel W. K. Evans of the Manchester Regiment, and as they also had a newly-appointed Second-in-Command, it appeared that a mistake had been made in sending me, and the Staff Captain went off to find the Brigadier (Brig. Gen. E. St. J. Pratt of the Durham Light Infantry). On his return he told me that Pratt said I was to go as Second-in-Command to the 11th Cheshires as the present Second-in-Command was not satisfactory. I then walked about a mile to find the 11th Cheshires who were occupying huts and tents in a wood. Evans there told me the whole situation and that the present Second-in-Command had only been with them a few days, but was quite unsuitable, being generally in a muddled state from drinking too much whisky. He told me that for the moment I should just be attached without any particular job pending the departure of this Second-in-Command.

The 11th Cheshires are in a very disorganized state. They only came out of the trenches four days ago and since the beginning of the offensive last month they have lost 75% of their strength. They began by losing 300 men from machine-gun fire in a few seconds in the original attack on Thiepval.[7] That disaster seems to have been the result of very bad staff work as they never got any orders as to the time of attack until 2 hours after it should have been and they 'went over' long after any surprise effect was any longer possible when they had seen the troops on their flanks make their attack. After this Thiepval affair they had been pulled out and then had further unfortunate experiences about Aveluy Wood where their then CO, Aspinall, had been killed. As a result there are only two officers now with the Battalion who had been with them on 1 July and the greater part of the officers and men have recently joined from various sources. The 11th Cheshires are one of the original new Army Battalions 'of the first 100,000'. Aspinall was formerly in the 15th Hussars and appeared to have made the 11th Cheshires pretty efficient but got himself cordially disliked by all ranks in the process. The officers of the Battalion now hardly know each other by name. Each Company messes separately and Evans wants at once to constitute a Battalion Mess while we are out of the line so as to try and remedy this state of affairs. The whole of the 25th Division seems to be in very much the same state as we are. General Bainbridge* who commands them only took them over from General Doran just before the present offensive and had not had the opportunity of training them. He has been very active in ungumming (i.e. sacking) many of the Brigade and Senior officers and Pratt has only had this Brigade for a few days. It is a curious coincidence that the Brigade Major, also quite new, is a Sapper called Martel* whom I met a few weeks ago at Elveden where he was laying out the ground for the new engine of warfare (i.e. the tank) which is there being tested. He is a great boxer and was Army Champion. He seems also to have done very well in command of a Field Company RE, having already got a DSO and MC.

14 August

Day was spent in training under Company officers. The officers seem a very mixed lot, most of them very uncivilized. There is one very nice Company Commander, Nares, a regular of the Cheshire Regiment who has lately been sent there after being badly wounded. Except for him they are rather an uncouth lot.

15 August

Marched in the early morning for about 6 miles to Raincheval where we were billeted. I shared a room with the present Second-in Command, quite a pleasant person who was formerly in a Cavalry Regiment and who was sent here by the favour of his old CO who now commands an Army Corps. His nerves, however, are certainly in a very jumpy state which may or may not be due to drink. He is to leave us 'on account of his health'.

15 August (Extract from Diary note)

Besides this Major and the CO, who are older than I, all the rest of the officers are boys between eighteen and twenty-five. All the intermediate generation have apparently been killed off. They are quite a nice lot but necessarily deficient in military knowledge.

16 August

The Second-in-Command handed over everything to me and departed. Towards evening it began to rain in torrents. I have become responsible for the Battalion Mess and am starting a Battalion Canteen, not with a view to making a profit for the Battalion funds, but rather to let the men have things at as cheap a price as possible when up in the trenches and out of reach of the larger Canteens to which they can go in the back areas. Those of the men who have been through the last weeks of fighting seemed very confident and say that the German is no longer the man he was. He will not now face our artillery fire, but lives in deep dugouts 25 feet below the earth in some cases. These tunnelled dwellings take, of course, a long time to dig, and if we could only take his last line of these he would have no means of escaping from our very heavy artillery fire. Many of the recent failures have been due to the over-keenness of our troops who, thinking them to be empty, have gone on far beyond the last line of German trenches directly after the curtain of artillery fire has lifted. The Germans have then emerged from the safety of their deep dugouts and cut off the attacking troops, being free from any bombardment owing to the uncertainty of our artillery of the exact positions held by either side. It is generally thought there is a fair chance of wearing through this year as we are undoubtedly knocking out many machine guns, and it is with these weapons and not with any weight of Infantry that the Germans now hold their trenches.

17 August

At 2 p.m. we got orders to be ready to move at 4.30, and marched about 6 miles to Forceville, where we occupied some very delightful billets.

19 August

Went on only about a couple of miles to Hedauville where we were in tents and huts and billets, all of them extremely dirty. The cleanliness and sanitation of these places through which troops are constantly passing on their way to and from the line are enforced by Town Majors. In this case the position is filled by a very inefficient 2nd Lieutenant. It would be an excellent reform to bring out some of the older officers who are unfit for the trenches and give them this work, on the efficiency of which the comfort of troops is largely dependent. Two Battalions of our Brigade are now bivouacked in Aveluy Wood and go up every night to dig trenches in front of the line. We are working hard at training. Even on Sunday there is little relaxation and we parade from 7–8, 9.15–10.30 and 11–12.45. On weekdays the afternoons as well are fully occupied.

21 August

Great encouragement is drawn from the attack carried out near here a couple of nights ago. Although four Battalions went over there were only 300 British casualties and, apart from Germans killed and wounded, 400 prisoners were taken. Although these were of a very good German Division, they put up very little fight. Their morale seems very bad and they say that they are left in the trenches for days without any rations and that the rear services don't worry about the men in the trenches but leave them unrelieved until most of them are blown to pieces. There is an abominable noise of bombardment which is especially disturbing at night, but I suppose one will soon get used to it.

THE BATTLE OF THE ANCRE HEIGHTS 13 September – 11 November 1916

Front line 1 July 1916
Front line 13 September 1916
Front line 11 November 1916
trenches
75 Bde *British positions on 21 October 1916*

0 1000 2000 yds
km 1

Beaumont Hamel
Grandcourt
Pys
Ancre
Le Sars
chalk pits
Hamel
mill
St Pierre Divion
10 Cdn Bde
11 Cdn Bde
farm
4 Cdn Div
Stuff trench
Regina trench
53 Bde
quarry post
117 Bde
Crucifix Corner
Schwaben redoubt
116 Bde
Stuff redoubt
75 Bde
74 Bde
18 Div
Courcelette
Zollern trench
25 Div
39 Div
Thiepval
Zollern redoubt
sugar factory
II CORPS
Wonderwork
Hohenzollern trench
Martinpuich
Aveluy Wood
5 ARMY
Authuille
Pozières
High Wood

22 August

Moved up early in the day to bivouac in Aveluy Wood. The weather was very showery, otherwise our new abode would be quite pleasant. To avoid casualties our men are dotted about the wood in small parties. Battalion Headquarters live on the back edge of the wood on the opposite side of the valley, two or three hundred yards away. There are many guns, some of them French 75mms, mixed with some heavy British howitzers. Day and night there is an ear-splitting din and one's candle is continually flickering with the concussions. The Boche fairly frequently shells these gun positions but a very large proportion of his shells do not explode. Actually in our wood they put very few shells. We are so hidden in the trees that they probably realize how little return they could expect from shelling so large a wood. In the evening I went up with a working party which was digging new 'parallels' or assembly trenches just in front of our line. The parties only consisted of about 50 men each and were working in different parts of the lines under their own officers, so there was really nothing for me to do except to look out the lie of the land. We first went down to a Royal Engineer dump on the right lying north and south from the eastern fringe of Aveluy Wood. Royal Engineer NCOs there met our parties to guide them up to the trenches and to show them what work was to be done. North-east of Aveluy Wood we crossed by a causeway the River Ancre which here spreads into swamps about a quarter of a mile wide. We then got into a communication trench which took us by a steep climb about 150 feet above the river. The communication trench ran on through what must have been a thick wood, though it now looks like a colossal harrow inverted, the trees being bare poles, and not one in fifty having any top. There being no moon, one could only see by the flash of the guns and star shells, but by these means it was quite easy to read the names painted up on the corners of the trenches. The fire trench was empty as its garrison was pushed forward to cover our men who were deepening the two new lines of assembly trenches which are being dug in front. These are reached by a new communication trench and I went along a sunken road and saw the bombing parties which lie out in front about 80 yards from the German trenches to protect the digging parties from surprise. As the Boche were also out digging in no-man's-land, no bombardment was going on while I was there, but the air overhead seemed alive with shells going to areas further back. Shortly after I left the working party the German party must have withdrawn as they began a heavy bombardment which caused our party several casualties.

23 August

The combined effect of the increased din and the wearing of a steel helmet gives me a permanent headache, but I am told that I shall get over it in time. One sees very few people except the officers of one's own Battalion. Under present conditions each Company and Battalion Headquarters necessarily mess separately. Our Mess consists of the CO (Evans), Hill, the Adjutant, the Signal Officer and the Intelligence Officer. I very much like Evans who is in command. He is a regular Major in the Manchester Regiment and only recently came to the Regiment from a Staff job with the Second Army. The Adjutant, Hill, hasn't an 'h' anywhere. In civil life he was a lecturer on Agricultural Chemistry at some Welsh University and seems to have won innumerable prizes and scholarships. He is very discontented with the favouritism alleged to be shown by the authorities both in civil life and the Army. He hates and despises all staff officers, feeling no doubt that he has far more brains himself, and says that there are many Double First men serving in the Armies who ought to be on the Staff. With all his cleverness, however, his manners are such that what the Staff might gain in brains, it would certainly lose in friction. This afternoon a terrific bombardment revealed four hitherto unsuspected rear big guns, 12 or 15 inches, which I was glad to find reduced other people's heads to the same state as mine.

24 August

Took up a gas warning to our working parties who were digging out in front of the central King's Own Yorkshire Light Infantry trench. I got back about 1 a.m. and found a Brigade wire warning me as President of a Court Martial but giving neither date, time nor place. At 4.30 a.m. another orderly found me with instructions that the Court Martial was to be this morning. The charge was malingering in that the man had counterfeited lameness on the way to the trenches for digging. The medical evidence was very clear and we gave the man 90 days Field Punishment No. 1.[8] It is rather anomalous that if a man wilfully absents himself when warned for duty in the trenches he is at the present time almost invariably shot for it, whereas if he achieves the same thing by malingering or a self-inflicted wound, he gets off quite lightly. Riding back from the Court Martial at Forceville I met for the first time Bainbridge, our Division Commander.

27 August

Yesterday we moved up to take over some support trenches. They were until recently an old British Front Line but are now so fearfully blown in that Evans induced the Brigadier to let us settle in Authuille Wood just behind. It came on to blow and rain and as the wood contained nothing in the way of shelter except slits in the ground, the men had a beastly night. Hill, Evans and I managed to cover in a hole which must at some time have been dug for a gun and, except for the little frogs which kept jumping on to one's head, spent quite a good night. This afternoon I went up to see the trench where we are to dig day and night with a view to fixing up details of the work and reliefs. I took up with me Nares, a subaltern called Anderson and some orderlies who would act as guides to the digging when it should come to the turn of the other Companies to supply them. We went through some very dilapidated trenches newly captured from the Boches a few days ago. There was a good deal of shelling on the way and a shrapnel took off the top of Anderson's head and put a bullet through the thigh of one of the orderlies. We all got covered with earth and Nares got a black eye from a large clod. We found a stretcher party nearby to whom we handed over the wounded orderly and then went on to the Company Headquarters of the Border Battalion which is holding the line. The Company Commander turned out to be a man who had been to us during our shortage of officers but who had just gone back to his own Battalion. He told us it was a very nasty place and that his Company had had 40 casualties from bombardment last night. The whole place was littered with Boche corpses and, owing to the great heat, very unpleasant. When we got back we found the medical officer, a very nice fellow called Loy who had only joined us two or three days before, and also the Bombing Officer (Salisbury) were missing. They had gone out in the evening to find a place near a bivouac in which to store bombs. We made a thorough search for them round the camp but with no result. During the night I supervised the stacking, as they were brought up by carrying parties, of several thousand bombs. We put these in a covered-in store which we had found and in the morning we found the bodies of Loy and Salisbury within about five yards of where we had been standing. The carrying parties had great luck; while they were actually drawing their bombs to bring them up here, a heavy shell took off the head of one of the men without exploding. If it had gone off it would probably have detonated the bombs and killed anything up to 40 or 50 men.

Lots of rain, which is trying, as of course none of us have any change of clothes with us.

29 August

Yesterday afternoon the 8th South Lancashires of our Brigade attacked and captured a bit of German trench but were afterwards driven out again. We were kept hard at work supplying carrying parties with bombs, wire, pickets, etc., besides digging at the communication trench, where we had been working for the last few days. At about 3 a.m. Nares, who had taken out a party of 60 men at midnight to dig the new communication trench, reported that he could not find the trench where he was to work, as the old German trench which used to lead to it had been completely blown out of existence. I therefore went up with a fresh party starting at 4 a.m. and going up the same way as Nares and Anderson had gone up a couple of days before. The trench became more and more battered and finally disappeared altogether in a wilderness of shell holes. It was only just dawn so we were able to search in various directions to find it. Finally we struck the remains of another trench running about parallel and, working along this, eventually we got back to the original trench beyond the part where it had been bombarded out of existence. Finally we got to the place where we were to dig. I brought down with me afterwards three German prisoners who had surrendered during the night. They belonged to the German Guards Division which had a few days previously taken over the trenches opposite. They said they had had nothing to eat for two days and that our bombardment had absolutely wiped out the trench where they were. One was a nice-looking boy of about 16 although he professed to be 22. I told them that Roumania had declared war, but I don't think they believed me as they merely laughed and said they hadn't heard.

30 August

Took over part of the fire trench with one Company last night. About 10.30 further orders to provide about 500 men in small or large parties up to over 200, to carry up 7000 bombs, ammunition, pick shovels, sandbags, etc., to various dumps in or near the fire trench. Owing to the necessity of keeping intact our Company for the trenches tomorrow, and also our 8 Lewis gun teams, we couldn't provide more than about half the number demanded. While Evans thrashed out details of trench relief with McKerrow, who commands the Company going in, I went off to the Brigade Officer to explain. General Pratt said we must have out everybody, including Lewis gun personnel for all but 4 guns, going to the trenches, officers, servants, etc., and carry up the things before daylight, if necessary in two journeys for each man. It was simply pouring with rain, but we managed to get the last party off by 1.30 a.m. Two journeys for each man were not enough as the Staff Captain had worked out the loads on a one-journey basis and it turned out a physical impossibility to carry up two boxes of 12 bombs each along a muddy trench with frequent holes, ankle- or knee-deep with mud. As it was, with only one box and the other hand free one man fell and broke his collar bone. Tried to sleep from 2 a.m. onwards after seeing the last party off, but every hour messages or difficulties came in, such as guides not being forthcoming, parties losing their way and unable to finish their work in the time. It is an odious business having to force men to do what you know to be impossible. The Staff Officer sits in a well-lit, warm dugout and works things out on paper assuming good conditions and everything going right. The Regimental Officer has to get the impossible done somehow with the men dead beat and no guides able to take them to the map references in the trenches which in many cases are absolutely obliterated and consist of a waste of shell holes. After breakfast I went to see how 'B' Company were getting on in the trenches. It was still pouring in torrents and I was absolutely covered with clayey mud from head to foot, though my waterproof protected from wet all except my knees and downwards. Since I saw the fire trench a couple of days ago it has been blown practically flat for about a hundred yards, and one bolts from one hole to another doubled up through a furrow which only covers one about up to the knees. This morning I saw two German heads looking at me from about 50 yards, but they didn't shoot! It is very lucky they are so fed up and peaceful as in the present state of our trench they could give us a much worse time than we could them once active sniping started.[9] Yesterday, according to the previous occupants of our trench, they were sniping pretty freely but they were also relieved last night and now we have another and more peaceful Regiment of Guards opposite us. When we get our trench deepened we'll begin shooting at their heads. The trench is in an indescribable condition, as lots of dead Germans who have been put away into the parapet are now lying right across the path. The reserves of ammunition, bombs, etc., are for the most part buried by the bombardment. These we can renew from a dump in the support line, but the provision of sandbags, etc., which are urgently needed and also of men for digging is impossible as, owing to the demands of the Brigade, we have no men available for carrying or digging. We are holding what was the Boche third line, and fortunately there are good dugouts, though now the trenches are turned about they are in the back wall and therefore more likely to be buried by the Hun bombardment. Rain only stopped late in the evening and it is so damp that I don't think our clothes can possibly dry.

31 August

Dry, sunny day. Delightful after the cold and rain. Most of the Battalion were again out last night carrying. Evans went up to the trenches and said that the Boche waved to him. Our men say the Boches sometimes make a signal with their hand to keep down. It is surmised that this means that an officer is coming and that they would therefore have to shoot. There is no doubt that if only they knew how well we treat our prisoners they would come over and surrender in large numbers. They express great surprise when captured at not being killed as their officers said that we always murder our prisoners.

2 September

Still very showery weather. We moved our Headquarters up to 'Quarry Post', some dugouts in a chalk pit on the eastern side of Authuille Wood.

3 September

For days past we have been preparing for an attack which was first to have been on the 30th, then on the 1st, then on the 2nd and finally took place this morning. It may have been put off originally because of the appalling weather but the last postponements must have been caused by its being part of a larger operation. This morning there has been heavy bombardment on both our flanks, though not actually next us, which is evidence that our push was part of a bigger one. As originally arranged, two of our companies were in conjunction with another Battalion to go out of the fire trench held by a third of our companies, following up an attack made by another Battalion but crossing over their objective and making for a line of trenches behind that and which we couldn't even see because it was over the skyline. Our Brigade was strengthened by a couple of extra Battalions and all the six were originally to be attacking at the same time. Late last night, however, we got orders cancelling much of the arrangements as applied to us and the other Battalion which was to attack the 2nd line. I suppose higher authority thought the scheme was too ambitious and thank goodness they did as the attack failed. Although the people who attacked from our trench got into their objective, owing to a misunderstanding on their part or that of the artillery, the barrage didn't lift, and they got knocked out of the trench by our own fire, without even seeing the Huns who were all snug in their dugouts. If our men had gone through them and into a trench beyond they would of course inevitably have been wiped out as they could not have got back over the first enemy trench.

Our people in the fire trench have had a good many casualties and indeed all our companies, as they have been continually shifted about for the last twenty-four hours and generally through very heavy shelling.

We had hardly any cover at the last place and they gave us an abominable shelling early yesterday afternoon and a worse one yesterday evening before we left. In the night they put a shell right into what was our orderly room. We are now in very safe dugouts in a chalk quarry with eight feet of chalk over our heads, and with strong wooden supports. I should think it would keep out anything smaller than a direct hit from an 8 inch. I fear our Brigade has been badly knocked about this morning, though we know nothing definite of what took place except on our front. At our new quarters we are away from our guns which is a great relief. Their blast used sometimes to put out one's light.

4 September

Had a very exciting time in the trenches, several HE shells dropping right in our fire trench. Our gunners seem not to be a patch on the French. It is of course impossible to train artillery in a few months and I suspect also that some of the trouble is due to bad work on the part of the FOOs (Forward Observation Officers) who don't go far enough forward and often deliberately turn fire on the bits of line held by us under the mistaken impression that they are still in Boche occupation. The artillery duels of which one reads too often mean that the Infantry are being blown to bits and the expression 'duels' might just as well be applied to a game of ninepins as to these one-sided performances.

5 September

Early this morning a Colonel with his four Company Commanders called to find out details in preparation for taking over our bit the day after tomorrow. The Division to which he belongs has lately come down from thirty or forty miles to the north of us, comfortably out of this 'push area'. Certainly after these two months of almost continual fighting our Division (25th) will not be much good until it has been rested, filled up and retrained, so I daresay we may be either given an easy time for a bit, or may be sent to a quiet part of the line. Just before I joined the Battalion, most of the Corps to which our Division then belonged were sent northward, but it was announced in Orders that our Division was kept back because it had done so well that it had earned a further opportunity. Personally I think it is a mistake to wear out Divisions as they have this one. In the attack the day before yesterday our Brigade had two COs killed and their Battalions have been knocked to pieces. I was up in the fire trench again this morning and found it was again being shelled by our field guns. The RE officer who was working there took his men away, saying it was not good enough to go on and that he really didn't know which side of the trench to make the parapet. These guns make a regular habit of bombarding our trench and last night knocked out one of our Lewis guns with five out of seven of the team. If only our guns were handled like those of the French we might succeed as they do. As it is, our Infantry get sacrified to the incompetence of our gunners.

6 September

Owing to fresh complaints that our own field guns were shelling our fire trench, I went up about 2.30 p.m. to see whether the Brigade had yet got it stopped and found that it had become far worse, as, although the field guns were no longer shelling us, some heavy high explosives were knocking in our trench in another place. I went along the trench to make sure they really were our own shells and saw one land within ten yards of a bombing and Lewis gun post about twenty-five yards forward of our line in an old German communication trench. I decided I had seen enough and was hurrying to get back and have it stopped when another of our shells covered me with dirt and a third nearly broke the drums of my ears. The RE had been working hard at our trench for the last few days, and were getting it well dug down and pretty safe against shrapnel. I found that for about thirty yards their work had been undone and the parapet and parados blown into the trench by our own shells. I went back as quickly as I could until I met the Staff Captain who went on post haste to the Brigade Headquarters to try and stop their infernal guns. The trouble is that we have the heavy guns of about four Divisions massed behind us and it is very difficult to identify the particular batteries responsible as we could only guess the shells to be about 6-inch. When I got back a Canadian gunner came in to ask where he could put an observation post. He happened to mention that he had seen our shells flattening out the Wonder Work. As this German trench is well over the skyline from the whole of our position, it was quite clear that they mistook the German front line for it, and imagined that the Germans were in the Hindenburg trench which we were holding. It was quite impossible to get the lunatics behind us stopped and about 6 p.m. we got a message down to say that our own shells had smashed up one of our Lewis guns. How the Germans must laugh when they see the performances of our artillery!

7 September

We were relieved after dark and moved down to a camp between Albert and Bouzincourt. I hope we may be taken away altogether from the push area. It is said that besides us only one other Division has been right through the offensive from 1 July.

Our Divisional General, Bainbridge, is said to be chiefly responsible for preventing us being removed to some more quiet part of the line. Everyone agrees that he's a horrible man who only thinks of his own advancement. It is believed that he has been much blamed for the failure last Sunday. Protests have been put in by some of the COs concerned and it is generally hoped that Bainbridge may lose his job for having thrown away so many lives by asking exhausted troops to perform an impossibility.

8 September

Marched about six miles to Lealvillers where we remained the following day while the men went over in relays to have baths at Acheux. Out of the line one finds this life very narrowing as one has no excitement to take one's attention off the fact that one has very few interests in common with those among whom one lives. Evans is a very nice fellow and a most efficient soldier, but one never talks of anything except the daily life out here. The Mess of the 10th London was less trying as there there were several people who took an interest in books and politics.

The Boche take advantage of an easterly wind to send over little balloons which before they come to earth scatter pamphlets making out that all the troubles of France are due to their Government being held in bondage by us.

10 September

We marched nine miles to Amplier just south-east of Doullens.

11 September

Marched a further ten miles fo Autheux, and on the *12th* reached Agenville, a nice little village not yet spoilt as are the villages further forward by the continual passage of troops. I am billeted in a spotlessly clean cottage belonging to an old woman. During the last three weeks the Battalion has lost about 100 killed and wounded, so we hope to have time to assimilate a draft of new men before we go back to the line. It seems rather uncertain whether I shall remain here, as the second line of the 10th London Regiment in England, with whom I have been in correspondence on the subject of getting my servant, Borley, sent out, have been told by

OC Records that I am shortly to be reposted to Egypt to command the 1st Battalion, 10th London Regiment. Nothing, however, is known of this by the Brigade or Division and it is said that officers under present conditions are only sent from the BEF to Egypt in the very rarest instances owing to the shortage out here.

15 September

When I wrote in my diary of the attack made ten days ago by the Division I ascribed its failure to the officers being knocked out and the lack of efficient NCOs after two months' continual fighting and heavy casualties, and also to our artillery barrage not lifting as arranged. I was the more able to believe the latter explanation from my own experience of the inability of our guns to distinguish between trenches held by the enemy and ourselves. It now, however, appears that after two minutes' intensive bombardment our barrage did lift from the trench to be attacked. For 25 minutes before our bombardment began, however, the Boche guns had been bombarding their own trench. When our men got into it at the prearranged time, the trench was already destroyed, being only a couple of feet deep, and from what the survivors say, they mistook the Boche barrage to be fire from our own guns. This is not altogether surprising as there was a terrific din from the bombardment in both directions. While the Boche bombardment of their own trench went on, most of the garrison were 30 feet down in the dugouts, up the shafts of which they sniped our men as they passed. Except for direct hits they were there absolutely safe from any bombardment and could easily dig out the entrances when the bombardment ceased in those cases where the destruction of the trench had buried them. A few Boches were lying in shell holes about fifty yards behind their own line and it appears that they picked off most of our officers with rifle fire. In deep shell holes they would be pretty safe from the shells exploding in their own trench. This new Boche method of smashing their own trench seems to make these pushes on a narrow front almost certain to fail. The attackers can't find the entrances to the blocked dugouts and are annihilated by the bombardment and close-range sniping before they can hope to dig a new trench. The Boches had been noticed to put a few high-explosive shells into their trench daily before our attack, and this was no doubt for the purpose of registering. The terrific bombardment of all our communications, Battalion Headquarters etc. on the day previous to the attack showed that they knew we were preparing for a push. His aeroplanes cannot have failed to spot the carrying parties working to and fro in the communication trenches like strings of ants, to make battle dumps of bomb ammunition, barbed wire, pickets etc. in our fire trenches. This information no doubt causes him to barrage his own trench in the expectation that just before dawn we should attack. Though our guns did not fail to lift their barrage in this attack, I am more than ever convinced that our casualties, enormous as they now are relative to the French, are due to the fact that the British infantry are the slaves of the British artillery whereas in the French Army the reverse is the case.

Our attack orders lay down beforehand exactly what the artillery barrages shall be in relation to 'zero' or the time of commencement. For example, 'From zero to zero plus two minutes, the artillery will barrage – trenches (the objective). The barrage will then lift and a steady rate of fire will be maintained until zero plus ten minutes on trenches from — to —. From zero plus ten to zero plus twenty an intense barrage will be put on ...'. Such a programme when laid down is always exactly followed. In many of the British attacks, such as that on Thiepval at the beginning of July, it was soon known that the original intensive barrage on the objective had not knocked out the Boche machine guns. In such a case the French would probably modify their artillery arrangements and go on battering those spots which were shown by the experience of the infantry to be of importance. Not so with us. In spite of the infantry being mown down, the forearranged artillery barrages must be followed: they are as the laws of the Medes and Persians. At the beginning of July the crack French 20th Corps under General Balfourier found themselves hung up by fire from a village which had not been sufficiently flattened by artillery fire. Instead of carrying out the programme as prearranged, the artillery were ordered to go on smashing the particular spot until the defenders were knocked out. As a result the French Infantry reached their objective with insignificant casualties. On the right of this Corps was the French Colonial Corps. They were held up in the same way, but the Corps Commander refused to modify the artillery programme and incurred very heavy losses in taking his village. Result, he was *dégommé* next day.

I don't know whether it is obstinacy or merely inefficiency which leads our gunners to stick their toes in and say that they cannot modify targets to suit the developments of infantry operations. Nor do I know by what method the French actually do communicate with their artillery when wires are cut by bombardment. This, however, is a mere matter of detail, as visual communication by signals to contact aeroplanes or by rockets on a method previously arranged with the artillery would present no difficulty if once it were admitted that the lives of the British infantry were more important than the prejudices or inefficient laziness of our gunners. One cause of the casual way in which they shell our own trenches is no doubt that the British artillery observation officer stays too far back where he can see nothing. If, as I believe is the case with the French, the FOOs did their observation from our front-line trenches they would soon find a to prevent their bombardment. One disadvantage of our comparatively amateur staff officers is that they cannot stand up to the superior technical knowledge of the gunner. When the latter say a thing is impossible the British Staff Officer is too ignorant to be able to do anything but collapse.

We remained at Agenville until the *25th*.

16 September (Extract from letter to his wife referring to the first employment of tanks in battle on the previous day)

The news seems very good and the 'caterpillars' referred to in our official reports seem to have been a great success. Perhaps we may still get through this year, though I fear there is still a strong line through Pys and Le Sars, which may cause a lot of trouble beyond Flers where, according to the wire, 'a caterpillar was seen walking up and down the street followed by cheering crowds of British troops'.

If they do get through I suppose we shall be on the move.

18 September

Evans went off for eight days' leave leaving me in command of the Battalion. We spent our time in hard training. The weather began to turn cold and there was a good deal of rain. One afternoon I rode over to Crécy to see the battlefield, and another day I presided at a Court Martial which tried five different cases. With these exceptions I spent my whole time training with the Battalion.

25 September

Marched seventeen miles to Amplier. It was a most trying march owing to the heat and dust, the men not having lately worn their packs and many of the drafts being quite untrained. A large number fell out from sore feet or exhaustion on the way. There must be bad Staff work somewhere to knock the men to pieces by such a march when by starting us a day earlier it might apparently have been avoided. At Amplier Evans rejoined us on his return from leave.

26 September

Marched ten miles to Lealvillers where we stayed for two days. While here Martel (our Brigade Major) left us to become Brigade Major to the new formation of tanks, and his place was taken by K.F.B. Gattie, a New Army soldier who started the War as a Territorial and who turned out a first rate Staff Officer. We had been apparently rushed up to the forward area in case we were wanted to follow up the successful attack[10] in which Guidecourt, Moraval and Combles were captured.

27 September

New methods of intensive digging were tried. Each Battalion sent a company in the morning to try one method and another Company in the afternoon to try the other. The results are to be checked by reversing the times tomorrow so as to make sure that the greatly superior worth of the morning method was not merely due to the greater energy of men at that time of day.

27 September (Extract from letter to his wife)

I don't for a moment expect that anything will come of Broadwood's recommendation but it was very good-natured of him to write. Of course if a Staff job turned up I suppose I should take it though I would rather have a Battalion, being aware that I have not the necessary training and knowledge for Staff work. As far as I know, pretty well all Staff Officers here are regular soldiers, and the standard of efficiency is certainly far higher than it was with MEF. One does not therefore feel bored at being second-in-command in the way I did there. Of course Staff work depends much on one's general, and it would be an awful gamble to go to someone whom one didn't know.

28 September

Was President of a Court Martial. One of the cases was a desertion charge. There was practically no doubt of the man's guilt but there was a half-witted youth prosecuting who never attempted to produce the necessary evidence. The accused had no one to defend him and therefore one had to be the more scrupulous not to do the work of the prosecution. It was a very difficult case as the man would of course have been shot if we had found him guilty. Finally we came to the conclusion that as the prosecution did not attempt to deal with the question of intention we could only find the man guilty of absence without leave. Furious as these muddles by the prosecution make me, I must say in this case I was profoundly grateful as it would have been a horrible job to sentence the man to be shot. Every few days in Army Orders there is published a batch of men who are shot for cowardice or desertion and I suppose with a conscript army this is a necessity. I am getting more than my share of Court Martials as for the moment I am the only Major with the Brigade and there is no one else available as President. It wouldn't be so bad if only the adjutants knew their job and didn't waste one's time by neglecting to warn witnesses or nominating members of the Court without necessary length of service and generally muddling their business.

29 September

At 2 a.m. we got orders to move this morning and started off soon after daylight in pouring rain. Our destination proved to be an empty field just outside Bouzincourt with only an old trench for shelter. Eventually we got fifteen tents, though the last five only turned up about midnight.

30 September

At 2 a.m. we received orders that at 10 a.m. we were to move up about three miles to Crucifix Corner on the right bank of the Ancre near Aveluy. We there took over some dugouts which provided accommodation for about 150. The rest of the Battalion had to bivouac in the open but were fairly well covered from shell fire.

1 October

Rode up to our Brigade Headquarters in what used to be the village of Pozières. The place is now quite flat and one could only recognize it amid the surrounding waste of shell holes as having once been a village by the few bits of wood sticking up which used to be trees. There is not a blade of grass to be seen anywhere and the ground consists of circular pits ten to twenty feet across with half-buried German guns and twisted bars and sheets of metal, the original shape and purpose of which is now unrecognizable. In Pozières we found a 'tank' which had been stuck for some days in a hole and had only just got out on to what used to be a road, and is now again being repaired. The officer told me he had been into the 'Sugar Factory' on the first occasion that the tanks were used.[11] He said he had destroyed very few Boches or machine guns, as they all ran away in all directions as soon as they saw his monster coming. He said that these tanks are not suitable for the shell holes and that the practice ground in England had not in any way calculated for these obstacles. There were two more just along the road which had had to be abandoned, and had been burnt out inside in case they fell into Boche hands. Actually, however, we saw a party of men round each of them, probably trying to salvage the remains. We didn't penetrate into Brigade Headquarters which was in a kind of pit with a sort of roof of beams and earth over the top. An attack was going on by the outgoing Brigade in the hopes of handing over to us the trench in a more satisfactory state, and both our and their

General were down below. Having found out what was going on from the Artillery and Intelligence officers who, with signallers and runners, were crowded under the roof, we departed home. The weather had cleared up and the sunshine is very welcome as four-fifths of our men have to sleep out without any shelter.

2 October

Incessant downpours of rain. Managed to get remainder of men under some sort of cover, chiefly tarpaulins, bivouacs, etc., stretched over unroofed dugouts.

3 October

Went up to see our digging and carrying parties at work. It was pouring with rain and rather muggy and such heavy going that I was soaked through with perspiration under my waterproof. I first went to Mouquet farm where we had 200 men carrying bombs up to a forward dump across the open. There was a good deal of shelling. Then I went to see 100 men whom we had digging a new communication trench about forty yards away from the old Boche one. Fortunately they were shelling the line of the latter so accurately that our men who were digging escaped. On returning I found orders had come for us to take over some trench from another Brigade tomorrow evening, and to send officers up to reconnoitre in the morning. It is in some ways better to be in the line than do this heavy carrying and digging work which knocks the men up quite as much and is almost as tiring to the nerves.

4 October

Evans, with the four Company Commanders, went off early to reconnoitre the trenches we were to take over in the evening. Everything was a sea of mud and there was a good deal of rain in the morning. Accordingly, about 1 p.m. I got a note saying that Evans could not possibly get back and I was to send off the Battalion and Company at a time to meet guides at a certain dump. Hill went away yesterday to have an operation on his foot, and I had a busy afternoon with Wilkinson who is acting as Adjutant in his place. He is quite a nice boy who was an Oxford undergraduate when the War broke out. I went up with the Battalion Headquarters party of bombers and signallers. We met the guides at the dump north-west of Pozières and then began our progress over the most appalling ground to Battalion Headquarters. The ground was pitted with shell holes, most of them half-full of water. Along the track, carrying parties had churned the ground to liquid mud in many places up to one's ankles, which in the dark of course concealed the slippery slopes of clay under the surface of the pools. Every few yards a message came up from the rear to halt in front and at the rate of about half a mile an hour we finally reached our destination, not without a man falling into a shell hole and breaking his ankle. I found Evans waiting in a dugout with the outgoing OC, 2nd-in-Command and Adjutant for the relief to be completed. The dugout was a German one sheeted with iron inside. It has four entrances but only consists of shafts twenty to thirty feet deep and a passage about four feet wide. Unfortunately we have to share it with another Battalion Headquarters and an artillery telephone station and with a first aid post. I came down to find Evans cramped up with our predecessors at our end of the passage. The staircase was crowded with the runners, signallers, etc. who have to be ready at a moment's notice. I arrived about 8 p.m. and we waited until 3.30 a.m. cramped up with the 49th Canadian Infantry Battalion until the relief was complete. The Companies for the fire trenches left the dump at 8 p.m., but such was the state of the ground that it took 7½ hours before the relief was complete in spite of the trenches being only about a mile away. One difficulty is that the guides provided by the outgoing Battalion always lose their way in the dark, not altogether surprising, especially when, as in this case, the outgoers had only held the area for 48 hours. The 7½-hour wait was odious as one had to sit in a cramped position, wet through above the knees. There was also continuous friction between the Canadians and the other Battalion with which we shared the passage and who had relieved another Canadian Battalion in a support line in daylight. The runners of this Battalion had encroached from their staircase into the aid post and, as Canadian wounded kept coming in, their CO was continually protesting. There was one unlucky case about fifty yards from our Headquarters. A party was bringing down a wounded man and one of the bearers must have kicked a dud shell or unexploded Stokes mortar bomb with his foot. Anyhow, without any shell being heard coming, there was a terrific explosion which killed the stretcher bearers but curiously enough only wounded in the head the man on the stretcher. We got very little sleep.

5 October

The Brigade Major of our Brigade and of another which will probably take over from us came in, and afterwards also our Staff Captain. We are to dig hard and also to try and carry up for battle dumps in the fire trench. With the ground in its present state these tasks are not easy, especially as last night the Boche blew to pieces not only the tramway to the dump from which carrying was to start, but also the dump itself. I then went off to tell the OC Companies what they were to do. Snell, the bombing officer, and Bingham, the signalling officer, came also. The communication trench was odious, up to one's knees in liquid mud in some places and over one's ankles in the stickiest of clay, which nearly pulled one's boots off, in others. We alternated between shortness of wind and dislike of having to play leapfrog over some extremely unpleasant corpses on the one hand and even stronger dislike of the shells which invariably came on to the trench as soon as we showed ourselves along the top. When we at last got to the fire trench we found it pretty good except for a gap of about eighty yards. With my prismatic compass I took a cross bearing of four Boche batteries of which we saw the puffs of smoke and flash. On returning we sent details into the Brigade.

6 October

We were relieved at night by the 74th Brigade and are going back a couple of miles to some dugouts from which we shall no doubt be used for digging and carrying until we are again wanted for this line. It is, I think, sound to shorten the period in the trenches to 48 hours as the conditions are very exhausting and the conditions of the ground make it impossible to get up enough water for the men to drink. Our artillery is outrageously slack. Although our fire trench is right up on the ridge and looks down on the German positions both sides of the Ancre, no FOO has ever come up. If they ran up a wire they could direct fire from our trench and knock out any number of Boche batteries of which we see the puffs of smoke.

The ground being dry we had a quick and easy relief by the 74th Brigade and were back in some good dugouts at Ovillers, about three miles back, by 1 a.m. We remained in this position until the 15th, providing digging and other working parties every night to help the 7th and 74th Brigades who were in the line.

On the *9 October* Stuff Redoubt[12] was captured. This involved us in finding a lot of digging parties for the consolidation of the line. During the last day or two we did some practices for the attack on Regina trench which is to take place as soon as we get back into the line. [Guinness contemplated allowing himself to be nominated for a staff duties training course and noted: There's no doubt that a Brigade Major's job is the most attractive to my taste. One never sets eyes on the staff of any bigger command anywhere near the trenches.]

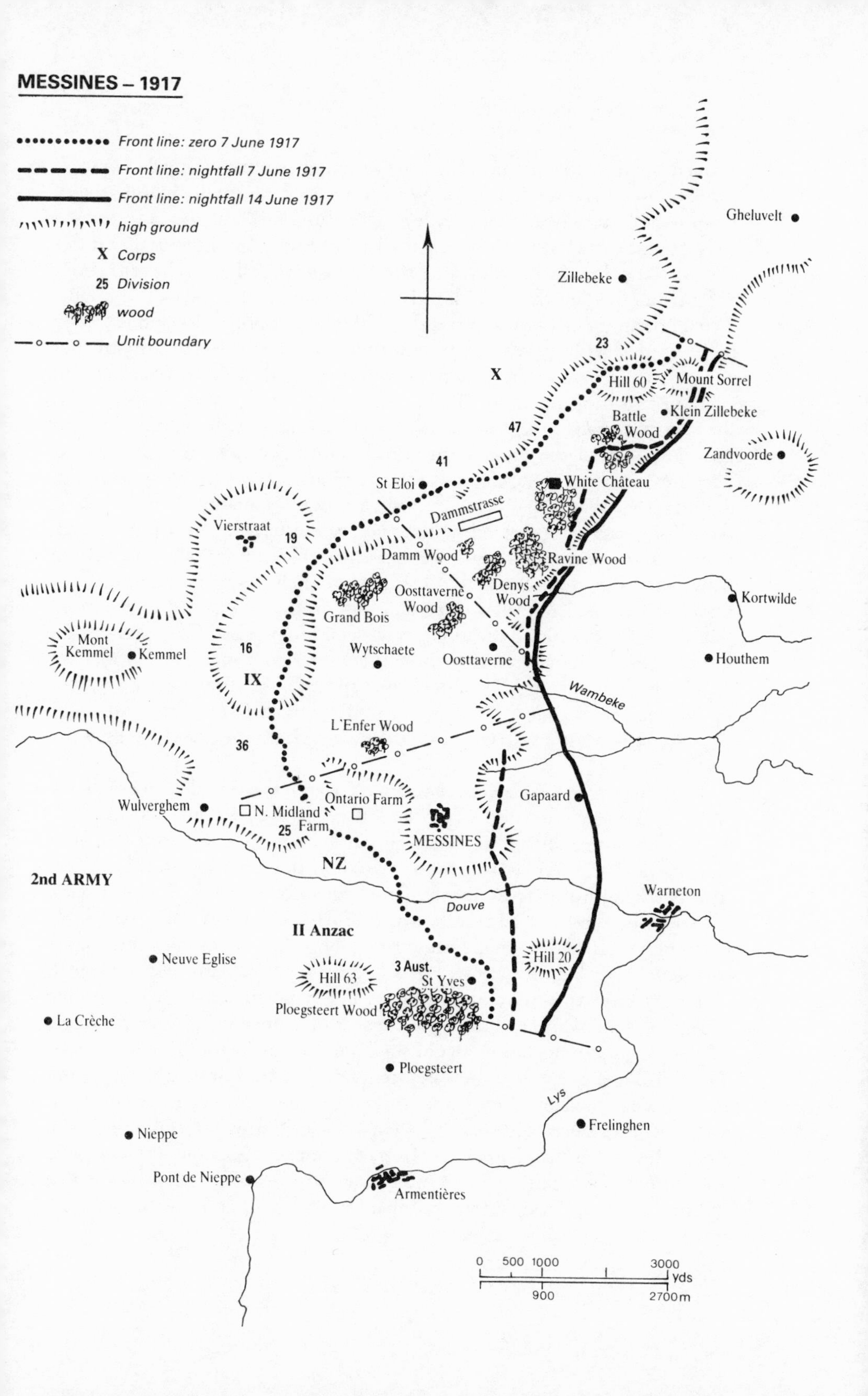
MESSINES – 1917
Front line: zero 7 June 1917
Front line: nightfall 7 June 1917
Front line: nightfall 14 June 1917
high ground
X Corps
25 Division
wood
Unit boundary
Gheluvelt
Zillebeke
23
X
Hill 60
Mount Sorrel
Klein Zillebeke
Battle Wood
47
Zandvoorde
41
St Eloi
White Château
Dammstrasse
Vierstraat
19
Damm Wood
Ravine Wood
Oosttaverne Wood
Denys Wood
Kortwilde
Grand Bois
Mont Kemmel
Kemmel
16
Wytschaete
Oosttaverne
Houthem
IX
Wambeke
L'Enfer Wood
36
Ontario Farm
Gapaard
Wulverghem
N. Midland Farm
25
MESSINES
NZ
2nd ARMY
Douve
Warneton
II Anzac
Neuve Eglise
Hill 20
3 Aust.
Hill 63
St Yves
Ploegsteert Wood
La Crèche
Ploegsteert
Lys
Frelinghen
Nieppe
Pont de Nieppe
Armentières
0 500 1000 3000 yds
900 2700 m

15 October

Moved up about a mile into the reserve trenches of the Brigade front on the left of where we last held. We are in deep German dugouts, very cramped. Yesterday afternoon very successful attacks were made on two strongpoints, the last from which the Boche could fire directly down our side of the ridge. In the attack of the Brigade which we relieved, about 100 prisoners were taken with only about twelve casualties on our side. The German infantry now surrender at the first opportunity and it is only their infernal artillery which prevents their complete collapse. Any further advances on a narrow front here, however, though they would no doubt enable us to mop up more Boche infantry, seem hardly worth while as they would again bring our trenches under direct artillery fire, whereas now just behind the crest of the ridge which we hold for observation purposes, they are very difficult for the Hun to hit. Our men were out digging all last night and have finished a new front-line trench; 200 of them will have to go out digging again this afternoon at 3 p.m. which doesn't give them much rest. There are two 60-pounder guns just behind us which are a great nuisance. One of their shells burst prematurely and knocked five men out who were standing on top of our dressing station. We sent over and cursed the gunners who said they'd had three prematures since yesterday afternoon. Each time these infernal 5-inch guns shoot, our candles flicker and one's head feels like splitting. Unfortunately I've lost my ear protectors and cannot get those for which I've written for some days. I lost my last pair trying to deaden some loud snores which kept me awake one night.

Took over reserve trenches at 10 a.m. Though the Battalion were pretty well all digging last night, we had to find another 200 for digging communication trenches in the afternoon. I went up to see Stuff Redoubt and the new fire trench which our Battalion dug running to the west of it; it is a beautiful narrow trench which the Boche so far does not seem to have discovered. I had quite a peaceful walk except for a couple of nasty black HE which made me hurry along the communication trench on the way up. Coming down I deviated from the communication trench and went over to look at a deserted Tank lying in what used to be the village of Thiepval but what now consists of branchless tree stems, heaps of rifles, equipment, fragments of shell and bits of former human beings. The Tank had been set on fire before being deserted. It had had a crump in the side which no doubt put it out of action. The engines and guns were missing. I was told that the occupants got out of the tank uninjured. Before leaving it they had clearly done much execution and just alongside was a covered-in blind sap end littered with traces of the shambles which it had enclosed. Tremendous bombardment began soon after dark and went on most of the night. Having lost my ear stops I filled them with paper.

16 October

Early this morning we got orders that the Brigade was to sideslip. The left-hand Battalion in our bit was to hand over to the Division on the left and we were to take over the left-hand Battalion frontage from the Brigade on our right. Our Battalion Headquarters and two companies remain where they were and the other two Companies went up and relieved the 11th LF (Lancashire Fusiliers) this afternoon with support in Sollern trench.

17 October

Our Companies in the line are being relieved today but we are stopping where we were, as meanwhile other troops had taken up the accommodation which they had vacated and it is a great difficulty to get them fitted in under cover. Owing to the attack we are now to make on Thursday, A and C Companies were brought from line in the evening. It was a trying relief as the Battalion relieving us didn't know how many Companies were required and sent up one too many, causing much congestion. Besides this they were hours late in reaching the rendezvous for meeting our guides.

18 October

Evans went up at 6.30 with half the Company Commanders and I at 9 with the other two to look at the bit of the line from which we are to attack. It came on to rain about 7 a.m. but didn't last more than a couple of hours. Very busy day with orders and amendments.

19 October

Very little sleep last night. Only got to bed about 11 and had just got to sleep at midnight when an officer arrived from the Brigade to get a map on which to alter artillery barrage lines. Just when we got to sleep again a Brigade Orderly arrived with fresh orders and woke everyone up because we had no light and he had no matches. We breakfasted at 3 a.m. and went up to the trench at 3.45. It had just begun to rain and we got up there absolutely wet through with our own perspiration under our waterproofs. We packed Battalion Headquarters into the dugout, a very small one where most of us have to sit on the stairs. At the other end and in the intermediate passage are twelve signallers and twelve runners. The other dugouts in our bit of trench are all broken down below as the Boches were burnt out with phosphorus bombs and, with the wood linings burnt, the roofs collapse. In about five places men can sit on the stair shafts. It rained incessantly all the morning and by mid-day the trench was knee-deep in mud and the men were shivering with cold. About 11.45 we got orders that 'zero', which was to have been at 2.07 was postponed for 24 hours. Great disappointment as the men were looking forward to 'going over' and ending their misery. Two Companies were sent back to avoid the dangerous congestion of the trench. As it was two shells which came in in one case killed six men and in the other wounded one and killed five. Orders were issued for the two Companies sent back to start again at 4 a.m. so as to be up at daybreak tomorrow morning. The misery of the men without greatcoats or blankets in the rain and mud and with no prospect of hot food or dry clothes for days is terrible. It stopped raining in the evening but continued icy cold.

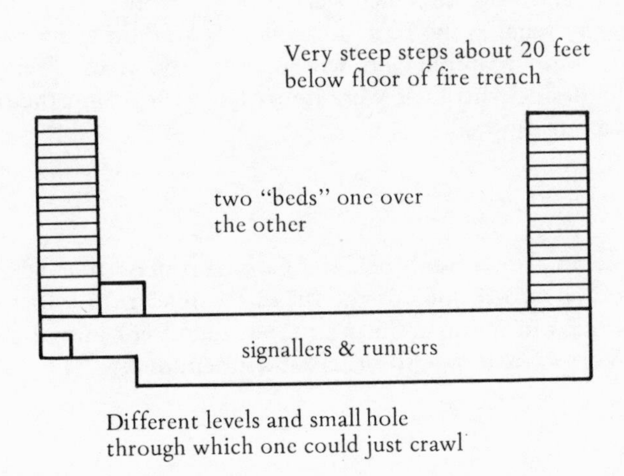

20 October

At 2 a.m. orders arrived that zero is again postponed 24 hours. It has no doubt been impossible to get the artillery ammunition up; already two days ago I saw field guns stuck hopelessly in the mud a couple of miles behind the line. It is not raining today but the mud is indescribable. I have just seen a man stuck in the mud up to his knees whom they took $\frac{3}{4}$-hour to get out. They first tried in vain with a spade but it was like trying to dig in treacle and finally they loosened the mud from his feet with their hands. An Artillery Observation Officer arrived up with one foot bare. First he lost his boot and then his sock. One of our men lost the sole of his boot but kept the upper. One poor devil from the Battalion who were taking over on our right last night got stuck in the communication trench on the way. He finally got into our trench where he remained for about two hours raving mad. We sent along for his officer who said he would attend to him, but as he did not do anything our stretcher bearers were sent for. Just as they were preparing to take him down over the top the man died. Our men being in 'assaulting order' have, of course, no greatcoats and have been shivering with cold ever since they came up. The Brigadier came up this morning and saw the state they are in. If we had assaulted yesterday as arranged it would have been much better, but heaven knows what they will be like tomorrow. At 6 p.m. an officer of the Border Regiment came up to say that they (who had been out of the line and under cover) were coming in to relieve for the assault our two Companies who would have been out for the two nights without warmth or shelter. Our two spent Companies were to hold the line while those we had sent down to be under cover were still to go over.

22 October

Attack on Regina Trench at last took place at 12.07 yesterday and was quite successful.[13] Hundreds of Boche surrendered and some even came out of the village of Grandcourt nearly a mile beyond the objective to give themselves up. At first we were endeavouring frantically to try to get information which was not easy as the bombardment was terrific and our wires were continually cut. Our Battalion Headquarters are the forward visual and wire signalling station and we soon knew that all along our Brigade front the objective was obtained. The day and night were a hideous nightmare as our Battalion Headquarters were also the only Advanced Dressing Station anywhere near the fighting. The three other Battalions had their three stations a good half-mile behind us with the result that we got all the worst cases. Evans and I didn't lie down until 5 a.m. It was a wild struggle of wounded up and down our steep dugout steps. Every half hour we sent through by visual or telephone to our Staff Captain as to the scandalous incompetence of our medical arrangements. Our single-handed Doctor (Chamberlain) dealt with 150 cases before midnight. Many of these were able to stagger on, but we were quickly swamped with over thirty men hit through the chest, stomach or legs who couldn't possibly walk. The assault having taken place at noon, we got six stretcher parties up between 5 and 6 p.m. and then not another until 4 a.m. when four more arrived. We simply couldn't get the wounded in and the outrageous failure of the Field Ambulances to carry out their duty to evacuate our Advance Dressing Station must mean death to many of the cases who would otherwise have been saved. The little corner which ought to have been our office was of course immediately full of seriously wounded officers. One who lay on our floor groaning from 1 p.m. until 4 a.m. would certainly have had a chance of life if he had been taken off immediately, but will no doubt die of collapse when after 24 hours' delay they open his abdomen. This is only one case out of scores. Our stair top was continually swept with shrapnel and HE until 2 a.m. this morning which killed many of the wounded before they could find room on our stairs. Unfortunately the Boche knows that this is an important centre of communication and keeps bursting shells continually right on to us. At 3 a.m. this morning we got orders that we shall be relieved some time today. I hope it may be soon as since the day before yesterday it has been impossible to get any food or water to our men and we've not got a crumb of any kind here as we gave all we had to the wounded.

Were relieved at about 3 by a very strong Battalion of a newly arrived Division. They are fine-looking men with apparently the most incompetent lot of officers. The Company Commander who took over from us seemed to know absolutely nothing as to where he had to go or what he had to do. They arrived in the most spick and span clothes and were heard criticizing the unwashed appearance of Evans and me, who, unshaven and coated in dried mud from head to foot didn't look our best. They asked the most idiotic questions such as whether they ought to put out posts! Nares, a regular Army Captain attached to us, was dressed as are most officers in the trenches in 'Tommy's' clothes and equipment and the incomers asked him if he was the Sergeant-Major, probably because they were so surprised at his superior knowledge. They marched in with packs on their backs, which no one else nowadays thinks of taking to the trenches as they are too bulky to allow of people passing each other and mean that they climb over the top and draw fire. They marched in contrary to all regulations closed up in Companies instead of big platoons with considerable intervals between. If any Boche aeroplane were up they could not fail to notice that a relief was going on.

24 October

The whole Battalion didn't get back to the tents, where it spent last night near Albert about five miles behind the line, until 1.30 this morning. Today we came on about the same distance to W— where we are in billets and where I hope this evening to have a bath. It is understood that we shall shortly entrain for another part of the line altogether. I hope we may get a bit of rest first but with the present activity probably troops cannot long be spared from the line. This evening it has begun to rain which is very unfortunate now that the Hun really seems to be on the run. Our casualties the day before yesterday seem to have been about eighty. Unfortunately the Orderly Room clerk of one Company with the Company rolls on him got blown to fragments by a shell. One of our officers, a boy who had only joined about ten days, was killed by one of our own shells in our own trench. As the barrage ought to have been 200 yards away at the time, it shows how inaccurate our artillery are. Our dugout was also continually being hit by shells from one of our 9.2 Howitzers on the previous day when they were presumably under the impression that they were cutting the Boche wire 400 yards away. The artillery observation officers whom one meets in the trenches often seem quite incapable of reading the map and one of them pointed out our position on the map quite 300 yards wrong, so it is not surprising that they kill a lot of our people.

25 October

Marched to Authuille, quite close to the village of Ampliers where we were recently billeted. In the afternoon Duncannon arrived in a motor and carried me off to Sir Henry Wilson's Headquarters at Vauchelles-les-Domant. It was a great change to find oneself in a civilized Château with linen sheets. Besides Sir Henry and his two aides de camp (Duncannon and Godfrey Locker Lampson), the only other member of the mess is Du Prée*, his BGGS (Brigadier-General, General Staff). Sir Henry strikes me as a man of great brilliance and width of view and it seems a pity that he should be wasted on the Command of the 4th Army Corps. It is said that those above him are afraid or jealous of his brilliant tongue. Both Lloyd George and Bonar Law wanted him to succeed Hunter (probably an error for Sir Charles Douglas*) as CIGS but Asquith refused on account of his attitude about Ulster just before the War[14] when he was the brain behind Gough.* Wilson has a letter from Haldane, (Secretary of State for War, 1905–1912)* written I think in 1912, to say that the PM wished his frequent visits with the French General Staff to cease as they were considered likely to offend Germany. Fortunately Wilson took no notice and elaborated plans of cooperation between the Expeditionary Force and the French.[15] Haig* is said to be jealous of him. When Monro was appointed to command in India, Haking* was appointed to command the First Army. The War Council, however, have to ratify Army Commands and signified that he would not be acceptable and that they preferred Wilson,

Cavan* or Horne* in that order. Haig, who has little gift of exposition when presiding over meetings of generals, appointed No. 3, the least brilliant.[16] Cavan, of course, has a great reputation and some people talk of him as the most likely successor to Haig. Wilson is gravely anxious about the lack of men. To win the war we must attack on a wide front and if we can keep going two offensives of the size of the Somme can hardly fail. If we attack with insufficient troops and a restricted front it means appalling waste of life, as it would enable the Boche to mass their artillery. As it is, we have hardly enough men for the Somme offensive. Divisions are from 2500 to 3500 below strength and the drafts arrive insufficiently trained and go over the parapet without even having had time to learn their officers by sight. To win we need another 1½ million men, not later than February. If Asquith only makes up his mind to take them in a few months time they cannot be trained by the decisive moment. The Boche coup in the Dobrudja will no doubt enormously increase our difficulty.[17] Constanza has no military importance. Until Rumania went to war Germany was getting all her available corn and oil and is therefore only thus better off that she may be able to take them without paying. Almost certainly we shall repeat our Gallipoli blunder and will divert forces now in Egypt, England or out here to Salonika, though this is the decisive theatre with 127 Boche Divisions.

After two most interesting nights with Sir Henry Wilson I returned to Authuille. I found that orders had just arrived for me to report for a six-week Staff course at Hesdin beginning on the 31st. The 25th Division are entraining on the 28th for Flanders but I shall of course not travel with them. The course to which I am going is the first which has been held out here. It is said that only those who have been through it will in future be given Staff employment and that it is to be made a permanent school owing to the growing shortage of men who had been through the Staff College.[18]

29 October

Having seen the Battalion off last night, I stayed at the Quatre Fils D'Aymon Hotel, Doullens, and explored the very interesting Vauban fortifications. Rising from enormous fosses, the brick or hewn stone walls are now covered with great trees growing from the green slopes above and now just turning to glorious autumn tints.

30 October

Left by an early train for St Pol. Met Clowes who used to be at Eton with me and who was proceeding from another Division to attend the same course. After crawling in the train all the morning we got to St Pol where we were lucky enough to hire a motor for the rest of the journey. Hesdin is a charming old town with an old Spanish Town Hall. The course is split up into five separate Messes each consisting of ten officers. Those in my Mess are a very nice lot, but as all except one other are already staff officers, I shall probably feel horribly ignorant when we start work tomorrow. I am billeted on a nice old lady in a spotlessly clean house about 300 years old.

I remained at Hesdin until *December 13*. The course was run by Brig-General R. C. Currie and was very interesting. The officers in the course were most of them Brigade Majors, the others Staff Captains or GSO3s and one learnt almost as much from discussing matters with them as from the lectures and exercises. In the morning we generally had certain actual operation orders of either Armies or Corps given to us and proceeded from them to work out our orders in syndicates in which we daily changed places and filled different posts In the afternoons we had conferences and criticisms of our own and the Instructors' productions and the evenings were generally spent at a lecture by some expert from outside. Towards the end of the course when things got organized there was perhaps a tendency to give us more to do than we were properly able to assimilate, but I certainly learnt a lot and had a very interesting time.

18 November (Extract from letter to his wife)

We have had some extraordinarily good lectures lately. The worst was on tanks from Colonel Elles who took them over out here recently. He was quite inaudible and didn't seem to know much about his subject. Perhaps he was frightened by the rows of Generals, from Army Commanders downwards, who had come over to listen to him.

The prevailing view is that in their present stage of development they are very little use.

They go so slowly (only about a mile an hour) that unless they go in front of the infantry they are never able to catch them up in time. If they go in front it prevents us using our barrage, and on the other hand gives away the attack and brings down a terrific barrage on our trenches which wipes out our infantry as soon as they begin to climb out.

Of course they may be able to improve them but at present most people who've seen them in action say they'd rather do without.

It was a great change again to be among civilized human beings of wide interests. E.W.M. Grigg,* whom I first knew as Garvin's associate on *The Outlook* and who afterwards became Editor of the *Round Table*, was in my Mess and used to produce very brilliant and unconventional work. Without ever having soldiered before the War, he turned out to have very great natural genius in that direction and shortly afterwards became GSO1 of the Guards Division. We did a good deal of practical work in the open air, writing out of doors, after having ridden to examine the ground. We also visited various salvage, supply ammunition and other depots to see the systems in force and also descended on the unfortunate Division who happened to be holding the line at Arras, so as to pick the brains of the various Staffs and to write attack and relief orders and various other exercises based on the actual position there. At the end of my course I went home on leave. I left England to rejoin the 11th Cheshires on Christmas Eve. I got to the Battalion at Romarin Camp close to Steamwork on Christmas morning after a very difficult journey. During a heavy storm on the 23rd, a rope had parted between a tug and a 4000-ton steamer which she was towing into Boulogne, with the result that the steamer slewed round and got jammed between the piers at the mouth of the harbour, where she broke her back and sank, effectually blocking the entrance. The result was that all traffic had to be diverted to Calais where there was great congestion and we did not get away from Calais until 4.30 a.m. after a very wet and cold wait. When I reached Steamwork I found the gale had broken all the telephone communications, so had to set off on foot to our transport lines to get a conveyance for my baggage.

The 11th Cheshires were very busy as fifty of them were making a raid in the evening to try and get some Boche prisoners at a spot SE of Ploegsteert Wood astride the Ploegsteert–Warneton road. They had been working out the details and practising on fake trenches some days previously. Just after dark the party started in lorries which took them a couple of miles to a point from which they would work up to the line. They went up with their faces blackened and hay tied round their heads to take off the sharp outlines against the sky. Evans went up to watch the raid from the fire trench where a special telephone was being laid. I was not allowed to go up and had to wait for news at Brigade Headquarters. I there made the acquaintance of our new Brigadier, General H.B.D. Baird* of the 12th Bengal Cavalry. The raid took place but we didn't get any news through until an hour afterwards. A good many Boches were killed and we succeeded in catching one alive from whom the necessary identifications were obtained as to what troops were opposite us. Our casualties were one killed and three wounded but the Battalion holding the line were rather heavily shelled afterwards and had four men killed.

28 December

We celebrated Christmas on the *26th*. The Battalion was at this time accommodated in some rather dilapidated and dirty huts.
We moved up and took over the Ploegsteert Sector with our Battalion Headquarters at Rifle House in the middle of Ploegsteert Wood. Our front-line trench runs along its eastern edge southward to the Ploegsteert–Warneton road. The line here is fairly quiet but during the Christmas night raid the communication trenches had got blown in at the south-east end of the wood, thus blocking the drainage and causing the trenches to be badly flooded. It is my job as Second-in-Command to organize the working parties on trench repair, etc. and I spent most of the first day wading about in water well over the knees, trying to find some way of getting rid of the water. The ground is very flat and the natural flow of the ditches here is eastward towards the Canal. We have got outlets under our front line parapet to let the water out into no-man's-land but the Boches seemed to have dammed it up so that it all runs back and floods our line. It is necessary to walk in gumboots up to the thighs, as many parts of this area are much flooded. Battalion Headquarters are in very comfortable elephant iron shelters piled up outside with layers of sandbags about ½-mile back from the front line. The wood is so thick that the Boches cannot easily see the inhabited patches and we are thus pretty free from bombardment though especially at night machine-gun bullets are apt to sweep across the tracks. In summer this wood would be delightful, but in winter conditions is so flooded and swampy that not only in the trenches but also throughout the wood one has to walk on the duckboard tracks.

The present system is that we are six days in the line and six days out either in close support or in reserve back at Romarin camp. About once a month we shall probably go right out of the line and get a fortnight's training while in Divisional Reserve. War here with only about one casualty a day is a very different business to what it was on the Somme where just holding the trenches in the same day the Battalion had perhaps thirty or forty men knocked out.

1917: Flanders. The Battle of Messines and the Passchendaele Campaign

2 January 1917

We were relieved in the line and moved back to billets about four miles back in Nieppe. It is a dirty, squalid little town with pretty well all the glass broken in the windows. Being on the main road from Armentières to Bailleul, there is a ceaseless stream of lorry traffic which throws up jets of black mud from the badly mended shell-holes and pools caused by subsidences in the *pavé* and covers everybody in the streets and the houses up to the first floor windows with great splotches of mud. Life from my point of view was far preferable in the trenches, where one got a pleasant amount of exercise walking round to supervise the works of drainage and repair. Here, however, one lives in absolute dirt and squalor and the whole Battalion Mess together in a small room which is good no doubt for our *esprit de corps*, but in other ways somewhat trying. During the day we train either close to Nieppe or else on a larger ground just east of Bailleul. This involves a very tedious march of five miles each way along a very rough and congested *pavé* road. In all this area there is great shortage of training grounds as the inhabitants like to keep their pastures for their cattle and already much of the land is taken up by hutments, transport lines, artillery horse lines, etc., etc.

6 January

General Baird and I went into Bailleul to dine with Sir Alexander Godley who commands the 2nd Anzac Corps. Bram Jackson is his ADC and Edward Greene is Staff Captain to the heavy Artillery of this Corps. We are in the 9th Corps commanded by Sir A. Hamilton Gordon.* He is said to be quite useless as a Corps Commander, having held big administrative appointments prior to the War and never having had any experience in commanding troops. I met our own Corps Commander dining with General Godley. Hamilton Gordon is not an attractive person and it is said that part of his gloom and depression is due to some defect which prevents him tasting anything and makes him incapable of distinguishing

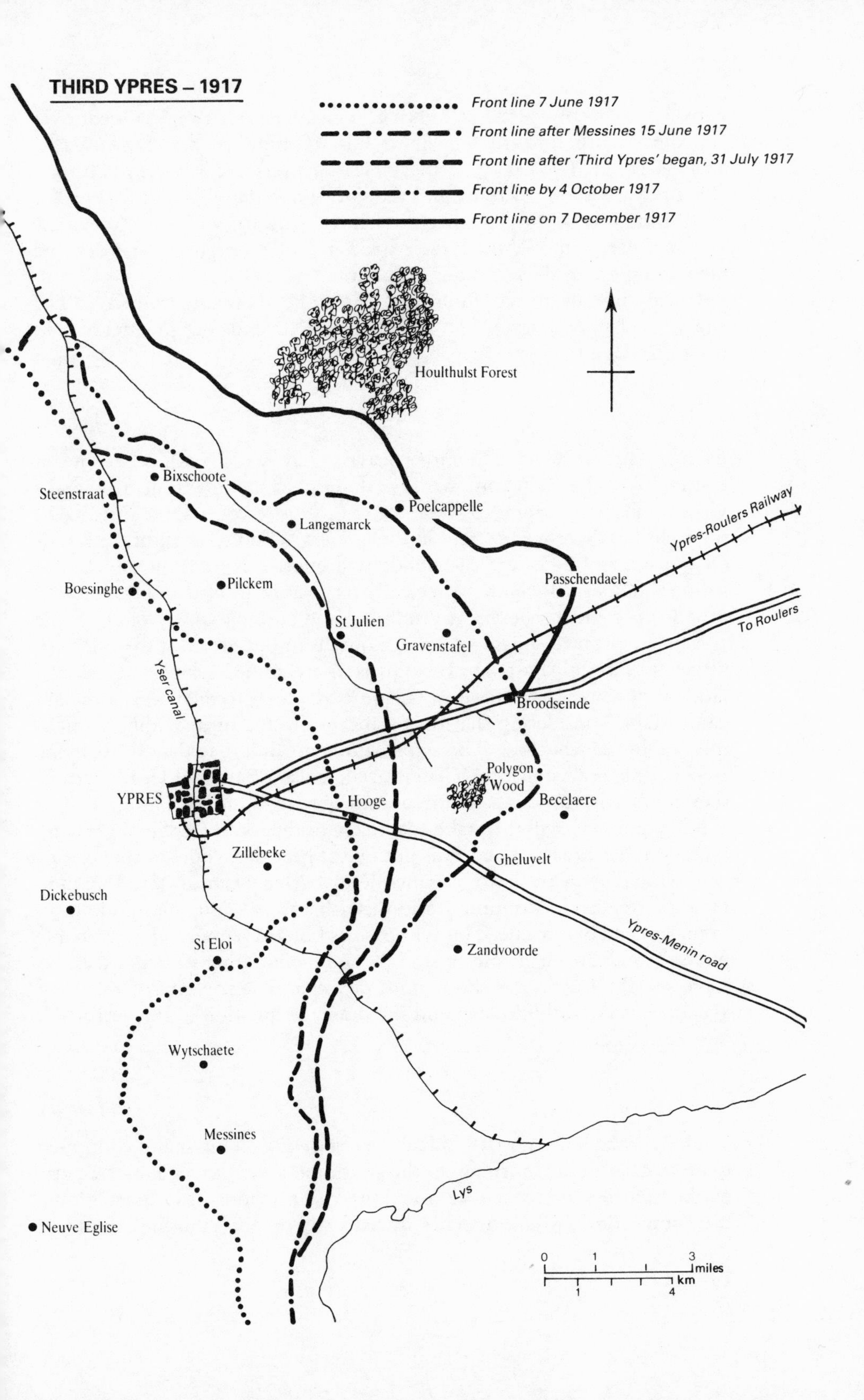
THIRD YPRES – 1917
Front line 7 June 1917
Front line after Messines 15 June 1917
Front line after 'Third Ypres' began, 31 July 1917
Front line by 4 October 1917
Front line on 7 December 1917
Houlthulst Forest
Bixschoote
Steenstraat
Poelcappelle
Langemarck
Ypres-Roulers Railway
Passchendaele
Boesinghe
Pilckem
St Julien
Gravenstafel
To Roulers
Yser canal
Broodseinde
Polygon
Wood
YPRES
Hooge
Becelaere
Zillebeke
Gheluvelt
Dickebusch
St Eloi
Zandvoorde
Ypres-Menin road
Wytschaete
Messines
Lys
Neuve Eglise
0
1
3
miles
km
1
4

between a glass of water and a glass of whisky. Another night I went over and dined with Edward Greene at Fort Rompu on the Armentières–Estavies Road. The heavy Artillery Headquarters live in a very comfortable brewery a long way behind the line where they have now been for several months. If they ever have to move, Edward will want a separate wagon for his kit as during their time at Fort Rompu he has collected beds and sheets and every kind of luxury.

During the latter part of our time at Nieppe, the weather got very bad and we had a good deal of snow and hail which made our practice attacks most unpleasant.

16 January

Evans went away on a month's leave today which will leave me in command of the Battalion. We are taking over the line tomorrow and I went up in the morning to reconnoitre it. Our sector is some distance to the right of where we last held in Ploegsteert Wood. Our right flank rests on the River Lys where the floods will effectively prevent any Boche from raiding us. Much of our sector is very badly flooded and the left end of it is very much battered by minnies and is unpleasantly close to the Boche. The ruined village of Le Touquet is in our area but there is very little left of it. Our Battalion Headquarters are in the back part of a ruined farm at the west end of this village and are extremely spacious and comfortable considering that they stand out in the open within about ½-mile of the Boche line. The explanation no doubt is that though the Boches fully realize that the farm is occupied as a Battalion Headquarters, they don't wish to knock it down until there is an attack on one side or another and they will then take advantage of their knowledge to blow up Battalion Headquarters and thus put out of gear the whole of the sector.

The old railway track from Armentières to Menin runs close to Battalion Headquarters and a communication trench has been dug alongside it up to the left end of our line. This is known as Long Avenue, and is a horrible place as, owing to its being so straight and having long stretches with no traverses, the Boche can shoot right down it. The top end of this long avenue is very badly flooded and the drainage question in this sector is a very serious one.

17 January

Took over the line by 12.30. It had been snowing all night and continued to do so most of the morning. In the afternoon I went to reconnoitre parts of the trenches which I had not done the previous day. Parts of the communication and fire trenches are half-way up one's thighs in mud and water. Though my long gumboots prevented me from getting wet I was splashed up to the shoulder with mud when I got home. Owing to the waterlogged conditions of the ground the line here consists in many places not of trenches but of a parapet. We do not hold the whole of the front line in strength but concentrate at certain strongpoints. The gaps between are at present very dangerous owing to the parapet being so low and we shall have to work very hard to heighten the parapets to repair the serious dilapidations and to drain the water away.

The Boches opposite this sector have got a large collection of Minenwerfer which throw anything up to 300 lb shells and blow enormous craters in our line. The big ones look rather like rum jars in the air and when they are active one has to keep one's eyes open for them so as to bolt round a traverse and lie flat if they come close. Owing to the softness of the ground here, unless they come almost on top of one, one has a pretty good chance as they bury themselves in the ground and blow a crater up to about twenty feet wide and six or eight feet deep.

The first days in this sector were rather bewildering as it is an absolute maze of old trenches and it took some time to get the hang of the defence scheme and artillery arrangements and to find out localities of the various machine guns and medium and light trench mortars which are dotted about in one's area, and of course under one's command for tactical purposes. In case any trouble should happen at night we always have an artillery officer sleeping at our Headquarters and responsible for good communication with the various Batteries of Artillery which cover our Section.

A great advantage of being in the trenches is that one lives in separate Messes and the whole Battalion is not cramped up together in one small room. I spend a good deal of the day with RE officers discussing means of getting rid of the water. Apart from the incessant snow and rain the great difficulty is that, when by days of labour one has got the water to run in a particular direction, a 'Minnie' arrives and blocks up the trench. We have got one communication trench fittingly known as Napoo Avenue which has been obliterated three times in six days. There are about twenty different Minenwerfer emplacements opposite our sector, each of which is known by a different name for purposes of identification. These emplacements are not continuously occupied but we have them marked down on maps and when the officer on trench duty can satisfy himself that the shells are coming over from a particular direction he telephones down to Battalion Headquarters that 'James' and 'Joan' are active and we telephone on to the Battery concerned to retaliate on the emplacements in question.

20 January

Yesterday I spent much of the day wading round the line with General Baird and today I took round our new GSO1, Colonel O.H.L. Nicholson, who seems to be a very capable and pleasant person. There is an extraordinary variety of Minnies in these sectors. Some of these projectiles are pointed, others blunt-ended and others are pear-shaped. Some turn head over heels in the air and others come straight. Some burst on impact and others several seconds afterwards, after being buried deep in the ground. It rather looks as if there is an experimental school opposite us for teaching the use of the various kinds.

22 January

Went round the line at 5.30 a.m. Went up again afterwards to have a quiet examination from an OP in order to locate trench mortars. The water in the left end of the sector is still well over one's knees in places, but we have managed to get some of it out by flooding parts further back which were previously dry. After lunch I walked down to Le Bisé, the Headquarters of the Battalion in support, for a Brigade Conference. Just before starting, a heavy bombardment began and I saw a truck on the station suddenly disappear from a direct hit. When I returned from the Conference I found things had become pretty hot. Our telephone communication with one Company was cut by a shell coming into their dugout, taking off the head of the man who was speaking and wounding the other operator. I sent up two more signallers who connected us up by the other wire, generally used for artillery work. Meanwhile the other two Companies on the right of the line were sending very disquieting messages – 'communication trench blocked in 10 or 20 places', 'one platoon completely isolated'. Joseph, Jemima, Jane, Charlie Chaplin, Gertrude and Constance were all hard at work, assisted by .77s and 4.2s. SOS rockets went up on both our flanks and the Brigade became very worried and kept ringing me up on the telephone to know what was happening.

I sent an Intelligence Officer down to a fort on our right flank to try and discover what was happening to the Corps on our right on the other side of the Lys, but we weren't able to get much information except that the Boche were also very active on that side.

By about 7 p.m. things got quieter in our sub-sector and I went up to the line to see the damage. I found that, though greatly exaggerated on the telephone, it was pretty bad. The communication trench up to our right Company was blocked in three places by huge Minnie craters, eight to ten feet deep and about twenty feet across, and the fire trench on the right was also obliterated in the same way in several places. The centre

Company had suffered very little except for a large hole through the parapet in one place which made a very awkward gap in our defence. This Company had probably got off so lightly owing to the fact that they are only from fifty to eighty yards away from the Boche and they probably cannot trust their Minnies to shoot accurately enough to risk shells dropping so close to their own trenches.

The centre communication trench was badly blocked and also that on the left but fortunately some way back where it didn't very much matter. The urgent need was to connect up to the Minnie holes so as sufficiently to reconstruct the trench for our relief tomorrow morning. I arranged therefore to have every available man of the three forward companies put on at once to the work of clearing and to get the Company in support who had been working hard all day to be up again at 3 a.m. after a short sleep. Owing to the fact that trenches were in many cases revetted with corrugated iron it was a very heavy task to get them clear as the torn and twisted sheets had got thrown across the line through which one had to cut and had to be dug out before the path could be re-opened. Relief orders only reached me at 1 a.m. – relief is to be complete by 11 a.m. Fortunately by tremendous efforts we got the trench opened up just in time to let the first relieving Companies through by 9 a.m. The Boche had apparently been plastering our line to distract attention from raids which he carried out on our right and on our left. Fortunately the Minnies generally speaking came clear of our actual posts and we got off very lightly with three men killed and as many wounded.

23 January

On relief two of our Companies moved into a line of strongpoints about 1000 yards behind the line and two more Companies went into support about one mile back at Le Bizet. This village has been a good deal knocked about by bombardment and is quite uninhabited so that we have it all to ourselves and there is any amount of room. There is not, of course, a pane of glass in the place but calico is generally stretched across the window frames and a good many of the rooms are fitted up with stoves, so in spite of the arctic weather one keeps pretty warm. The men are fearfully tired and when I went round their billets I found most of them fast asleep. There is, however, so much urgent work to be done that they will, all the same, have to go up to work tonight. I spent the afternoon reconnoitring the routes to our assembly position in the event of an attack. The ground now is frozen quite hard so that all such work as filling sandbags has become almost impossible.

24 January

In the morning I went round all the forts which we are garrisoning, a long walk taking about four hours. On the map one gets very little idea of distances. All the communication trenches, of course, are so traversed and have so many bends that one walks two or three times as far as it would be in a straight line. The ice in the flooded trenches is now about three inches thick.

27 January

The Kaiser's birthday. Passed quite quietly though we had expected the Boche to celebrate it by raids.

29 January

Came back to the trenches to take over the same Le Touquet sub-sector that we held last time. The trenches being frozen solid gives a great opportunity for snipers, as instead of walking as before two feet deep in water and mud, one now goes on the frozen surface. This morning, largely owing to this, one man was killed by a sniper and four men wounded by rifle grenades.

30 January

Still freezing hard and some more snow. Living as I do in a dugout with plenty of clothes and blankets, I can realize how much the men are suffering in this weather with no blankets in the trenches and no dugouts owing to the wind being in a dangerous quarter for gas. Blankets in the trenches are of course quite impossible as they get immediately sodden with water, and to use dugouts in the front line when the wind is dangerous means that the men inside would be suffocated in their sleep in case of a gas attack. In spite of the terrible conditions, the men are wonderfully cheerful.

31 January

Where the Minnies have burst in the ice on the old shell holes the fragments are at least six inches thick. We are hard at work trying to improve our wire but it is quite impossible to drive in pegs and wiring is therefore limited to the preparation by day of 'knife rests' which are thrown out into no-man's-land during the night and the ends attached together so as to form a continuous line. A Boche sniper has been very troublesome at the nose of our salient ever since we came in last Monday. That morning he killed one of the Battalion whom we relieved and since then he has cut the sandbags at one of our posts to ribbons so that the sentry had to be moved into another bay. As he had been located about fifty yards away from our trench, just where the Boche trench runs nearest to us it was not easy for our artillery to knock him out without making a hole in our parapet at the same time. He became such a nuisance, however, that I finally decided to risk it and moved our people to a flank while the 18 prs put about 20 HE shells on the spot. They burst one shell within a yard of where he had apparently just been shooting and we have had no more trouble with him since.

1 February

'Fish-tails' and rifle grenades were troublesome in the morning. The 'fish-tail' is a grenade about eight or ten inches long with fins projecting from a central rod behind and is fired by the Boche off a kind of stick apparatus. While I was up in the line they hit two of our stretcher bearers who were just inside a dugout sorting out men's socks to take them down to be dried, and the fish-tail burst just in the entrance to the dugout almost in the same spot where another fish-tail had burst two days ago and knocked out two of our Lewis gunners.

After dusk I went off to see a post which we hold 400 yards away on our right flank and separated from our line by a complete gap. One can only go there after dark as it is important that the Boche should not know that we occupy it. On my way out I felt rather uneasy at the number of Minnies that were exploding and I had no sooner got there than I saw SOS rockets going up along our line. It was impossible to tell how far off they were, so I ran back as hard as I could to the telephone of our right Company and rang up Battalion Headquarters. McKerrow, the Adjutant, told me that an SOS signal had gone up from our left Company and also further along the line on the front of the Brigade on our left. Unfortunately our left Company are far away from their telephone, because we can't get the mile of wire required to run the Battalion and artillery lines on from the previous Headquarters which they occupied but which I thought too far back from the line. It was therefore difficult to get information but by the time I reached Battalion Headquarters an officer had got down to their telephone and said that after being bombarded for a quarter of an hour by six Minnies (they counted that number of shells in the air at once) a terrific barrage of Field guns, 4.7 Howitzers and rifle grenades opened on them. At the same time men were seen moving some way off on the left of our line and the Company Commander, feeling sure that the Boche were attacking, put up the SOS. This end of our sub-sector is very nasty, as we are separated by a gap about 400 yards wide from the Battalion holding the other bit of our Brigade front. There are battered-in trenches between, but in many places they are quite obliterated. It seemed likely that the Boche had gone for this gap in which case we could only shoot at his flank, and trust to the machine guns and strongpoints behind to stop him going any further. After our SOS barrage had been going on for about half an hour, seeing that the bombardment of our left had quieted, I got the Artillery liaison officer to ask the Artillery Group to stop firing. Later on in the evening I heard from the Battalion on our left that they had sent out a patrol into the gap and about sixty yards from our post had found two Boche helmets, one full of brains, one officer's cap covered with blood, and some Boche bombs, left in the trench, also three German rifles. I ordered our Company to send a patrol out from our end, warning the Battalion on our left that they would be out after 3 a.m.

2 February

I went up myself at 4.30 a.m. and found that the Sergeant who took out the patrol had heard people moving about and breaking through the cats' ice about twenty yards away. Asked why he didn't go for them he said he had thought they might be a patrol from the other Battalion. As he told me they afterwards heard a voice saying '*baronfa*' (?) this was of course absurd. (Perhaps what they really said was '*Wer ist da*'.) Anyhow, there was nothing to be done now except to see whether any traces remained, so I took the Sergeant and told him to guide me to the place where this happened. With a couple more men we scrambled along for the most part behind the trench where it had been blown in. Finally we got to a place where he said he had stopped when he heard the noises. We went on in the direction from which they had come, found some broken cats' ice in a Minnie hole, and close by a big black patch right across the trench. It was too dark to see what it was, but there were either bits of mud or bits of bone frozen into it. I kicked off a chunk of the dark ice and wrapped it up in a handkerchief with some snow. Failing to find anything more we went back another way. As soon as it got light I found that the chunk of dark ice was chiefly blood. I put it in a tin and sent it down the Brigade as evidence of what had taken place. Apparently the Boche had raided the gap. The officer had probably been killed by the Lewis gun of our left post (which had fired into the gap when the Boche put his barrage on). The rest of the party then probably decided to go back. Whether or not the patrol from the other Battalion had found the officer's cap, helmets and grenades in the same place as our pool of blood I don't know. Possibly the party whom our patrol heard may have been a stretcher party or men sent over to remove traces of their failure.

Last night I found the advantage of the Artillery Liaison Officer, who always sleeps at our Headquarters. The artillery arrangements are now certainly much better than they were on the Somme. Experiments in England have shown the gunners that their range tables were quite unreliable with the new ammunition, and they now realize that they must inevitably drop a lot of shells short and that when the infantry tell them so it is no reflection on their shooting. In the SOS barrage last night they were dropping shells behind our trenches. I brought one of the shrapnel cases down with me and gave it to the liaison officer with the result that the officer whose guns were firing on that particular bit of line came up to see me and find out details. A few short shells were of course inevitable as the SOS brought on a barrage at six rounds per minute from a whole Brigade of Artillery concentrated on quite a narrow front, besides the Heavies behind. To do any good they had to fire at the Boche trench which is so close to us that the 'error of the gun' (4% of the range) would inevitably on the average, quite apart from defective ammunition, cause a few shells to drop short. Artillery fire is an expensive amusement. The liaison officer who has just come up says that last night his battery alone fired about £700 worth of ammunition. Our little SOS must have cost £3000 or £4000 at least.

3 February

We watch the weather very anxiously. It still gets colder and colder and I hope the frost may last for another twelve days as after that we shall be clear of this sector for about six weeks and may thus avoid the terrible conditions of mud and dilapidation which will come with the thaw. The idea is that after a month in this wet sector we shall do a fortnight's training (if the Division is still in the same Corps) and then go back for a month to the other and drier sector of the Divisional front.

4 February

We were relieved by the Borderers in the early morning and went back to Pont de Nieppe, a grubby little suburb about a mile west of Armentières, nominally inhabited by factory workers. Under ordinary conditions, while here we should be sending up working parties every night to the trenches, but the ground is now so hard that all digging is impossible. I have got quite a good room with a chimney which enables me to keep warm with an improvised stove made out of an old bucket.

7 February

It now turns out that I was sent to this Battalion by mistake. There is another W. E. Guinness who is a Major in the Manchester (Regiment) but recruited in the Cheshire area. I only had the original gazette in *The Times* showing him as Second-in-Command in a Cheshire Battalion but we now got 'Part 2 Orders from the 3rd Echelon' quoting the gazette of this other W. E. Guinness and thus showing that the Cheshire Battalion to which he was to be posted as 2nd-in-Command was indeed this one. I believe, however, that the mistake is not likely to make much difference as my namesake is said to be out in Mesopotamia and the AG's Department is continually mixing people up in this way.

8 February

We moved up at short notice relieving the 2nd South Lancashire Battalion in the support position at Le Bizet and the line of forts. I found that the Second-in-Command of the South Lancs Battalion, who was also commanding in his Colonel's absence, is in just the same position as I; having seen a lot of service in Egypt he left the Yeomanry there in response to an invitation to Senior Officers to transfer with a view of commanding Battalions in the BEF. Like me, he has been stranded for the last six months as Second-in-Command of a Battalion in which he has no sort of local interest.

10 February

We moved back into the line which has become much noisier than when we first took it over. During the actual relief we had three men killed and two wounded and the Battalion we relieved had two killed and one wounded. Our Battalion Headquarters are much less comfortable than they were before, as the Boche planted six shells into them a couple of days ago, probably in retaliation for our having shelled what is believed to be one of their Battalion Headquarters. Many are now laid up with colds and influenza which I am staving off with quinine.

13 February

Busy day. Went all round the line between 5 and 8 a.m. Just as I had finished breakfast the GSO2 of the New Zealand Division turned up to reconnoitre the line in case they have to take it over, so I went round again with him. After lunch I went up a third time to try and get our Stokes (mortars) on to some Boche snipers who, owing to various contretemps, only succeeded in getting a very unpleasant half-hour from Boche Minnies, fish-tails and rifle grenades which chose the moment of my arrival to come to life. My rendezvous with the Stokes officer was in vain as heavy trench mortars had unexpectedly arrived and put six into his emplacement, so blocking it up with their own ammunition as to make it impossible for him to shoot.

15 February

During the day the enemy were very active and we had a good many casualties. In the evening, however, it became very quiet and I feared some trouble must be brewing.

16 February

At about 3.25 a.m. I was awakened by the explosions of heavy Minnies in rapid succession. I had often heard it other nights but generally on the front of the next Division. From where I lay I could see all along over their trenches which are separated from ours by a deep river. This time their line was dark except for the lazy drop of an occasional Verey light. I ran in to the signal dugout next door just as the operator wrote down the names of seven different Minnies which were active. I got through straightaway to the Brigade and asked them to put the Howitzers on at once. The telegram was from our centre company but the noise was more from our left. I found the Adjutant trying to ring up that company, but, as usual when they start shelling, the line was broken. He got through to the centre company and told them to send an officer along to get in touch with the left to clear up the situation. As soon as our Howitzer retaliation came over the Minnies quieted down. I went out to where the sentry was watching for the SOS and where I had fixed four iron rails pointing to our three Company Headquarters and the right of the Battalion on our left. It was bitterly cold but a beautiful night without a star in the sky. For the first time I had absentmindedly taken off my waistcoat to go to bed, and though I had thrown an overcoat over my shirt my teeth were chattering. I watched the red trails of sparks left by the 260 lb Minnies as they toiled up and drooped down again, each being followed by a terrific roar and mushroom of yellow flame. One saw them even better than in daylight and I went in to the Orderly Room to verify from the map the particular members of the family which were active. I found there a messenger from the left company to ask us to send the SOS to the Artillery as their lines were broken and the Boche was in the trench. I went to the liaison officer's dugout. He was sleeping like a log. I prodded him until he woke and told him to get the batteries on. We then turned out our Support Company and Headquarters details and waited for the Company Commander to report. Meanwhile another messenger arrived with a bloodstained scrap of paper and nothing on it but C 4.1./C 4.2. I rushed to the liaison officer and got him to switch all the batteries on to the left. The Adjutant meantime was talking to the Brigade and trying to get news of the line. At last the Centre Company Commander rang through. The officer he had sent had found an officer of the left Company and reported that they'd had a heavy shelling but that there were no Boche. We therefore shut off the guns, sent off the signalling officer to get the line mended and to trace the runner who had brought the verbal message and who had meanwhile vanished. It was then nearly 5.0 a.m. and we went into the Mess to warm ourselves up with cocoa. It was extraordinary that the Company should have sent such messages about nothing and now that it was quiet I would go up and clear the matter up.

The first pink of dawn was showing as I started. A white frost had made the duckboards like glass. About 200 yards from the front line there was a chasm in the communication trench, then a blown-in dugout and a dead Stokes gunner. The rest of the way was littered with fragments. I was told at the first Lewis gun post I came to in the line that there had been no Boche and that our shells had been worse than those of the enemy. I went along round the corner and found the whole place blown in. It was then too dark to see details but on the way back I found the remains of three men, two of whom could only be collected in sandbags. Clambering round the piles of débris which blocked the trench I found the Company Commander and his officers. Certainly the Boche had been; the trench was littered with about 40 of their stick grenades, but he didn't think they had got in. The next post (a Lewis-gun post) had seen Boche crossing no-man's-land and fired, but only about twenty-five rounds as the gun then jammed owing to an explosion driving earth into the mechanism. The Boche had apparently wanted to raid but had quickly turned back owing to the rifle fire. Further along and right to the end of our line they'd seen and heard nothing but the Minnies. I went back to where the bombs were and cross-questioned one of the sentries who had been on duty at the time of the attack. Yes, the Boche had come in. He suddenly saw about eighty of them. They threw bombs at him and he at them from behind a traverse but he didn't seem clear as to what had taken place. It was now getting light and we saw a dead man lying close by in the trench. We looked into a dugout and found another, sitting up with a bag of Boche bombs and his head blown in. There was no doubt about it. The Boche had most certainly been in our trench. To cut short what was long in discovering, they had rushed the post under cover of a box barrage. Probably they didn't stay more than three minutes altogether and then cleared out. Five men were dead, four wounded and three missing, and the only trace of the raiders were stick grenades and a Bavarian cap. They had chosen their place very well. When we took over the line there had been two little houses one on each side of this post. Persistent shelling by Minnies had reduced them to mounds of masonry, screening the ground in front from enfilade Lewis-gun fire from either flank. The front was so churned up, a tangle of beams and corrugated iron and sandbags, that men could crawl out from the Boche line eighty yards away and creep along under cover of Minnie holes to within five yards of our post. What could they do when, suddenly, on the lift of the barrage, these shouting Bavarians, four or five to one, leapt down upon them? The wire entanglements in front had been mended by us night after night but day after day had been blown away.

I went down to the Dressing Station and saw one man with a broken head. He said that suddenly two Boche landed on his back. They were all round him and he only remembers a violent struggle during which they kept shouting '*Kamerad*' before he lost consciousness. He also remembered seeing one of the missing men bayoneted. The other wounded were too bad to question. One had a hand and a leg smashed.

I don't know how such raids can be prevented. If one has a standing picket out in no-man's-land to cover a weak point of this kind, night after night lying out without any permanent defence they are almost certain eventually to fall an easy prey. If one sends out continual patrols to watch and spot the small area to which their movements are restricted they become an easy ambush. On the whole the safest course seems to be to keep the men in the trenches and to rely on their alertness to foil a raid. In this case they were apparently caught by the Boche coming over so quickly on the lift of the hurricane barrage that they had no time to get out of the shelters in which some of them had sought cover from the shelling.

In the afternoon we were relieved and returned to the positions which we previously held when in support. I was to have gone on the 18th, when Evans would be back from his month's leave, to the CO's course at the 2nd Army School which takes a week and consists chiefly of discussions. Division, however, telephoned today that as Evans would be back he was to go himself instead.

17 February

Evans and Baird walked up in the afternoon and told me there was a probability that I should be sent as Brigade Major to General Bethell* who commands the 74th Brigade. It is already so far fixed up that a new Second-in-Command (a Regular of the Cheshires) was being sent up from the 10th Cheshires in the 7th Brigade to take over from me. In the evening Borley turned up, having for the last six months been struggling to get to me as servant. In the evening I went down from Support Headquarters at Le Bizet to dine with General Baird at Pont de Nieppe where Evans was staying for the night before going off to the CO's course.

18 February

I had not seen Bethell previously and was struck by his great restlessness and energy. He wanted me to come in at once so that if Thompson (his present Brigade Major) was suddenly ordered away I should be on the spot to take over. I had, of course, to go back to hand over, but even then he was continually telephoning to know how soon I was going to turn up. I came to him at a very bad moment as I had got an abominable cold and high fever as the result of my early morning alarm in scanty attire two days previously, and I gathered later that I looked so dilapidated that Bethell had grave doubts about taking me and thought that my health would collapse under any strain. I moved over in the afternoon and sat up with Thompson till 1.30 a.m., working out march tables and other arrangements for our three-days' march to the Quelmes area where we were being sent for a few weeks' training.

20 February

Began our march through a downpour of rain, spending the night at Caestre. In the afternoon Thompson and I rode out to reconnoitre routes for the following day's march as some of the roads marked on the map are quite unfit for transport.

21 February

Marched on again to Peblingham where I developed a violent attack of fever, but by means of drastic remedies got it under control and went up by motor on the *22nd* to our destination at Quelmes, a delightful little village about six miles west of St Omer.

23 February

Rode all round our training area which offers exceptional opportunities, being quite close both to the 2nd Army Infantry School and also the 2nd Army Musketry School with very good facilities for rifle shooting. Thompson left a day or two after our arrival at Quelmes but the 2nd Army proved very recalcitrant about my appointment as they wanted to promote the GSO3 at our Division (25th) whom neither Bethell nor Bainbridge wanted. I found life pretty busy as Bethell was like quicksilver and had none of the usual hangers-on to a Brigade Staff. Instead of the usual Brigade Mess of about ten, we were only five – Bethell, Marriott* (the Staff Captain), an Orderly Officer (Dobbin of the 2nd Royal Irish Rifles), a Signalling Officer (Reynolds), and I. Though one had hardly a moment even to look at a newspaper, I found life infinitely more interesting than with a Battalion and no longer felt that my brain was turning into wool from lack of exercise.

3 March

We motored over with Kincaid Smith, the CRA (Commander, Royal Artillery) of the 25th Division, to see the 8th Cavalry Brigade where Bethell used to be Brigade Major. General Bulkley Johnson seems rather like Bethell in character and I should imagine they must sometimes have knocked their heads together. On the way back we dined with the Blues at Fruges. Tweedmouth was in command and the only others there were Pembroke, Harrison and George Meyrick.

We were at Quelmes until *18 March*, training hard and doing a lot of musketry. The shooting takes place across a valley against some terraced banks. Across the top along an upper terrace runs a road with sentries at either end of the danger area to stop people passing while we shoot. One day when the 2nd Royal Irish Rifles were on the range, Plumer,* the Army Commander, came motoring along until he was pulled up by a whistling ricochet bullet. He went back to the sentry and asked why he had not been warned. The sentry answered, 'The officer's after telling me to stop any person using the road, but he said nothing about stopping Generals'!

20 March

We started back to join the 2nd Anzac Corps under Sir Alexander Godley, staging on the way at Lynde and Strazeele on the way to our destination at Brune Gaya only half a mile from our previous home at Romarin. The Brigade are not in the line but are hard at work every day digging the trenches for the Third Australian Division who are holding the line. We went over and lunched with their Commander, General Monash,* on *23 March*. He is a typical old Jew, in civil life an engineer. He was not much thought of as a Brigadier at Gallipoli and was given a Division because the Australians don't like being commanded by British professional soldiers.

27 March

General Broadwood, commanding the 57th Division, sent for a motor to fetch me. He seems very well and it is most unlucky for him that Douglas Powell (his doctor) forbade him coming out at the beginning of the War. As it is he has come out with a second-line Territorial Division consisting of good men but a very poor lot of officers and an absolutely inexperienced Staff, all three of his GSOs having only had Gallipoli experience and knowing nothing whatever of the conditions here. He wants COs for two of his Battalions and is trying to get them from us. I told him that I found, as an amateur, that, though it was comparatively easy to run a Battalion in the line, one was much handicapped by lack of necessary experience for training it. Staff work under present conditions is almost as new to the regular soldiers as to anyone else, whereas the organization and machinery of a Battalion is very little changed by a war. I was inoculated for enteric and, having foolishly afterwards ridden a pulling horse for about ten miles and then walked another two miles, became so stiff that it was great pain to move at all.

29 March

At last my definite appointment as Brigade Major has come through. Plumer was extremely obstinate about the matter in spite of repeated interviews with Bethell and Bainbridge.

6 April

Moved about eight miles back to a disgusting little village called Steentje about two miles south of Bailleul where we stayed until sent back to the line at short notice to take over the Wulverghem sector on *13 April*. We then for the first time held that sector from which we were a few weeks afterwards to make our attack on Messines. We are very busy working on the sector and beginning to work out plans for the great attack. Our Brigade Headquarters are in the village of Neuve Eglise from which one has a horrible walk of a couple of miles along a cobbled road down to Wulverghem before one gets into the trenches. We live in quite a comfortable house and it is extraordinary that, within three miles of the line, the Boche have allowed it to stand so long. The explanation may be that many of the inhabitants of the village are still here and probably give useful information to the enemy. After abominable cold weather an improvement took place about *23 April*.

During this time I began to see Bethell's defects. He becomes frightfully impatient and unreasonable when things don't go right. For instance he constantly ordered 1000 to 1500 men to put out wire, in the dark of course. This involved huge carrying parties along trenches which quickly became blocked and a great amount of organization was needed to arrange the necessary parties to put it up when these carrying parties had got it down to the line. As everybody concerned knew beforehand, the whole plan miscarried. The forty or fifty wagons which were detailed to convey the material to Wulverghem got stuck in the mud and upset into ditches, and apart from this were blocked from reaching the appointed place because of other wagons unloading ammunition etc.

When Bethell went up the next day, he of course found the whole country littered with dumps of wire which the parties naturally had been unable to find in the inky darkness. No-man's-land was wired in places, but not the places which we had ordered. Vesuvius in eruption couldn't compare with Bethell. I had to send for the Transport Officer and pack them off to the trenches for 48 hours to ensure that they did some work. Finally he cooled down and was satisfied with sending two of them to work at collecting all the dumps together.

The following day I went up with our Field Company Commander and found that a good deal more of the wire had been put up wrong, very easy in the dark when, as in this case, the work had to be done by troops who were not holding the trench immediately behind and were therefore not able to work out all the details thoroughly in daylight. On reporting the position to Bethell he told me to send for the Colonel, the 2nd-in-Command and all the Company Commanders to be here in half an hour, explain things to them and send them up to see their mistake in daylight. I pointed out that they only got home to bed at 7 a.m. and were probably just then getting up, and that if they were to start on a three-mile walk in the afternoon they couldn't possibly explain things to their men and make their arrangements for the evening. Finally after an awful struggle I was allowed to send half the officers down to reconnoitre before dusk and to leave the remainder behind to organize the working parties.

It is very annoying to have to deal with Bethell in this sort of mood as one could get infinitely more work done if he would realize the need for less haste and for giving an opportunity for working out things carefully beforehand. Still, it is probably better to be with a man who in his impetuosity decides wrong rather than with one who waits and sees until it is too late for any decision to be right. Undoubtedly the War has made one realize that the man who takes the second-best course immediately has a great advantage over the man who finally does the right thing when it is too late. Bethell is a great enigma but he seems able to get most unreasonable demands. People generally refuse what he asks flatly at first but finally give way and do what he wants.

The Division was very keen at this time to get fresh identification of the Germans holding the line opposite the Brigade centre. Several unfortunate attempts were made by the 2nd Royal Irish Rifles and others which entailed a good many casualties and no result. We then worked out a really detailed trench raid and got the wire methodically cut by 2-inch mortars. I used to go and watch their shooting from a rise in the ground about 300 yards behind our front line. Our 2-inch mortars are so called because they shoot a 2-inch iron cylinder with a ball about the size of a large football at the end filled with HE. One felt quite sorry sometimes, watching these shoots, to see the Boche running out of their flattened trenches with these things landing among them in the open and sending them up into the air. The most remarkable part of the performance used to be the complete lack of Boche retaliation. It must have been very demoralizing to their infantry who were thus subjected to the most infernal bombardment without a single shell coming from their guns. Probably they have learnt that nowadays they get two and three times as many shells back for every shell they send over. The raid, however, which we were preparing for never came off owing to our sudden relief.

We remained holding the Wulverghem Sector until *30 April* when at very short notice we were relieved by an Australian Brigade and went back to our previous quarters at Steenje. During the ten days that we remained there, we carried out strenuous training at the Mont de Lille ground just south-east of Bailleul. I marked out with flags the German trenches as nearly as possible to scale and, the Battalions having taken it in turn to do their own parts of the attack separately, finally did it together. We had got the plan worked out in considerable detail and represented the barrage by a line of drummers moving back at the scheduled times.

Edward Greene was in Bailleul as Staff Captain of our Corps Heavy Artillery and I saw a good deal of him. I also had one or two aeroplane flights in machines of the PE8-type belonging to the Squadron working with our Corps. I went up the first time with Kinneer, the Squadron Commander, a very nice fellow who was later killed in Italy. Afterwards I went up with a boy who had gone straight into the Flying Corps from his school and had got a DSO for an extraordinary flight through a snowstorm to drop a bomb on Hindenburg one night when he was reported to be sleeping in some house a long way behind the Boche line. His Squadron never expected him to come back, but by some extraordinary chance he did so, having dropped a bomb on Hindenburg's conservatory according to the reports which afterwards came from our secret service.

Our training schemes and working out details of our equipment and methods of attack kept me very busy at Steenje. There always seemed to be about ten things to do at the same moment and it was a perpetual anxiety not to forget one of them.

5 May

I went over to see General Broadwood. He seemed in great spirits and looking very well. This was the last time I saw him before he was killed. (He died of wounds on 21 June, 1917.) After a wet Spring the weather now became very hot and dry.

10 May

We went back to the Wulverghem Sector. I found the daily walk to and from the trenches in this broiling weather very trying. The Boche had begun to put a good many shells into the village where we live and our reserve Battalion which shares it with us (at this moment the 2nd Royal Irish Rifles) have found it safer and more comfortable to bivouac in a field.

I spent from *11 May* to *18 May* in Paris, Nares, the 2nd-in-Command of the 13th Cheshires, coming in to do my work. On my return I found a Brigade Conference was just assembling. We had by this time worked out our forthcoming attack on the Messines Ridge in very great detail. We were very busy too trying to catch Boches, as it is very important, in view of the forthcoming attack,[19] to get information as to the German Divisions in the line and the Reserves behind them. On *22 May* Bethell and I motored over to the Recques area and looked over the ground there with a view to having our final practices for the attack. We found the 58th Brigade practising their attack at the moment and I came across Alex Thynne in command of a Wiltshire Battalion. We found the Brigade Commander, General Glasgow, on the ground and fixed up for me to go over the following day and stay with him while marking out the ground for our work. I went over again on the following day with a party of officers and men to help me and spent a real hard day on the *24th* pegging out an exact model of the trenches with the help of a prismatic compass. This was a very big job as there were eight different lines of enemy to be marked on a width of 700 to 800 yards and to a depth of over a mile, besides our own front line and support system which were to be used as Assembly trenches. Our Brigade arrived early on the morning of the *26th*. The weather was broiling hot. We practised on the training grounds the whole evening until 9 p.m. and then began again at 3 a.m. the following morning (*27 May*). There was no sleep in between as we were working out details and I had to be up on the ground at 1 a.m. to supervise the practice of marching up in dead silence to the Assembly trenches. We got a couple of hours, however, in the morning before doing another practice that afternoon.

28 May

In the early morning we did our final rehearsals, and I suppose the Brigade really did it extremely well, as I never before heard Bainbridge, our Division Commander, praise anything. Sir Alexander Godley, the Corps Commander, was also very pleasant and astonished us all by talking quite openly in his speech to the men about our attack during the next few days on the Messines Ridge. These days at Recques would have been delightful if one had had time to enjoy them, as our Brigade Headquarters were in a very nice Château.

29 May

We went back to the forward area being packed very tightly into huts and tents just round La Crèche village. The following week was an absolute nightmare – orders and counter-orders as to details in the attack and the exact number of men to be taken over; also working out and leaving behind those who were selected as B teams. Bethell insisted on meticulous control of the B teams and made every Battalion send in rolls to show the exact qualifications of each of the 100-odd officers and men thus left out to enable the Battalions to be quickly reformed after casualties. Bethell was in addition continually changing his mind on matters of detail and driving not only me but also the Battalion Commanders nearly mad. Altogether there was very little sleep to be had all this week as, in addition to difficulties owing to Bethell's nerves, there were incessant messages day and night from Division and also from our own units.

At last on Tuesday, 5 *June*, at 2 a.m. orders came through that we were to move up to our prearranged bivouac area between the hours of 7 and 9 a.m. It was less than three miles away and it was necessary for the whole movement to take place between these hours, as many aeroplanes were then to be in the air to keep away the Boche machines and protect us from observation. All details as to approach marches had naturally been left out long beforehand. Our Headquarters remained for the night of the 5th at La Crèche, but we spent practically the whole day in the bivouac field in conferences with Commanding Officers, etc.

6 June

We spent the morning again in conference. A broiling hot day. Bethell moved up about midday to our battle Headquarters at North Midland Farm, leaving me to see the units off on their march to the assembly positions. They began going up in the afternoon at long intervals and the last had left our concentration area by 8.15 p.m. It was a busy day and I had a tremendous lot of writing which had to be done in my message block over and over again with carbons, clerks and typewriters having gone to battle Headquarters. Just before our first Battalion moved off I received the time of zero, namely 3.10 a.m. on the *7th*. It was dusk as I saw the last of the Brigade off the ground and I walked over to our Divisional Headquarters a few hundred yards away in their huts on the Ravelsberg to see whether they had any further communications for us. I found Legge, the AA and QMG in a terrible state that he had failed to deliver a huge consignment of wire cutters for which Marriott, the Staff Captain, had asked him. He had them and various other stores for us in two lorries, and though I assured him that it was quite out of the question when men were already in their assembly trenches to distribute anything of the kind, nothing would satisfy him but to send them to our Brigade dump just beyond Wulverghem. I then rode up and intercepted the head of our column just before they got into the trenches by Wulverghem. They had made a five-mile march up there by special tracks which we had marked out across the field and we had elaborate arrangements for giving them hot soup etc. as they passed. It was an anxious job until they were over the last bit of the road as the Boche had a habit of shelling the corduroy diversion track round Wulverghem. However, this particular evening it was fortunately fairly quiet and the men got up with very few casualties in spite of the very crowded state of the roads. I got up to our battle Headquarters by about 11.30. They were in a newly constructed dugout on high ground at North Midland Farm, about 600 yards behind our front line. One got a wonderful view of the ground from here but it was such an obvious place for an observation post that the Boche was rather fond of putting bursts of shells on it. In this way Bowyer, the QM of the 11th Lancashire Fusiliers, got his head taken off as he was just coming into the door of our dugout.

7 June

All troops were reported to be in position by 1 a.m. and were served out with hot tea and rum in the trenches. From 1.45 to 2.45 I got an hour's sleep. Then we all woke up and waited for the crash. At 3.10 a.m. there was a most terrific concussion from the explosion of the mines all along the Boche front line. The one nearest to us under Ontario Farm contained 200 tons of explosives. The explosions were simultaneous, being fired by electricity, but the ground went on rocking as if it was made of india rubber for several seconds after the explosions and the earth poured down through cracks in the planking over our heads.

With the explosions of the mines our barrage came down and our assaulting Battalions went over to the attack having eight separate lines of objectives to take on, one behind the other to a depth of a mile. The assaulting troops also were formed up, line behind line in assembly trenches specially dug for the purpose. The barrage of the Boche trenches was terrific, a greater collection of artillery than is said ever before to have been concentrated. As soon as the attack went forward the dust and smoke was so dense that the observers near the top of the dugout could see nothing. As the barrage rolled back we got more and more impatient, telephone lines run forward from our cable head were cut by the Boche bombardment and the power buzzer jammed. All we knew was that the Brigade had all advanced into the black fog; our cable line operators in our front line could see nothing else.

Bethell sat with a volume of Shakespeare open in front of him, shouting to me in the next room every minute or two demands for information which of course we couldn't get. We picked up a certain amount from wounded and prisoners coming back and heard from Brigade on our flank that they had got their first objective. Finally, hearing not a syllable ourselves, the General thought we must be hung up and sent me out to find out and do anything possible. With another officer, Massey, who was attached as a Staff learner, and some runners, I set off, going by compass as soon as I was over our parapet, as the whole ground was changed. Trees and hedges, reduced to poles and sticks before, had now nearly disappeared, and the ground was like giant pumice stone, huge pits and craters up to ten feet deep. Streams of wounded walking back and a certain number of bewildered men wandering about not knowing where they were. We collected a good many of these and made them go forward again. The Boche shelling of their own former trenches was not very heavy and there was little machine-gun fire. We found the two advanced Battalions in their final objectives, those in the rear having just passed through to go on. I scribbled a message and sent it back by runner to the General and then went on to the top of the ridge where our other two Battalions were just reaching their objective. Up here there was considerable enemy shelling, MG fire and sniping. While I was taking a bearing with my prismatic compass to find out whether we were in the right place, they told me to look out for a sniper who promptly put a bullet through the head of a man who was crouching next to me.

After having a look at the line and strongpoints which we were consolidating, I went back to Brigade Headquarters, calling on my way out at a position in the Boche line to which we had intended to move our Brigade Headquarters. I found the dugout so blown in that it was out of the question.

The rest of the day was very busy. Bethell went up in the afternoon and got hit on the way down by the base of a spent shell. Fortunately it only raised an enormous bruise and made him very stiff.

After we had consolidated our final line, another Brigade of our Division went through us and twelve hours after zero an Australian Division went through them. The latter did not get their final objectives but spent their time in the first looking for souvenirs. Though fine men individually they have no cohesion, discipline or organization, and are in these respects far behind the New Zealanders. Our men were digging in hard all the time though as it turned out the Boche was too beat to do much counter-attacking. Every few hours, however, came reports of enemy concentrating in various places and much ammunition was spent by the artillery on both sides.

8 June

Went up early (3.30 a.m.) to try to disentangle position of units who are dug in on rather irregular lines. A good deal of excitement in the evening owing to counterattacks real or imaginary on some very disorganized Australians. Though it is only at the time of writing two days afterwards, I cannot clearly remember the details of these days. In our deep dugout we live by electric light and one is hardly conscious as to whether it is day or night. On this and the following day we were shifting the Brigade about and readjusting our boundaries, and producing a good many orders which were cancelled owing to changes of details by higher authority before ever reaching units. There has been a good deal of shelling, especially in the top of the ridge and in the village of Messines, chiefly enfiladed from heavy Boche guns and over 1/3rd of the Brigade are casualties. Fortunately the proportion of killed to wounded is remarkably low.

10 June

Went round our Battalions at 4 a.m. Very misty morning and things pretty quiet. On the way back went to see mine craters just to our left. They are astounding, 50 to 70 yards in diameter and about 40 feet deep. Our artillery was extraordinarily good and nothing could possibly live under its fire. The ammunition is very different now to what it was on the Somme and the ground this time is not littered, as was usual at that time, with unexploded shells.

11 June

Came back for 24 hours' rest in bivouac, a couple of miles back in a delightful green field by the River Douve. It is difficult to remember details of what happened on the intermediate days. One never got more than about three hours sleep in the 24. There were incessant things to attend to, battalions moving to different bits of ground owing to redistribution of the front and every day some part or other of the ground to be reconnoitred for moving, siting of trenches, etc. The '24 hours' rest' for me consisted in going down with the Brigade while the General stayed for the night up in our Battle Headquarters dugout with the clerks. Correspondence all came to me and I was woken up just six times during the night.

12 June

Had a fearful rush. No clerk with me and stacks of paper pouring in from both sides, Division and Advanced Brigade. It was a blessing when the 24 hours ended and I saw the troops off back to the line where we are in close support.

14 June

We are going back up to our bivouac again tonight but it may again only be for another short rest. It will be nice to get a good sleep. Otherwise we've been living in an extraordinarily civilized way in our dugout thirty feet below the surface. We've got endless passages, five entrances and eight rooms down here, also electric light. One only hears a very dull thud when a heavy shell lands on the top.

15 June

We went back into Divisional Reserve in the same field on the banks of the Douve to which we went on the 11th, and stayed there until the *17th*. I spent most of the time compiling the history of operations and getting the Brigade reformed by the re-absorption of B teams, etc. We went over about 2600 strong and had something over 1000 casualties. Bethell did not come back with us into the line but went off home on leave. Craigie Halkett,* who commanded the 9th Loyal North Lancs, came in and took over the Brigade. We had a pretty strenuous time in the line until *June 23rd*. We had our Brigade Headquarters in a concrete pill box just east of Messines, and were holding our front line on the Ridge at Gapaard village. We were instructed to worry the Boche as much as possible. Originally we were to have done quite a big attack, not with a view to holding the ground but just to kill Boches and shake their nerves. Bainbridge, however, was very firm about the matter with the Corps and said that in view of the short time we had had for reconnaisance and the obscurity of the Boche positions, we couldn't do it. Every night, however, we were patrolling in considerable force, trying to cut out machine-gun posts, etc.

We also continually knocked their line to pieces with artillery. We were holding nothing of course in the way of a continuous line, just isolated posts on the salient features of the ground. It was very unpleasant walking up to these posts, as one had to go straight for the open and there was always quite a good chance of missing one's way and walking into the Boche post instead of ours. The enemy infantry, however, seem to be extremely demoralized. This can be the only explanation of the way that time after time one was able to walk up to our forward posts in broad daylight and in full view of the Boche without a single shot being fired at one. On the other hand, his artillery was extremely active and one's walks used to be most unpleasant owing to his habit of suddenly plastering the ground with a heavy bombardment.

Battalion Headquarters, like ourselves, were in concrete pill boxes constructed by the Boche. The enemy who made them were of course fully aware of their exact position and kept them under almost continuous fire. It was all right once one was inside, but in going to see the Battalion Commanders one always had a very unpleasant job getting in at the entrance which was naturally on the Boche side of the pill box and subject to very accurate fire.

Some of these concrete buildings were really wonderful structures. The larger headquarters often consisted of several rooms made of reinforced concrete and covered up with earth. Some of them were very nicely fitted up and had electric light. The biggest one not far from our Brigade Headquarters had been used as a hospital by the Boche and had in some way got on fire. I never smelt anything so disgusting as the roast corpses.

Many of the best dugouts in Messines had been blocked up by the bombardment and during the nights we were in the line we had them searched and opened up. They were absolutely full of dead Boches and indeed before we left the line the whole of this ground became extremely objectionable from the unburied corpses. During the day it was impossible to go into the ruins of Messines as the Boche artillery kept on to them all day long.

The most unsatisfactory feature of the kind of harassing in which we were engaged during these days is that the Divisions on their flanks who are pursuing the same tactics are apt to provoke very violent and sudden retaliation all along one's own front. Thus on the night of the *22nd*, as one of our patrols was just going to rush an enemy machine-gun post which they had successfully surrounded, a neighbouring Division began a violent shoot which brought down heavy retaliation and killed both the officers who were out in charge of the patrol.

We were very nervous, too, about our relief because our Australian neighbours insisted on carrying out an attack at 1 a.m., by which time it was a physical impossibility for our men to get out of the line if they were to wait in the ordinary way for relief. Bainbridge, I must say, was very good in this kind of case. He was much worried about the position and rang me up personally on the telephone a couple of times during the evening, finally authorizing me to send a good proportion of our men down as soon as it was dark so as to get them out of the shell area before the inevitable retaliation started. It was a very anxious relief because one of the orderlies whom I sent up with orders to the Battalion Commander completely disappeared, and though, on finding that the orders had not been received, we tried to discover what had happened to him, we could get no evidence as to whether he had been blown to pieces or had walked into a Boche post carrying my message. Months afterwards it turned out that he had been taken prisoner, but he must have destroyed his message in some way before they caught him, as otherwise our line would inevitably have been plastered during the relief. The relief was reported complete at 2.30 a.m. and Craigie Halkett and I got out about 3 a.m., having sat as usual with the incoming Staff in our tiny dugout since 11 p.m., both parties nodding with sleep and longing for the relief to be over so as to be able to settle down. It turned out very lucky for us that we were delayed for a couple of hours as the Boche retaliation had then died down, though, judging by the dead Australians on the road and the descriptions of our grooms who had hastily decamped with our horses from the place where we had arranged to meet them, it had been very hot just before we came down. The Brigade got into buses in Wulverghem and were taken down to the Caudescure area by the Forêt de Nieppe, our Brigade Headquarters being in a little farm at Verterue.

I there learnt about General Broadwood's death (on 21 June), which was a very great blow to me. Bainbridge told me that Broadwood had been going along with his GSO2 and ADC to see his Artillery group. The Group Commander told him they were shelling a particular Battery and that it was most unwise to cross the railway bridge which was the only way to get there, as it was quite certain that the Boche had it under observation, and on seeing him get on at one end of the bridge they would have time to fire a shell and to catch him before he got off the other end. Broadwood, however, insisted on going, but left behind his Staff. As foretold by the Group Commander, the Boche put a shell on to the bridge and knocked out the Group Commander and Battery Commander, besides Broadwood himself. Both Broadwood's legs were blown to bits, and he died that afternoon in the ambulance.

During our last spell in the line there had been a good deal of rain but the weather was now again very hot and we did all our marches to the Fruges area by night. I got out all the march tables at Verterue before we started so had an idle three days and much enjoyed the marching on the summer nights. Our first stage was to Ham-en-Artois, the next to Laires, and the third to Fruges where we had our Brigade Headquarters in the same house where three months previously I had dined with the Blues.

The 25th Division remained in the Bomy area and we were at Fruges from *June 26th* until *July 23rd*. I spent the first few days riding round the area fixing up for the hire and construction of rifle ranges and training grounds.

Bethell returned in the early morning of Friday *30 June*, having been recalled from his leave on the orders of the Division. He was in a great rage on finding that the recommendations for immediate awards on account of the Messines attack had in most cases been thrown out by either the Corps or the Army. The whole of our Brigade received fewer immediate awards for this battle than one Battalion (1st Wilts) in the 7th Brigade, although the whole Brigade of which that Battalion formed part had only had one half of the casualties that we had. Bethell made a tremendous fuss about it, as he suspected that it was due to someone in a higher formation, whose business it was to allot the total number of immediate awards, giving a preference to the Battalion in which he took an interest.

30 June

We went over to a Conference of all COs at Divisional Headquarters at Bomy, where Bainbridge told us that we had been brought back to train for a big attack on the Passchendaele Ridge and gave us a rough outline of the work we should have to do.

1 July

I went on leave to England, returning on the *11th*. I found the scheme for our attack had been worked out in considerable detail during my absence. The function of our Division was to go through on the third day of the attack and to push on to the final objective. Our Brigade was to do the last stage of the advance and to advance about three miles in an open formation and to take the village of Passchendaele. We went several times up to the Bomy training area to rehearse our part of the scheme. It was a very different task to what we had had at Messines, being practically open warfare with no trench lines to capture and only sufficient artillery to deal with strongpoints and to fire at fleeting targets over open sights. We found the Brigade very ignorant as to the conditions of open warfare. Though they had reached a great pitch of efficient organization in set-piece trench attacks, all ranks showed great ignorance as to the use of ground and little of the initiative which is imperative in this kind of warfare. We used to bivouac up on the training area, Brigade Headquarters sleeping under the shelter of a haystack. Our practice attacks used to take place through the standing corn, very costly in the way of compensation and very annoying in spite of the compensation, to the farmers, who, in spite of the difficulties of getting labour, had managed to cultivate their land.

23 July

The Brigade moved by bus to the Lynde area, marching on the next day to Hondeghem, on the *25th* to Godesaervelde, and on the *26th* to Wippenhoek West. We were here among the hop gardens, very pretty but much enclosed country and a pleasant contrast from the dull flat Flemish surroundings. Brigade Headquarters were at a little inn on the Poperinghe–Steenvoorde Road, where the Belgian frontier leaves that road and bends up to the north. The march, however, was quite pleasant in spite of the heat. Bethell and Marriott had gone away to stay with the Fourth Army. Bethell returned in an extremely bad temper and was most abusive to the COs for having misunderstood the instructions which I had sent out about B teams. We had a conference on the *27th* on which he generated a great amount of unnecessary heat. It adds enormously to the work that he should in this way for no conceivable reason put sand into the wheels of the machine as everybody is rushed with work and trying to do their best. We were at Wippenhoek until the *29th* when we moved up to Dominion Camp, about three miles south-east of Poperinghe. During these three days we were all busy reconnoitring routes and getting to know the forward area. The march up was very unpleasant, the roads being fearfully dusty[20] and much congested with lorry traffic. For the purpose of the forthcoming attack we had been put into the 2nd Corps (Lt Gen. Sir Claud Jacob)* in the 5th Army. Jacob is a very good soldier but there is little confidence in our Army Commander (Sir Hubert Gough). After the wonderful organization and devotion to detail which one found in the 2nd Army, the 5th Army struck one as very haphazard in its methods.

While we were at Fruges, Jacob came and addressed us one day and talked the most arrant nonsense I ever heard about the function of the 5th Army, who in the next few days were to drive the Germans right out of Belgium. He told us that we should go on living in shell holes until the War was brought to an end by the complete defeat of the Boche.

Bainbridge had of course suffered from 5th Army methods the previous year on the Somme and lost no opportunity of rubbing in the inadequacy of our plans and arrangements. None of the lessons taught by Plumer's success seemed to have been learnt. The signal and RE arrangements were fearfully sketchy, nothing was thought out beforehand and everything was apparently left to be decided at the moment. The plan of the attack

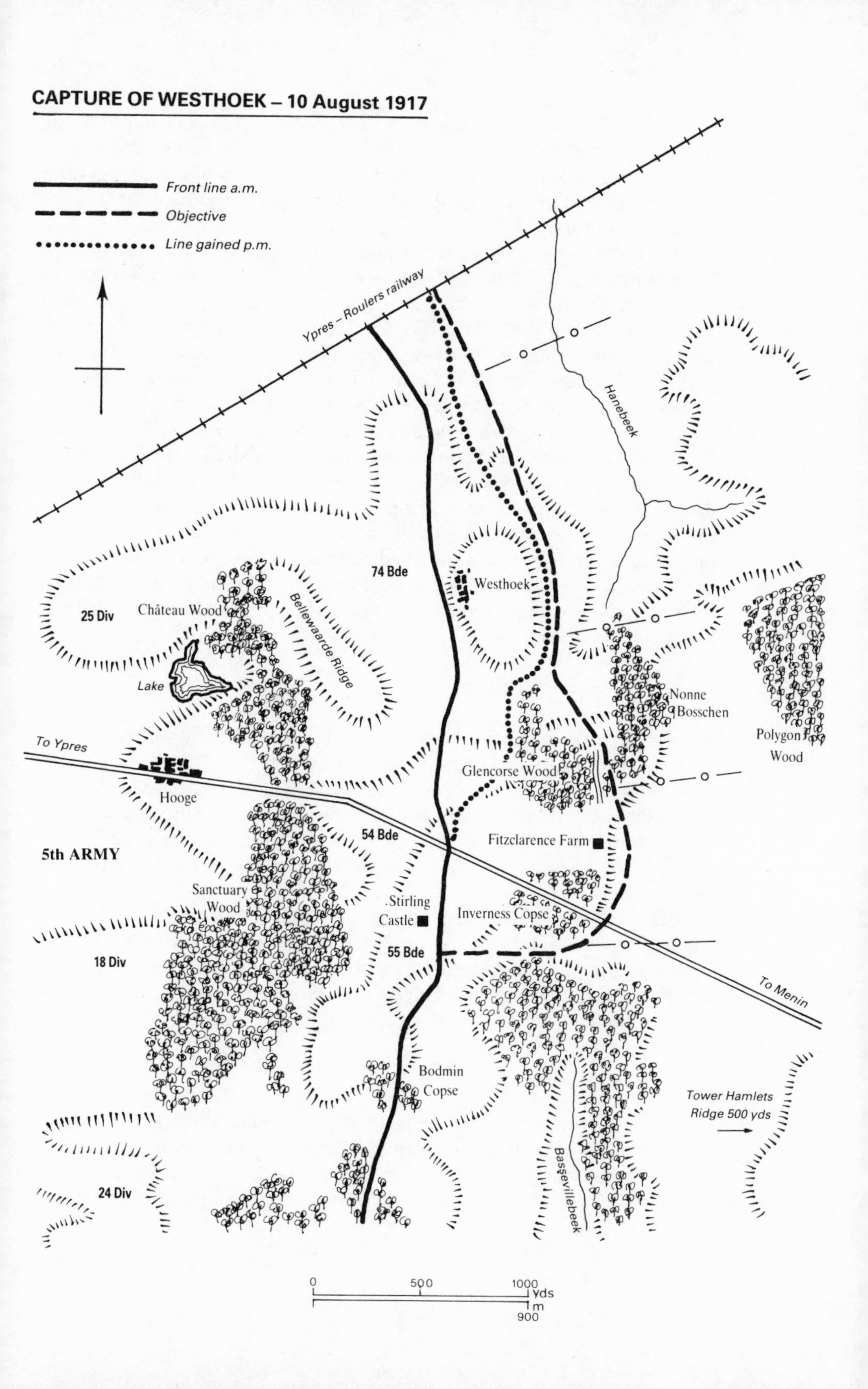
CAPTURE OF WESTHOEK – 10 August 1917
Front line a.m.
Objective
Line gained p.m.
Ypres – Roulers railway
Hanebeek
74 Bde
Westhoek
25 Div
Château Wood
Bellewaarde Ridge
Lake
Nonne
Bosschen
Polygon
Wood
To Ypres
Hooge
Glencorse Wood
54 Bde
Fitzclarence Farm
5th ARMY
Sanctuary
Wood
Stirling
Castle
Inverness Copse
55 Bde
18 Div
To Menin
Bodmin
Copse
Tower Hamlets
Ridge 500 yds
24 Div
Bassevillebeek
0
500
1000
yds
m
900

on the Passchendaele Ridge was in itself ill-conceived, as it ignored the strength of the Zandvoorde position. In these days before the attack, Bainbridge showed great insight by foretelling that, without first getting the southern end of the high ground, it was quite impossible for our left wing to push forward.

At 3.5 a.m. on *31 July* a great attack was launched.[21] Our function on the first day was to fill in shell holes through the Boche front line system at Hooge Château, so that during the following 24 hours a broad wooden road might be laid for getting up food, ammunition and guns. The attack was, however, hung up on the right owing to the faultiness of the plan. Our four Battalions who had been told off for this road work were none the less ordered up. The RE officer who was to tape out the exact line on which they were to work was, however, killed before he had time to do it, and it was typical of the inefficient methods of the Corps RE that no other officer had been told off as his understudy or had any idea as to the details of the work. Our men had practised the exact method of filing on to the work and exactly how to fill in the shell holes while we were back in the Bomy area, but after they had been up on the ground a short time, the Corps decided that the work could not be done, and sent them back to Ypres. Unfortunately they had pretty heavy casualties getting back along the main road.

1 August

It came on to rain in torrents and the ground became indescribably muddy. Never before had I any conception of what stiff clay can produce in the way of an obstacle to movement. Everywhere off the main roads became an absolute quagmire in which one sank over one's ankles in thick, clinging mud which almost lugged the boots off one's feet. At the same time if one tried to go at all up hill, it was so slippery that one was continually on one's hands and knees.

Following on the failure of the original attack Gough reverted to the old disastrous tactics from which we had suffered on the Somme. Instead of waiting to work out an ordered plan he kept flinging in troops on a narrow front, enabling the Boche to concentrate his Artillery on the attackers as from the periphery of a fan on to the centre.

2 August

Part of our Brigade having been up in Ypres since the *31st*, we moved the remainder with Brigade Headquarters to Pioneer Camp. On the *3rd* we moved up to Ypres and lived in a tunnel in the old ramparts. We had great difficulty in getting in at all as the whole of the accommodation was taken up by the Artillery. I had been up reconnoitring the line and rejoined Bethell in the new quarters, to find that there was a tremendous controversy going on, as the Artillery had had no orders to go out and flatly refused to move. They pointed out that it was quite impossible at a moment's notice to change the signal communication of three Artillery Brigades, and after Bethell had rung up Division and used some extremely violent and most uncomplicated language about the gunners down the telephone, every word of which was heard through the canvas partition of our hosts, it was decided that we should double up somehow and share the accommodation with them. As a matter of fact we were very lucky to get in anywhere. All the underground dwellings of Ypres were filled to overflowing, and the Area Commandant was nearly distraught with having to keep the peace between the various units and formations. Though our tunnel was very smelly and airless, it had the great advantage of having withstood showers of heavy shells for the last three years. Eventually, after we cleared out, the wooden partitions were somehow set on fire by an incendiary shell and a complete Brigade Staff was burned to death.

We were only in Ypres for a couple of days and then relieved our 7th Brigade who were holding the line north of the Ypres–Menin Road, and between that road and the Ypres–Roulers railway. This was a most unpleasant relief, as for some unknown reason, Bethell refused to let me go up in the ordinary way to fix up the details on the spot and insisted on working out the details not so much to suit the outgoing Brigade as for our own convenience. The result was I had a most unpleasant night of it being cursed down the telephone by General Onslow of the 7th Brigade. Finally at about 3 a.m., no one in the tunnel being able to sleep owing to my incessant conversation on the telephone, Bethell came and seized the receiver from my hand. He went on arguing with Onslow for about half an hour and they generated so much heat and talked so openly that if the Boche had had a listening set they would have known every detail as to the time of the relief and the routes.

During the night of *5/6 August* we took over the line, Brigade Headquarters moving into a deep dugout at Birr crossroads about half a mile west of Hooge Château. The dugout was one of the most disgusting places I ever lived in. It was only kept habitable by continual pumping and when the pump broke down one was generally up to one's ankles in water. Besides ourselves in the dugout, there was a dressing station and a good deal of accommodation given up to signals. The result was that our quarters were fearfully cramped and Marriott and I had to do all our work on a table about two feet by three on to which water was continually pouring down from the ceiling. Bethell had another little cubby hole on the opposite side of the passage and the five days which we spent before the attack were, I think, the most unpleasant of the whole of my time in France.

Owing to the closeness of our quarters Bethell's temper became absolutely impossible. He was asking everybody to do about six things at once and hardly gave us time to sit down and start on one of them before he called them back and asked them to do something else. The climax came when he accused me of losing a particular paper which I knew I had given him. Not only I but also the clerk agreed that we had seen it on his table. He used most violent language and said that he had never had it. Having caused us to waste about three hours searching for it, it turned out to be in his pocket the whole time. Finally things got to such a pitch that Bethell had to have his meals alone, as neither Marriott nor the Signalling Officer nor any of us could stand it, and insisted on feeding in our office. Fortunately, however, before the attack took place, his voice completely gave out and he could only speak in a whisper which we could no longer hear across the passage.

Our greatest difficulty at Birr crossroads was to keep in touch with our Battalions. Although their Headquarters were less than a mile away on the Bellewaarde Ridge, it was a good hour's struggle to get to them through the mud. Owing to the continual shelling of all the ground around Hooges, the wires were incessantly being cut, power buzzers were useless. After very great difficulty in getting the heavy Batteries up through the mud, for some unknown reason, possibly to do with the laterlogged and continually shelled state of the ground, they proved quite ineffective. Owing to the inefficiency of the 5th Army there were not even any decent buried lines back to our Division, a great contrast to the wonderful signal arrangements to which we were accustomed in the 2nd Army.

10 August

Owing to the impossibility of keeping communication, the General decided that I was to go up to our Advanced Report Centre for the attack. Accordingly at 3 a.m. I went up to an old German concrete pill box which we had decided on for our Forward Brigade Headquarters. It was right up on the Bellewaarde Road commanding a view forward to the Westhoeck Ridge on which was our Brigade objective, and also back to Brigade Headquarters at Birr crossroads. A British shell had fortunately knocked a great chunk of concrete off the western side and made a slit which proved invaluable for visual signalling when the atmospheric conditions were suitable. I was hardly ever in communication either with the Battalions in front or Brigade Headquarters behind, and most of the time I was only able to communicate with either of them by runner.

At 4.25 a.m. the Brigade advanced to the attack under a heavy barrage.

GERMAN OFFENSIVE AGAINST THIRD ARMY 21 – 27 March 1918

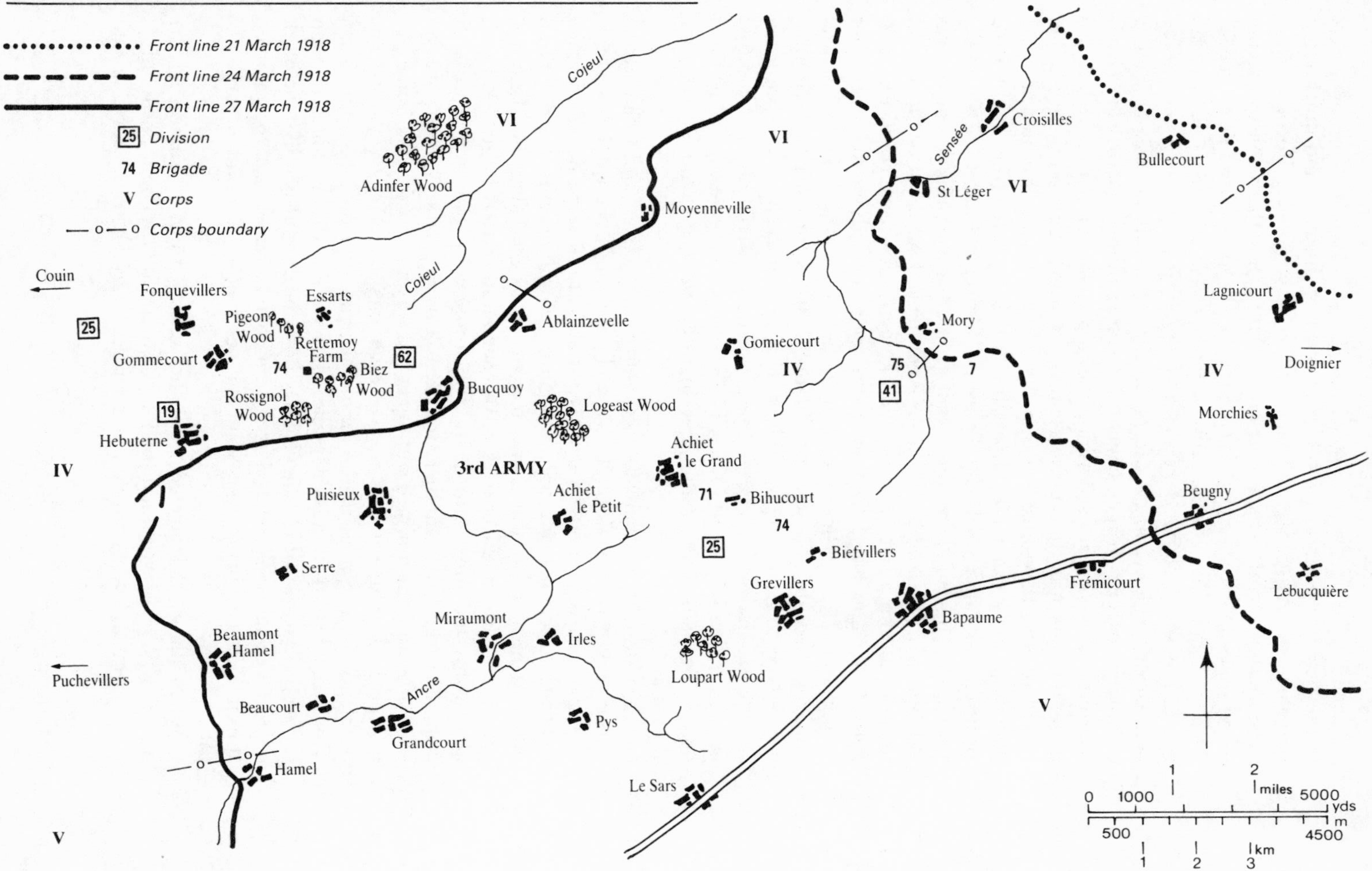

In the first five minutes we took hundreds of prisoners and quickly got our objective. As soon as we had done so, however, the Boche began a most stubborn fight to regain the ground and I spent the whole day trying to get quick information of his counter-attacks so as to be able to get the Artillery on to his concentrations. During the day our pill box and indeed the whole of the Bellewaarde Ridge was subject to a very heavy bombardment. Early in the afternoon for a few minutes the ladder line or power buzzer (I forget which) got connections with Brigade Headquarters. A message arrived asking me to prepare guides to take forward mules with ammunition, rations and water which were on their way up. I answered that they must be stopped as a heavy barrage had just been put down and the ground was impassable. It was too late – they had started already. Soon afterwards the Transport Officer in charge of the mules arrived, having left them about half a mile back (I think his name was Whingates, of the 2nd South Lancs Regiment). I went out of the dugout to speak to him as we were packed like herrings and he could not have got in. The Signalling Officer in charge came out with me to fix up about letting units know where the things would be dumped. I had just told him to go straight back and get the mules off-loaded where they were as if they were to go on they would inevitably be knocked out or stampeded and the Battalions would get nothing, when a big shell burst and knocked us all over. The Transport Officer had an eye out and one knee all smashed up, the Signalling Officer fragments in his shoulder and hand and I escaped altogether.

Just at this moment an SOS went up from in front and I had fearful difficulty in getting it through as visual [signalling] was quite impossible owing to smoke and dust. I sent two runners to stop the mules and then had to face the horrible problem of getting ammunition forward with no mules or men to carry it. For a few moments the ladder line held and I arranged with an officer back at Brigade Headquarters to get 200 Lewis gun drums and more ammunition up tonight by 250 men who were being lent to us from another Brigade to carry up rations. There was no hope of getting the dumped stuff up in this way and I had to ask Battalions to send back which in all but two cases they were unable to do. The problems about guides to the dump (which could only be approached over ground churned into shell holes filled with mud) sound little enough but were also a horrible difficulty. By now the dugout was like the black hole of Calcutta and while I went out to find out where the dumped ammunition etc. really was, someone put a pool of blood all over my papers.

When things had quieted I got the wounded out by some stretcher bearers who were working for a Regimental Aid Post about one hundred yards away and was then in a better position to cope with the incessant problem of communication. We couldn't use visual forward as we were in full view of the Boche and each time we showed our flash he put shells right on to us, sending earth in through the slit and knocking out all our candles. Just when shells were landing the observers couldn't see the SOS rockets, and this in our case at least caused delay which might have been disastrous. From 6 p.m. onwards until 8, SOS went up in turn from three Battalions. Sometimes one got a definite target – enemy massing in wood by Hanebeek for counter-attack – and in several cases we knocked them to pieces with Artillery before they could come on. In one case delay was very lucky as two Battalions collected in a wood before the [British] Battalion threatened could get through to me, and I to the Artillery liaison officer. When at last they did open, we learnt from prisoners that the Battalions had been absolutely annihilated, being by that time all assembled in quite a small area.

At about 9.30 p.m. things got quieter and having eaten nothing but one small slice of bread and butter since 2 a.m. (which I had got from the signallers) I felt it was time to get some food. Fortunately the Brigade Intelligence Officer who lived nearby was able to provide me with bully beef, bread, tea and rum of which I consumed a huge quantity. It was a great relief to get out of the signal dugout where I had sat all day except for short excursions out to parties of wounded or captured Boche, from whom in my sadly inefficient German I tried to obtain information as to available local reserves and probabilities of counter-attack. I found that one of the Battalions holding the line opposite us had been relieved only the previous night and by means of a captured confidential map showing the local German trench and encampment names was able to send back a good deal of information about Battalions within a few miles of our bit of line. The signal dugout (an old Boche one on top of the ridge which was captured on the 30th) was marvellously resistant to shell fire. It was so packed, however, with runners and operators that one couldn't move one's elbows without jostling the checkers next whom I sat and there was nowhere to put the papers which came in on one like flakes in a snow storm except on one's knee, when they were continually slipping on to the muddy floor. One also had great difficulty owing to breakdown of other means of communication and casualties in keeping enough runners to take messages. I got a message late at night to go at dawn and see Battalion Commanders, then to return and report the position to the General. I couldn't start for an hour after that, however, as our right centre battalion began blinking 'SOS, SOS, SOS' on its visual. Brigade visual proved to have been knocked out, and no other means being at the moment available, I had to send a runner back. Meanwhile I was flashing forward 'Are you OK?' and getting back only 'SOS, SOS, SOS'. Finally, seeing there was only moderate Artillery fire bursting on our line, I felt I

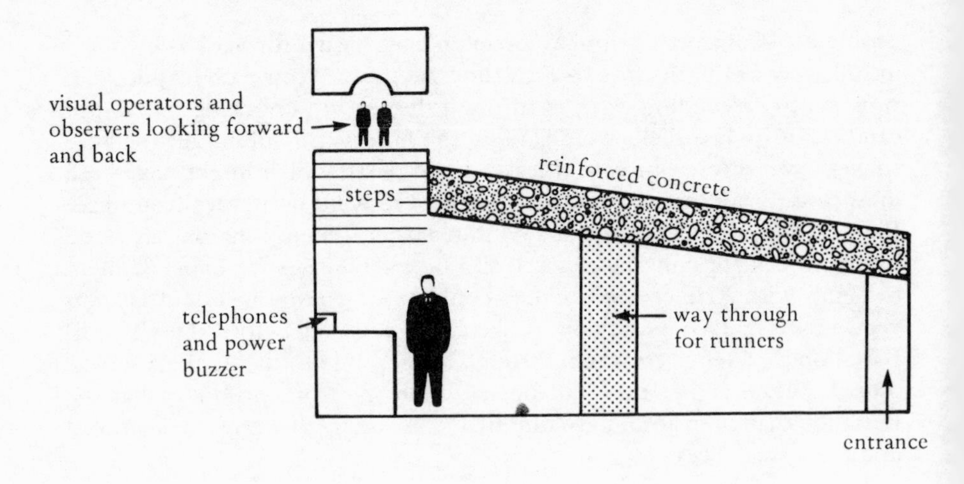

must find out what had happened and went up to the newly captured ground near our two right Battalion Headquarters from which I could look down on the ground held by the Boche. They weren't attacking us at all but I saw them going up, a few men at a time by rushes, and collecting just on our right, where the next Division had been held up the previous day. I therefore stopped the guns on our SOS lines and went back to Brigade Headquarters whence Bethell got through to Division and got the place dealt with by artillery.

I was quite sorry to get in as the Headquarters dugout was absolutely suffocating. Deep below the ground down about thirty muddy steps there wasn't a breath of air. The office where I worked with the Staff Captain had only room for one tiny table on which about six other people kept sticking down their papers on top of mine, so that we all got very irritable and the General's temper quite unbearable. His voice had completely gone as a result of the continual drip of water from the roof and the fact that for four days our feet had been wet continually owing to the impossibility of keeping the water down by pumping. As by this time we had got five other Battalions lent to us and as Bethell was continually moving companies backwards and forwards and sideways it became a nightmare to know where they all were. All the time more and more orders in from Division 'ref my GS so and so (which one couldn't find under a minute or two) – so and so is cancelled, etc.' On top of it people continually coming in to ask questions and crowding us so that one couldn't move.

None of us had had more than two or three hours sleep in the 24 for the previous five days and our heads were like wool.

Somehow, however, I managed to work out some relief orders with the Brigade Major and COs of another Brigade and on the morning of the 12th we finally moved out after a most anxious night wondering how many units would lose their way in the darkness. As it was we managed to get everybody out except half a company whose relief lost its way and who had to remain until the following night. Our bit of the battle was entirely successful and our Battalions all got further than we had told them to go and had to be pulled back. Unfortunately the (18th) Division on our right was not able to get forward owing to enfilade shelling from the direction of Zandvoorde, thus leaving the line which we gained very open to the south.

On relief we moved back to Halifax Camp near Ouderdom on the Vlamertighe–Reninghelsten Road, whence on the *14th* we marched back to Steenwoorde. On the *15th* and *16th* I compiled the history of our operations on the 10th and 11th which proved rather a complicated matter, as we had borrowed Battalions from three other Brigades and it was not easy to trace all our movements among the masses of messages and orders which had come in and out. Bethell was in a different mood since the strain was over. We were all in a very bad temper with him and he solemnly sent for Marriott and me and made a little speech, saying that we were not to think he didn't appreciate our work and no doubt we thought him very exacting and unreasonable but that he would long before have evacuated most Brigade Majors and Staff Captains. [As the following citation for the award of the DSO indicates, the diarist had played down his personal part in the action on 10th August and Bethell had good reason to be pleased with him.]

THE DISTINGUISHED SERVICE ORDER

Maj. The Hon. Walter Edward GUINNESS,
Suffolk Yeo. (T.F.)

As Brigade Major, the services of this Officer were invaluable to the Brigade throughout the preparation for the attack on, and capture of, WESTHOEK RIDGE on the 10th Aug. 1917.

Previous to the attack his reconnaissance and arrangements for the assault were excellent. At the commencement of the attack he was on BELLEWAARDE RIDGE, and as soon as Runners had reported attack to have reached and passed beyond its original objectives, he made a complete and thorough reconnaissance regardless of enemy shelling and rifle fire, and checked the whole situation in addition to finding out the requirements of the units. He remained on BELLEWAARDE RIDGE throughout the 10th and 11th, keeping in close touch with the situation, and by his prompt action on his own initiative he staved off at least one counter attack.

BELLEWAARDE RIDGE, was continuously shelled throughout the 10th and 11th, at times very heavily.

The personal example of this Officer was of great assistance throughout the operation and his reports were very valuable.

On the *17th* we moved to Reck but on the *20th* came back to Steenwoorde.

21 August

Sir Douglas Haig and General Kiggell* (his Chief of Staff) came over and inspected us. The weather had now cleared up and was very hot, but it would take a long time for the ground satisfactorily to dry up on the ridges east of Ypres. We stayed at Steenwoorde until the 1st September. Bethell seemed very much in need of rest, but Bainbridge said that under present conditions he couldn't be spared. He talked of trying to get a Brigade at home.

25 August

The weather broke again and must again have made operations extremely difficult. Time at Steenwoorde hung rather heavy on one's hands. The Battalions were busy with their organization and only needed to be left alone. Our Brigade Office was in a tent not very pleasant in the downpours of rain which made the envelopes all stick together and caused heavy drops to come down on one's papers. One day I found two large pigs in the office. They had managed to pull down a large bundle of papers which had been hooked up on to the walls and to trample them into the wet ground. The final disaster to the office came when after torrents of rain, the tent blew down and caused great havoc to the papers inside.

1 September

Bethell and I were intending to drive over with Bainbridge to the Cavalry Corps Horse Show. Fortunately the motor went wrong just before we started and kept us long enough for orders to arrive by which on the night of the 2nd/3rd we were to take over our old line east of Hooge. I went on at once to reconnoitre by motor and found that the line was considerably changed since we had left it, and the relief was much complicated by a readjustment of boundaries with our neighbours. I came back in the evening to meet the Brigade at Halifax Camp.

I went forward and looked after the relief, Bethell and Marriott only coming up early the following morning. They had, however, a very disturbed night as after my departure an aeroplane came and dropped bombs on them, knocking out one of their huts and wounding Reynolds (the Signalling Officer's servant) and several of Brigade Headquarters. I found our old dugout at Birr crossroads much more habitable. Some of the Field Ambulance who shared it with us previously had moved out, giving us more room and we were much less crowded up with liaison officers than when we tenanted it before. Even the drips from the roof had for the most part been covered up by waterproof sheets, though this was of doubtful benefit as it involved severe shower baths when the sheets gave way or someone touched the ceiling with his head. The chief trouble was the electric as the dynamo had broken down and we depended on the current from another dugout about ½-mile away, a cable from which was continually being cut by shells. We remained in the line until the *9th* and had a fairly quiet time. The ground too was drying up quickly which made communications much easier. The 5th Army was now being pushed out of the battle and the 2nd Army was taking over the front. The most noticeable result was the complete change in the signalling arrangements. Australians came up and buried lines along the Ypres–Menin Road, as ought to have been done weeks previously before the attack was ever attempted.

On *7 September* Bethell went off with General (Sir Archibald) Montgomery,* Major-General, General Staff, of the 4th Army to spend a week or ten days with the French Army, and Craigie Halkett again came in as his *locum tenens*. I expected quite a quiet time as we were not ourselves preparing for any attack. We were, however, incessantly being called on by Australians who were to take over from us, quite remarkable for their absolute ignorance about the country and generally unprovided even with maps. They wasted hours of one's time by idiotic questions and sat on the bed in my office most of the day in a revolting state of perspiration waiting for guides to take them on to their destinations. I covered acres of papers with reports for the incoming Corps as to what they could do and where they could do it, most of it absolutely useless as one was largely in the dark as to their intentions.

We got out with extraordinarily few casualties and the place was very different to what it had been when we were previously there. We were attacked one evening but it was not very serious and was stopped by our machine-gun fire almost before the Artillery could get on to it. The night of the relief was very unpleasant. Just when the relieving troops were well on their way up a great bombardment opened up on our flank on the boundary between us and the 2nd Army. The 'overlap' of SOS lines of course involved our flank Battalion, but the CO thought it must be our Division and told his Artillery liaison officer to try to stop it if so. This idiot sent back by visual 'Stop SOS' with the result that the Artillery Signal post saw the last three letters flashed through and not the first word and got the guns to open. By the time I had got through to the Battalion and found out what had happened the Boche was thoroughly frightened and though we stopped our SOS within five minutes he went on bombarding fairly heavily for about four hours with very disturbing effects to the relief of our troops in the line. The CO of our Battalion involved was very tired and jumpy and went on ringing up every half-hour or so to ask me to stop our guns in spite of my assurances that they were not shooting and that anything which came over from behind was from the artillery of our neighbours.

We were relieved on *9 September* going back to a camp on the Reninghelst–Poperinghe Road. General Baird (commanding the 75th Brigade) came over there to see me and asked whether I would come back to command the 11th Cheshires, as Evans was about to leave them to get command of a Brigade. I had no hesitation in refusing, as in my opinion they are far the worst Battalion in the Division, and I felt it would be a mistake to leave my present job just as I was beginning to get the hang of it.

11 September

We sent the Brigade off in 124 buses to Meteren. The enemy aeroplanes had lately become very troublesome in these camps behind Ypres. Almost every night they dropped bombs somewhere fairly close. The night before we left it was really a very beautiful sight: one of these raiders was caught in the beams of seven searchlights, while anti-aircraft and machine guns were shooting at it. The aeroplane looked like a great silver bird and the tracer bullets made a triangle of fireworks as they shot up into the sky. Lately in the line, too, low-flying aeroplanes had become a great nuisance. Every morning they used to fly quite low over our trenches and to shoot into them, while our planes, if there happened to be any within sight, seemed quite unable to do anything. It is probably impossible to swoop down on an enemy flying close to the ground in time to avoid a crash.

From Meteren we marched up by two stages to Auchel, a little mining town about eight miles west of Bethune. The country here is black with the mining industry and in every direction dumps and pyramids of black waste material, brought up to the surface of the mines, stand out as landmarks. At Auchel our Brigade Headquarters were billeted in the house of the Mine Manager and I had one of the most luxurious rooms in which

I ever lodged during the War. The owner of the house had been taken prisoner by the Germans but his wife was extraordinarily hospitable and almost overpowered us by her attentions, insisting on our using her linen and china and glass and taking control of our messing arrangements. We were now in the 1st Corps, commanded by Lieut-General Sir Arthur Holland. The fosses in this area made admirable stop butts and the whole Brigade was set hard at work on musketry practice. Craigie Halkett got bored at Brigade Headquarters and went back to his Battalion. I had a very quiet time at Brigade Headquarters as Battalions only needed to be left alone.

19 September

Bethell returned and sent me off on the 20th for a week in Paris, to the great indignation of the Corps who pointed out that three days' notice was the rule in asking for Paris leave. They haven't yet realized that Bethell once he decides on doing anything can never wait to observe any regulation.

27 September

I returned from Paris. On my journey back to Calonne Ricouart I for the first time came across a batch of newly arrived American officers who had been sent on ahead to be attached to various of our Corps and Army schools to learn something of the conditions before the arrival of their troops. This batch were all university men and seemed to be of an excellent type. They said that there were already about 80,000 of their professional Army now in France and that by the Spring this number would be raised to about half a million with the new levies. The Americans seemed to have avoided the mistake which we made in the early days of the War in allowing what would have been invaluable material for officers to get killed in the ranks of the Territorials who first went out to France. From its entrance into the War the US has dealt with its manpower on the broadest lines and in connection with the compulsory levy has separated out from the start and put through a special training that material which is most suitable to train as officers for the new Armies.

28 September

As the GSO1 of our Division (O.H.L. Nicholson) was going off on leave, and as Hamilton, the GSO2, would be doing his work, I was ordered to go and take over his job temporarily as two of our Brigades were going into the line and there was a lot to do. I therefore joined them in a very pleasant château at Labeuviure. The 7th and 75th Brigades went in and held the line in the north-west outskirts of Lens, and we got to work on a plan for the capture of Lens in conjunction with the Australians. They were to have seized the high ground to the north-east and south-east of the town, while our Division were to go at it in the middle. It was a horrible place to take on, being an absolute network of cellars. I made several visits in connection with this attack to our line at Lievin and Cité Saint Pierre. It was remarkably quiet, very different from Flanders; the one object of the Boche is probably to be left alone and he probably has no ammunition to waste in knocking down houses while practically everyone is living underground in the cellars.

3 October

A sudden change was made in the plans. The proposed attack was definitely cancelled and the 25th Division were transferred to the 11th Corps in relief of the 2nd Division. All three Brigades were put into the line, the 74th and 7th Brigades taking over the Cambrin and Canal Sectors respectively on *5 October*, and the 75th Brigade taking over the Givenchy Sector on *6 October*. This side-slipping of two Brigades from the line at Lens to another part of the line east of Bethune involved very complicated staging and relief arrangements. Bethell asked for me to come back on the 74th Brigade returning to the line. Bainbridge said he wished to keep me until Nicholson's return.

On the morning that the 74th Brigade left Auchel, while I was dressing at about 8 a.m., I heard Bethell's voice pouring down torrents of abuse. He was outside the front door, having arrived in a towering rage, and sent for Legge the AA and QMG of the Division, who, like me, had not yet come down for breakfast. When he got hold of him he said that some buses which he had asked for to take the advance parties forward to reconnoitre had not arrived and that all his COs were waiting out in the road in consequence. He said that the Division had known that this would happen the previous midnight and had never thought of telling his Brigade and that it was most damnable, etc. etc.! By this time Bainbridge was also on the scene in very bad temper at being kept from departing, as he had arranged, for a visit to GHQ. It turned out that Bethell had left Auchel before the buses were even due, that before he left he had rung up Division and asked, 'Why aren't those buses here?' A half-witted clerk replied, 'Q. heard last night at midnight that there were no buses available for your party,' thinking that Bethell referred to another party who were being sent up to bury cable and whom I had then ordered to proceed by road on hearing that Q. couldn't get buses for them. Bethell then of course jumped into his motor and came straight up to Divisional Headquarters.

I carefully avoided the torrent, and waited while they telephoned to verify Bethell's statement that the buses hadn't turned up. It proved that the buses had turned up quite all right and up to time.

I found Legge at breakfast in a state of collapse after Bethell's violence and it was said that Bainbridge had been very angry at such a storm being raised for no reason. Although I didn't like the life of GSO2 half as much as that of Brigade Major, this early morning example of Bethell's temper for the moment quite reconciled me to the peaceful life at Division Headquarters.

7 October

Division Headquarters moved over to Locon, the relief by our three Brigades now being complete. While at Division I got to know the Northern and Central Sectors of our Divisional Front. The 74th Brigade part is probably the most quiet of the three but abominably complicated with miles of tunnels running forward from the support line to the posts in front. As only two or three posts are served by each tunnel and one cannot possibly get by daylight from one post to another above ground, one spends hours stumbling about these underground passages which are nominally lit by electric light but where the lamps are so few and far between owing to the bends, one spends a good deal of the time groping about in pitch darkness. Connecting with these tunnels is an elaborate system of mine borings and it is said that nowadays our underground defence is so well worked out that it would be very difficult for the Boche to get under and blow up our line in the way that he used to during the early part of the War. General Baird, who commands the 75th Brigade, was in former days Haig's ADC and is now away staying with him for a few days. A telegram arrived saying that his wife had had twins and Gattie, his Brigade Major, rang up GHQ and got Baird on the telephone. On hearing the news Baird only said 'My God' and put back the receiver!

13 October

I went back to the 74th Brigade at Beuvry. Things are going very smoothly and Bethell's temper much improved. Batches of Portuguese are being attached to us to learn their work in the line and this has given me a good deal to do, working out their movements and what they are to do when they get to the line. We arranged for them each to be told off as understudy to a British soldier and our men showed great aptitude in getting the Portuguese to dig and do their work in the trenches. The great difficulty, however, was the overcrowding in the line which was necessarily caused by the double garrison. Life at Beuvry was quite pleasant with no unreasonable amount of work to do.

24 October

We had an unfortunate occurrence with a patrol of the 13th Cheshires, in which they apparently lost a couple of men whose bodies could not be found and who were presumably taken prisoner. Such episodes in trench warfare cause a great commotion and there are stringent orders that they are immediately to be reported owing to the danger of information in this way being obtained by the enemy. On this occasion Bethell went up to the line to try and straighten things out, telling me not to make any detailed report to Division until his return. Division, however, spent the day cursing me for not sending them more information as to the details and saying that the Corps Commander was in a great rage about it. Whenever I tried to get details from the Battalion concerned Bethell came to the telephone and told me not to fuss. He is the most insubordinate person that I have ever come across, but, though I continually hear him talking most violently to Bainbridge down the telephone, everybody for some reason puts up with his habits.

Bethell went on leave on *29 October*, Craigie Halkett again coming in to command the Brigade. He is a very nice person to work with but knows nothing whatever about Regimental work and he used to get me to set him problems of the kind we used to do at Hesdin to work out, never having in his life before even drawn up a marching table.

About the middle of October we lost the 2nd Royal Irish Rifles, who transferred to the 36th (Ulster) Division. They were a great loss to us and were I think as sorry to leave us as we were to see them go. Since the change was first suggested a few weeks before, Colonel Goodman had done everything in his power to prevent it and finally asked me to write to Carson who was staying at GHQ. I pointed out the disastrous effect of always segregating Irishmen in separate formations as if they could not work with Englishmen and suggested that to encourage such an arrangement was an encouragement of separatist tendencies. Carson, as I expected, wrote back to say that he was not able to do anything to help. The 2nd Royal Irish Rifles did admirable work in the 74th Brigade and, from having been rather a rabble in the early days of the Somme, became a first-rate Battalion after Goodman took over the command. They were very unhappy in the 36th Division and were almost wiped out in the attack on 21 March, 1918.

During the time at Beuvry I made friends with a one-legged kite balloon Section Commander and used to go up in his balloon to have a look at the line and observe shoots. It was abominably cold as one was generally up for about three hours at a time and, though I borrowed heaps of clothes, gloves etc. from balloon officers, one was always frozen by the time one came down. The observation of shoots was, however, very interesting; the man with me used to telephone how many minutes to the right or to the left of their target each shot from the heavy guns was striking. The basket in which one sat swayed about, however, so much that I found it very difficult to keep my glass sufficiently steady to measure the angle of the graticules.† It was all rather exciting watching the aeroplanes as if an enemy aeroplane went for the balloon it was necessary to jump out pretty quick, and before going up one has a parachute ready fixed on to a rope harness arrangement round one's shoulder and between one's legs so as to be absolutely ready. One man who lunched with us had in a single month parachuted seven times, three of which were from balloons in flames. If the Boche begins shelling a balloon seriously it is also necessary to jump as if one were to pull down it would merely draw a fire down and cause the probable loss not only of the balloon but also of the 100 men who wait below with a winding machine and secure the balloon on its return to earth. Though in this area I continually saw balloons in flames and the occupants parachuting I had no experience of the kind myself and no enemy aeroplane ever approached us. Each time a cloud came we pulled down below it, as enemy aeroplanes are apt to lurk up above the clouds where they can destroy balloons without being shot at by our AA guns.

One of the objectionable features of the Cambrin Sector was that it was commonly used for gas attacks. We had an RE Company which used to fire off projectors of gas, that is, great capsules of gas blown out of a kind of mortar sunk in the ground and fired several hundred simultaneously, and we also had a Company which used to discharge gas from cylinders. The latter form of attack was an infernal nuisance, as placing the cylinders in position under the parapets involved a lot of damage to our trenches and their presence was always a danger owing to the possibility of their being hit by a shell. When after weeks of work the cylinders of gas were in position and ready to be discharged one generally had to wait for several nights until the wind was suitable and one had to send off night after night endless code messages to our own units and to neighbouring Divisions to say whether or not the attack was coming off. Finally the Sappers got so tired of waiting that they let off their cylinders on a night when there was so little wind that they succeeded in gassing fifteen of themselves, probably largely owing to the carelessness of these very scallywag Gas Companies in adjusting their box respirators.

Bethell returned on *13 November*, but went for a day or two to take Bainbridge's place in command of the Division, the latter being away at

†A plan divided into squares to facilitate its reproduction in other scales.

a machine-gun demonstration. He upset all the relief arrangements which I had worked out for the Brigade. They had been made to fit in with the arrival of the Portuguese, and just as we had to change it all, the Portuguese Brigadier and two of his Staff descended on us to stay for a week. General Battista was a dear old man, who unfortunately could speak no known language. As I talked French, however, he insisted on addressing his conversation to me and I had to look as though I understood and retaliate. He continually said that the War would go on *'douze ans'* but it might be his way of saying *'deux'*. He always insisted on keeping his toast on my plate and altogether was rather trying at meals.

14 November

We carried out a raid which had involved a good deal of work and had been most troublesome to arrange while the Brigade office was a pandemonium of interpreters and other jibbering Portuguese attachments. We succeeded in taking no prisoners but each side had a good many losses. I saw that Lambert, who was both my successor and predecessor in command of the 10th Londons, was killed in Palestine. Mallinson from the 10th Cheshires who took my place as 2nd-in-Command of the 11th Cheshires was also killed shortly after relieving me, and as this took place in his dugout in the early hours of the morning there was every probability that I should have been in the same bed had I remained with the 11th Cheshires.

17 November

Bethell returned from Division and I went home on leave. Owing to Parliamentary work I remained an extra week and on reaching Boulogne on my return I found the Division had been sent south by train. I stayed the night at Boulogne and reached my destination at Bapaume at 10 o'clock on the night of *8 December*, after a very cold journey as there were only three panes of glass in the windows and such a crowd in the train that we had to sit facing the windows. Fortunately my wire from Boulogne had brought my horse to meet me at the station. I had a long ride through drizzling rain to a dugout on a sunken road about ¾ mile south-east of Lagnicourt on the Lagnicourt–Beugnie Road. I found Brigade Headquarters waiting to be able to report relief complete. Bethell was in a furious rage that it had taken so long. He had just dictated a 'strafe', saying that it was the most disgraceful muddle of which the Brigade had been guilty for over a year. As, however, it was very wet and muddy and pitch dark and the men were taking over trenches which they had never seen, besides having to put two Battalions where one had been holding before, there was really not much to grumble about. Craigie Halkett was most indignant at this message and wrote back: 'As I marched up the whole of the way with my Battalion, I know the distance and the state of the roads and am in a better position to understand the difficulties than an officer of the Brigade Staff who ordered the relief to be completed by 7 a.m.' Subsequent experience showed that in this sector it was quite impossible to get relief through before about 2 in the morning. Except, however, for occasional outbursts of this kind, Bethell at this time was quite reasonable and easy to deal with.

The Division had been sent down at a moment's notice to reinforce the 4th Corps (Lieut-General Sir Charles Woolecombe*) of the 3rd Army as a heavy counter-attack was expected after the unsuccessful and disastrous attack on Cambrai[22] the previous month. We remained in the same Headquarters in the sunken road south-west of Lagnicourt until 11 February. It was a well-concealed place and although the Boche from time to time used to shell close by, he hardly ever put anything actually into our Brigade Headquarters. We were very busy making proper defences. When we took over there was little except a chain of outposts and one had to go over the top in full view of the enemy up to the support line. The front-line trench was in places only about four feet deep and the support line consisted only of isolated posts. While we were in the sector we dug Leech Avenue, Bear Avenue and Lynx Support, that is, between 2000 and 3000 yards of excellent communication trenches. We also did a lot of work on the support line and supplied very large working parties for making deep tunnel dugouts in the new Reserve line dug by our Division Pioneer Battalion (6th South Wales Borderers). We also constructed much dugout accommodation in the line and throughout the sector at various Battalion Headquarters, besides cook houses, ammunition dumps and a well where Lynx Support joined Bear Avenue. When we took over the sector there was practically no British wire. We put out very nearly two miles of wire to cover our front line, all of our usual Brigade pattern of two rows double apron and three rows of knife rest or concertina in between. In addition to this we did a lot of wiring further back.

The country here is rolling downs with the chalk close to the surface. There was hardly a landmark anywhere as all trees close to the line had been cut down by the Boche to avoid their use as ranging marks. Unfortunately the Boche was on the higher ground in a very strong line covering Queant and Pronville and looked right down on us as far back as our Reserve line from the Ridge which covers those two villages from the south-west.

One of the first days we were in this new country I asked our messman, an old ship steward, how he had got on on his catering expedition to the Divisional Canteen. He answered, 'All right, except that it feels like an imitation of Christ in the wilderness.'

Fortunately the Boche, during the first part of the time at least, was very quiet and one walked backwards and forwards to the line every day without any trouble. We were holding the right sector of our Brigade front. The 40th Division was on our left and at the beginning of the time Charlie Willoughby's* Brigade, the 120th, was holding their right sector and was thus next but one to us. They were shortly afterwards, however, relieved and from his rest billets some way back he picked me up in a motor and took me over for a night at Amiens where we did some Christmas shopping for our respective messes. Amiens was at this period quite untouched by war and we found the Hotel du Rhin most comfortable. During the first part of our time, we had continual alarms of a Boche attack. He did make a fairly strong attack on our left at Bullecourt but this did not affect our own front. Towards the end of the year we had a lot of cold weather with a good deal of snow and when the thaw came we suffered much from mud in the shell holes along roads, but generally speaking the country dried up very fast.

1918: The German Spring Offensive and the Final Allied Advance

11 January

I received a wire from Evelyn saying that the Ministry of Munitions were going to commandeer 11, Grosvenor Place. Bethell at once fixed up for me to go off on leave, which was very good-natured as it involved delaying his own leave owing to the rule that we could not both be away at once. While I was just fixing up about my journey another wire arrived which had come quickly through official channels, although it had been sent off two days after the original one, saying that after all the house would not be wanted.

14 January

I learnt that the matter had been reopened again on the 12th, and telegraphed both to Mond* and Winston Churchill protesting against commandeering the houses of officers serving abroad and turning their families out into the street at a few days' notice. Finally on the 17th I got a wire from Winston Churchill to say that it had been decided that houses belonging to people serving out here would not be commandeered. The Office of Works were extraordinarily inconsiderate about the whole business and by threatening to commandeer the house with only two days' notice caused Evelyn endless worry and trouble. She had packed up practically everything in the house when the final reprieve came and got such a chill on her lungs tramping about in the streets looking for a flat that she brought on again her old trouble and had to spend most of this spring and the following spring in a warm climate.

After all, Bethell's leave didn't come off as he wanted to get away for a month and the Division could not spare him for so long. Rather than destroy his claim for the longer leave by going for a shorter period, he decided not to go at all and I went off for four days' leave in Paris at the end of January, not being of course yet eligible for English leave and there being little prospect of my being able to get away when the necessary period had expired.

At the end of January we had to reorganize the Brigade as three strong Battalions instead of four weak ones. We broke up the 13th Cheshires and they were distributed among other Cheshire Battalions. Our remaining Battalions got drafts from other units of their own Regiments being disbanded elsewhere. A lot of work was involved in the drafting of individuals but this of course affected the Staff Captain much more than me.

During the end of our time in the Pronville sector it was decided that when our Division came back after their rest the Divisional boundaries should be reorganized and we should take over some way further to the right. Our Brigade Headquarters were thus to be allotted to the left Brigade and we therefore had to provide ourselves with a new home. We chose a site for this on a sunken track running from Morchies to Beugny and worked out details of accommodation with Colonel Done, the CRE (Commander, Royal Engineers), who arranged with the incoming Division to carry out the work. As things turned out we only occupied this new dugout for a short time during the early stages of the battle beginning on *21 March*.

Our boundaries were from time to time modified while we held the Pronville sector and this meant a good deal of trouble as to Battalion and Company Headquarters. Several times I had to go up and do a deal with our neighbours about dugout accommodation and on one occasion when we had Scotch neighbours to deal with, we found them so unreasonable that we had to get GSO2 up from the Corps to settle between us and to make them give us dugout accommodation behind to correspond to the extra front which in accordance with Corps orders we had taken over. When we had four Battalions we normally held the line with two, having one in support to find working parties etc. and another back in huts near Beugnatre, about four miles back. I was not much concerned with the Battalion back at Beugnatre, as, when Bethell went to inspect them, Marriott used to go with him, since all our transport lines were back there and their organization came of course into his department. My daily walk used to be about two miles to the left of our front and about three miles to the right of our front as the crow flies but very much more when one allowed for the circuitous routes by which one had to walk; and one's normal prowl up and around the trenches involved a daily walk of anything from eight to ten miles.

5 February

I motored down with General Baird who commands the 75th Brigade to Camiers to see a machine-gun demonstration lasting two days. This was a new departure and either the Brigadier or the Brigade Major of each Brigade with someone from each Divisional Staff was ordered to go to one or other of these demonstrations. The Camiers School was commanded by Ironside* who afterwards made a great name in command of the British Force at Archangel. The two days I spent at Camiers were rather amusing as I met many friends, among others Charlie Willoughby, who was on his way home on leave to England. The lectures and demonstrations of the effect of a machine-gun barrage fired on to the smooth sand just after it had been uncovered by the tide were quite interesting, but one couldn't learn much in so short a time. While we were in the Pronville Sector we carried out several small raids but with very little success. The Boche line was very thickly wired and it was quite impossible to get through far enough to make certain of catching a prominent post. The forward areas were chiefly defended by posts and by machine guns lying out in the wire, but hardly ever occupying the same place twice. We had a great controversy with Division over one attempt for which I was responsible. Bainbridge had told Bethell he must get identification. Bethell was going away for the day and told me to fix up something with the 3rd Worcesters who were in the line. I worked out a beautiful scheme with Whalley and our Group Commander by which we put a box barrage round a place where the Boche almost invariably had a post and then rushed in to pick up the pieces. The show did not come off very well and the Division were very angry because without asking them we had fired off about 4000 rounds of field gun ammunition. Bainbridge wrote a personal letter to Bethell which made him so angry that he drafted a letter back to say that in future no patrol should go out beyond our wire without the consent of the Divisional Commander. I had the greatest difficulty in preventing him sending it. He said that Bainbridge couldn't possibly do without him and that within three days he would be begging him to do as he liked as no other Brigade in the Division could ever bring off anything. Finally, however, the letter did not go and Bethell vented his rage down the telephone instead.

11 February

We were relieved and went back to huts on the north of the road between Achiet-le-Grand and Achiet-le-Petit. We put the two forward Battalions on to a light railway which ran up to our Brigade Headquarters within a couple of miles of the line and from there they were taken right down to the camp, about eight or ten miles back. It was an abominably cold night and the men were nearly frozen in the open trucks as the journey took anything up to four hours. We remained at Achiet until 12th March, spending the time in hard training.

14 February

I was sent off with all the COs and Seconds-in-Command to a tank demonstration which involved a very long and cold drive on top of a motor bus. On returning at about 3 p.m. we found everybody had gone. Bethell had carefully arranged to send us all away so as to see what would happen in case of a sudden alarm. At about 1.30 he sent out orders that the whole Brigade and Transport were to move off in fighting order in an hour and a half. The atmosphere was very explosive on my arrival at the rendezvous, as Bethell had dictated the orders to a learner and had given him an indefinite map reference of crossroads in such and such a square with the result that as there were two crossroads in the square, part of the Brigade went to the wrong place. He never admitted his mistake and was very angry not only because several units were in consequence late, but because many men had forgotten to fill their water bottles. They were told that next time they came out without water they would be kept on parade for 24 hours to teach them to remember such things. Though such tests are no doubt very valuable, they are very inconvenient when one has had no lunch as we couldn't get any tea and there was no soup for dinner as the cook had thrown away the contents of the stock pot. One of the Battalion messes had collected a ham out of their bacon ration and were boiling it when the order came which caused them to throw it away.

16 February

I spent a long day reconnoitring Louverval spur and the ground by Doignier with a view to the possibility of our being put in there to counter-attack. We went round the latter area with the GSO2 of the 51st Division and I found the knowledge which I then got of the geography of Beaumetz very useful when I had to go up there to find out the position in the battle of 21 March. There wasn't a cloud in the sky and we saw an air fight at tremendous height. A Boche plane was flying at about 12,000 feet and the usual Archie bursts. Suddenly they ceased and we heard a faint sound of machine-gun fire up in the sky followed by the Boche plane falling. Obviously the pilot had been shot and lost control. As it fell the wings came off, probably from the strain, and fluttered down while the body came straight down like an arrow. It seemed a very long time in reaching the ground and appeared to fall just over a ridge about half a mile away. We thought it had fallen quite close, but after going over the first ridge we were told that it was beyond the second ridge some way away so we weren't able to find it. I went up once or twice to the forward area and we worked out a scheme of counter-attack on country of very much the same configuration between Bucquoy and Gommecourt. After we had worked out the plan as a Brigade we finally rehearsed it with the whole Division. While I was at Achiet I went over to see Charlie Willoughby who was somewhere up near Boiry.

25 February

I went over to give evidence in a Court Martial arising from the behaviour of an Artillery Liaison Officer belonging to the 59th Division but who had been attached to us for our attack on the 10th of last August. He was clearly guilty of desertion in the modern sense of having absented himself from dangerous duty. For some unexplained reason, however, he was only charged with drunkenness at the time of his disappearance, 3 a.m. on the morning of the battle, and the lawyers showed out of evidence as to his condition a few hours before that there had been ample evidence that he was drunk. To the astonishment of all of us who had seen the episode, he got off altogether, by pleading that he was not drunk, but virtually admitted the even graver offence with which he had not been charged, as he certainly never reported to the Battalion to which he was to have been attached and slipped away in the darkness from the orderly who was to have taken him up there.

While we were at Achiet I had a fly with the Corps Squadron whose aerodrome is only about three miles away. Another day we took the whole Brigade out for a route march to see our old battlefields of the Autumn of 1916, marching through Miraumont and Beaucourt-sur-Ancre and then crossing the river and going by Thiepval to Mouquet Farm. After halting for dinner we marched straight up north across Regina Trench to Grandcourt. The old trenches were hardly recognizable, having already fallen in owing to the weather and the whole country being overgrown with rank grass and weeds. I found the site of the dugout where I had spent the night after we captured Regina Trench. It was now a great hole about thirty feet deep and had obviously been blown up by a delay action mine, though there was no evidence to show when this had taken place. It blew a gale throughout this march with blizzards of snow and the going was so bad that we didn't take our horses and walked the whole way, about sixteen miles.

18 February

I went off in answer to an urgent telegram from the Whips who expected a critical Division, but was only in London for two or three days.

4 March

An order came that all Brigadiers, GSOs and Brigade Majors who might be away were to be recalled, no doubt in view of the expected Boche attack, so all prospect of normal leave faded away. The rest of the time at Achiet was devoted to reconnaissance and practice for counter-attack on the Louverval Spur.

12 March

We moved up to Frémicourt which was the Headquarters of the 51st Division, the Battalions being accommodated in huts close by. The German attack was expected from day to day and we had been detailed for immediate counter-attack in case the line was broken immediately north or south of the Bapaume–Cambrai road.

During the following week we more than once arranged details for relieving the 18th Brigade in the line, but owing to the fear that the attack would catch us in the act, these were cancelled. Meanwhile we were working hard at burying cable and connecting up our future Headquarters on the sunken road north-east of Beugny. We had glorious hot weather at this time and on the whole I had a quiet time as we had to be ready to counter-attack at an hour's notice, which meant that the order that both Bethell and I were not to be out together had to be strictly observed. Our own opinion was reluctant to expect the great German attack, doubting whether the enemy would take the gambler's throw of an attack on a sufficiently large scale to be worth his while. In view of the enormous reserves of manpower which the Allies could draw upon in America, the failure of a big attack was bound to mean complete disaster to Germany.

On *17 March* I wrote, 'I think the Boche is much more likely to try for peace now while he has still some manpower left, and if we can get what we want in the West, I cannot see how we should gain by going on fighting about Russia; if the Boche husbands his manpower and stonewalls us we can't hope to break him yet for several years.

'If he can keep up his civil morale it will be possible for him to prevent us gaining a real military decision by withdrawing his line whenever we have gone through the slow and exhausting process of preparing a great attack. If the Boche plays his cards well he can afford to offer the Allies such terms that their refusal would probably be represented by Allied public opinion as a case of committing suicide like the Chinaman on the threshold of his enemy.'

19 March

The weather broke and it began to rain in torrents. Nerves in high places seemed to be settling down and we issued orders to take over the line on the night of the 21st/22nd.

On the *20th*, however, there were renewed expectations of a German attack, though no orders were yet given to cancel the relief.

21 March

At 3 a.m. a heavy Minnie bombardment opened, and I thought it must be a big raid which, however, did not sound to be exactly on our front.[23] As it went on steadily for a couple of hours, I began to feel anxious and to think that it was a serious wire-cutting operation. At exactly 5 a.m. there was a long roar and whistle as if thousands of gas projectors were simultaneously being fired and this was immediately followed by a terrific burst of drum fire which had me out of bed and listening in my pyjamas at the door in a couple of minutes. It was a thick, foggy morning, and one could not have seen the flash of a gun more than a couple of hundred yards.

At 5.07 a.m. we warned the Brigade to stand to, eat their breakfasts and be ready to move off at a moment's notice. The incessant fire went on with little change all the morning. We couldn't get any news; although there was doubtless a very big attack on our immediate front, it might merely be a blind to distract attention from the real places the Boche intended to go for. At about ten I sent up a note to Pickering, the Brigade Major of the 18th Brigade, asking for news and he answered that so far they had only been bombarded without any attack developing.

At about 11.30 a.m., however, a motor arrived to take Bethell to see the Division Commander whose Headquarters were close by. He came back shortly afterwards saying we had been put under the 51st Division to counter-attack, (our own Division being some way back). I sent out orders to units to move off up the Bapaume–Cambrai Road and galloped off accompanied by a motor-cyclist to get in touch with the situation and to send back word. A good many wounded were already trickling back but I didn't wait to ask them what had happened and made straight for 18th Brigade Headquarters with whom we had worked out our counter-attack arrangements. They told me their reserve line was still holding and from there I was able to telephone to the left Brigade of the Division on their right (51st). General Beckwith told me his support line had completely gone and that the Boche were well down on the forward slopes of the ridge i.e. well west of where we had expected to counter-attack. I galloped off to Beetroot Factory where I had told the motor-cyclist to meet me, scribbled what I had heard of the position north of the road and sent it off while I went to find out what had happened to the south.

When I had left, it had been thought that the Boche was in Beaumetz or at least into the 'Corps line' which runs along its eastern side. I therefore had some doubt about finding the 153rd Brigade Headquarters in that 'village'. The valley was being a good deal shelled and, owing to the wire and trenches, I had to follow the light railway track which ran along the bottom. Beaumetz was still full of our people and very unpleasant with flying bricks and ammunition dumps on fire and blowing up. I found General Buchanan in his dugout and he marked the then position as far as he knew it on my map. I then went back, met the Brigade just west of Beugny and a message to say that I should find Bethell at 51st Division Headquarters.

I found him at the bottom of the dugout stairs with the new Division Commander who had only taken it over the previous day on Harper* getting command of the Corps. General Carter Campbell (Commander of 51st Division) said he wanted me to go up to his left Brigade Headquarters and settle about counter-attack with his Brigadier on the spot. He asked whether we could get our barrages fixed up by 4.30 p.m. Bethell said we certainly couldn't as our own two Artillery Brigades couldn't possibly be up in time, whereas the Artillery of the 51st Division would necessarily want more time as they did not know our plan. However, it was too late to go in without a barrage as we might have done at about 10 a.m., so there was nothing to be done but to try and fix up things with whatever Artillery the 153rd might still have at their disposal, and I sent off orders to COs to meet us at the Headquarters of the 153rd Brigade and to move their Battalions up to a line just behind it. It was impossible to ride nearer than about ¾ of a mile from it as one was in full view of the Boche as soon as one got over the ridge east of the Beetroot Factory–Morchies road. Bethell, Marriott and I sent back our horses and went on on foot. It was a very hot walk in a double sense. I was like a Christmas tree with a huge map case, glasses, pistol etc. and at 3 p.m. the afternoon sun was like a summer day. The Boche too was shelling the whole ridge and putting a very stiff barrage just round the Brigade Headquarters for which we were making. About 100 yards short of it an 18 pounder shell passed between Bethell and Marriott who were walking a couple of yards apart and went into the ground about three yards behind them and about six in front of me without exploding. It was the only 'blind' shell I noticed all day, but no doubt there were lots of them; in a bombardment one doesn't see or hear them in the dust and noise.

We found General Buchanan's artillery was mostly knocked out, one battery had had all its six guns destroyed, and from what he told us, an attack at that stage without artillery support was hopeless. There being a great crowd at Buchanan's Headquarters, it was decided that we should make our attack about a mile back with our friends of the 18th Brigade (6th Division) to which we at once proceeded, leaving, however, two of our COs to make their Headquarters with the 153rd Brigade which was in touch with us by wire.

We spent the night of the 21st with the 18th Brigade. Bethell at once took charge of everything and Pickering began taking down his orders without bothering about his own Brigadier! (General Crawfurd).

The 18th Brigade had put up an extraordinarily good fight and there was very little of them left. Finally, the next morning Bethell pushed the other Brigadier out altogether and would have calmly kept the remains of his Brigade if almost at the same time orders had not arrived from the 51st Division for all three Brigade Headquarters to move back to Frémicourt. Crawfurd seemed much relieved to have someone so violently sure of his own mind and what ought to be done. He is a nice little man, an oriental scholar and linguist, but by this time was very tired.

We spent a feverish evening and night on the 21st organizing defence against successive attacks and arranging to dig in new lines for the attacks on the following day. Gradually as the night wore on we got things straightened out. We were able to re-establish the Corps line and strengthen it up round the north of Morchies and down to the Bapaume–Cambrai road.

22 March

We went down to Frémicourt and established ourselves in the deep dugout out of which the 51st Division Headquarters were just clearing. Four Brigade Commanders were collected in this dugout and again Bethell ran the whole show. The day was spent in countering incessant attacks on one or another part of the Corps line astride the Bapaume–Cambrai Road. In the afternoon our 9th Loyal North Lancashires did a very good counter-attack and re-established the position, only to find their right flank turned by the 51st Division breaking and letting the Boche in behind them. They had very heavy losses, losing in this phase the bulk of their casualties of seventeen officers and 400 men, over two-thirds of the Battalion. Generally we were able to maintain our line but it was getting very thin.

In the evening (22nd) we heard that the 123rd Brigade of the 41st Division were coming up to relieve us and I went up to the Battalion Headquarters concerned to arrange about readjusting our boundary etc. I took up two of their COs and fixed up all about their relief of one of our Battalions (3rd Worcestershires) who had suffered heavily and whom we were pulling back into reserve.

I then went on to our right Battalion (11th Lancashire Fusiliers) who had dug themselves in chiefly south of the Bapaume–Cambrai road and who, owing to the break of the 51st Division in the Corps line in front of Beaumetz, were certain to be heavily attacked. I took up also one of the Machine Gun Company Commanders and we fixed positions for some extra machine guns to strengthen their right flank. They were in quite a strong position looking south to Lebucquière and north across the Bapaume–Cambrai road, but much open to enfilade machine-gun fire along a sunken road from Beaumetz to the Beetroot Factory. It was a bright moonlight night but very cold, the ground crisp with frost. I saw Massey (son of the Prime Minister of New Zealand, the 2nd-in-command of the 11th Lancs Fusiliers) who was then commanding the Battalion and got all his dispositions. He was shot through the heart by machine-gun fire an hour or two later, but was still alive when they got him down to the Field Ambulance.

23 March

I got back to our Headquarters about 5 a.m., riding from Beugny where I had left my horses. I there found that a Brigade of the 19th Division had meanwhile arrived to stiffen our right, that the COs were already up at our advanced Brigade Headquarters and that in the absence of their Brigadier Bethell had seized on them and was ordering their dispositions. When I came in he was using very violent language down the telephone to Alec Thynne, who commanded one of these Battalions (9th Wilts), for not having got into better touch with the 11th Lancs. Things woke up early that morning and before long it was clear that our people were being overwhelmed by the weight of numbers. What were left of the 11th Lancs Fusiliers gradually fell back to the south of Beugny as their position was impossible as soon as the Boche got into Lebucquière. From all accounts they had killed an enormous number of Boche and probably the enemy paid at least fourfold for their casualties (over 300 or half the Battalion) as he came from the east and south-east in close formation across the open.

The 'Army line' was the next system of defence, running north-west and south-east between Frémicourt and Beugny. This was strongly held and we sent up to tell our units to withdraw behind it. I went off to tell our two Battalions who had got back (3rd Worcestershires and 9th Loyal North Lancs) to dig in on the high ground just west of Frémicourt. I found they had left all their tools forward and were just searching the camps round to find dumps which might have been left by the Labour Battalions who had been there until a day or two previously, when I met Bethell who told me the whole Division was to withdraw on to a line east of Bihucourt and there to dig in. By this time Fremicourt had become very unpleasant and I sat down on the high ground to the west of that place and wrote out orders for units to rendezvous at Bihucourt. We concentrated at Savoy Camp between Biefvillers and Bihucourt.

I got very little sleep that night (the 24th/25th) owing to incessant messages coming in. A terrific bombardment from the direction of Morchies caused us to prepare for immediate action long before dawn. During the day we dug in on a line round Biefvillers on the south and east joining up with the rest of our Division northwards. At about 6.30 p.m. we learnt that the 'Army line' had been broken and we got further evidence that the Boche was pushing in on our right flank. We then moved our Brigade Headquarters back to Achiet-le-Grand where again I was continually called up.

25 March

By the afternoon the people on our right flank towards Loupart Wood (41st Division) had fallen back so far that it became necessary to readjust our line in touch with them and to fall back on to a line covering Achiet-le-Grand and Achiet-le-Petit from the south-east. Orders to that effect reached our own Battalions all right but we were not able to find the 5th Entrenching Battalion who seemed to have been shelled out of the place where they said they would be. This Battalion was a composite unit made up of men surplus to the new establishment when the three-battalion organization had been brought into force. It was commanded by Finch who had previously had our 13th Cheshires, now disbanded, and though we had no sort of authority for taking them along, finding them the previous day at Bihucourt (where they were digging a new line) left without any orders from Corps, we ordered them to join us. Not being able to get a messenger through to them when our Brigade Headquarters moved back at about 2p.m. to Bucquoy, I rode off myself to find them. They turned out to be holding a line just west of the railway, east of Achiet-le-Petit. I there met a Staff Officer from Corps with a line marked on a map which he said we were to hold until relieved by the 62nd Division who were being brought up from behind. This line was west of the railway and I told him that we were going to continue holding a line east of the railway on the high ground, parallel to the railway and running roughly along the line Irles–Bihucourt.

Meanwhile the 41st Division were steadily coming back, followed by a certain amount of artillery fire and I found Colonel Finch very reluctant to leave the good line on which he was dug in (and of which the officer from Corps had approved) and to advance to the next ridge with the risk of being caught in the open between. In this rolling, treeless country of chalk downs one could see for miles from the ridge west of the railway and obviously many of the units which were falling back in turn were simply doing so because their neighbours had set the example and because under the circumstances they had no means of protecting their flanks. I therefore told him that his advance would probably stop the retirement and that the people coming towards us over the sky line were not Boche but British.

Meanwhile the 41st Division were streaming back on our right and soon after one of our own Battalions (the 3rd Worcesters) also crossed the railway and took up a line between Achiet-le-Petit and the railway. Traill, who was in command, told me he had come back owing to anxiety as to his right flank and further that the Boche seemed to be round our left rear as bombardment all day had come from that direction. I reassured him on that point and then crossed the railway myself to find out where our line ran. Our right (9th Loyal North Lancs) proved to be entirely in the air owing to the departure of the 51st Division and our left (11th Lancs Fusiliers) also seemed weakly held where it joined the next formation on the Aichiet-le-Grand–Bapaume Road. I got the Worcesters up to protect our right flank and part of the Entrenching Battalion to strengthen our left.

After four nights without sleep the men were now in a state of very great exhaustion. On the other hand they were holding a strong line from which it seemed a pity to withdraw. The artillery fire of the Boche had quieted down (after my horse which was being held by my groom had got two small pieces of high explosive shell in the neck) and except on the right from Loupart Wood we were not getting much machine-gun fire.

I rode back to Bucquoy to find Bethell, passing through the 62nd Division who were digging in just east of Achiet-le-Petit. On reaching Bucquoy I found orders had come for us to withdraw behind the 62nd Division and we therefore got the Brigade back into Biez Wood and Rettemoy Farm west of Bucquoy where we ourselves remained with patrols out to watch our right flank towards Puisieux. We spent the night and most of the small hours of the morning talking to COs and then to the Brigadier of our 7th Brigade and again only got a couple of hours' sleep.

26 March

At about 7 a.m. we found that the 62nd Division had now withdrawn through Achiet and were holding a line just east of Bucquoy. Bethell sent Reid (our Signal Officer) along the road for half a mile to see what the position was, and half an hour later his servant came back and said he had

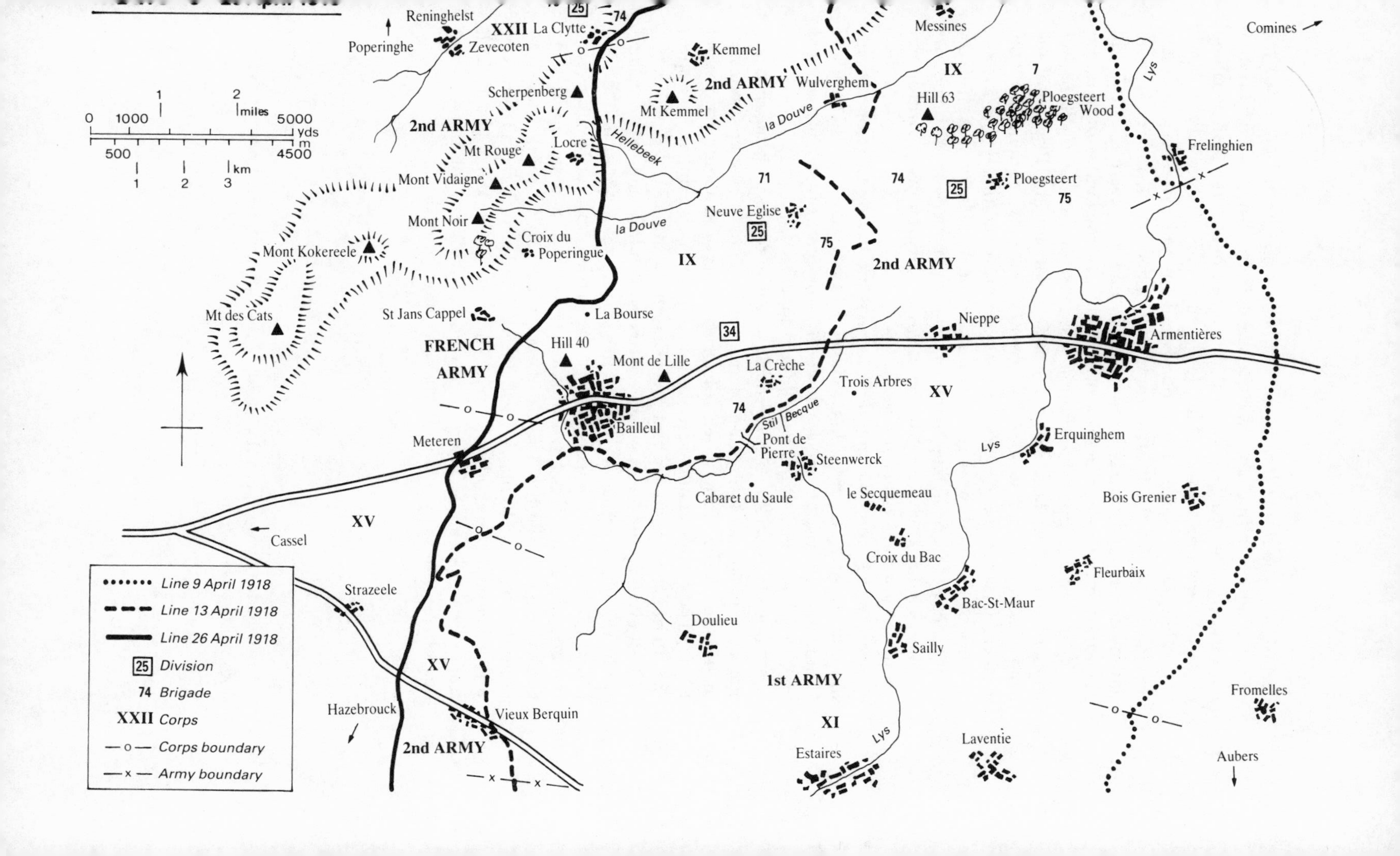

Reninghelst
Poperinghe
Zevecoten
XXII La Clytte
74
25
Messines
Comines
Kemmel
2nd ARMY
Wulverghem
IX
7
Hill 63
Ploegsteert Wood
Lys
Frelinghien
Scherpenberg
Mt Kemmel
0 1000 5000 yds
1 2 miles
500 4500 m
1 2 3 km
2nd ARMY
la Douve
Locre
Hellebeek
Mt Rouge
Mont Vidaigne
71
74
Ploegsteert
75
Neuve Eglise
Mont Noir
Croix du Poperingue
la Douve
75
IX
2nd ARMY
Mont Kokereele
Mt des Cats
St Jans Cappel
La Bourse
34
Nieppe
Armentières
FRENCH ARMY
Hill 40
Mont de Lille
La Crèche
Trois Arbres
XV
Bailleul
Stil Becque
Pont de Pierre
Steenwerck
Erquinghem
Meteren
Cabaret du Saule
le Secquemeau
Bois Grenier
XV
Cassel
Croix du Bac
Fleurbaix
Strazeele
Bac-St-Maur
Doulieu
Sailly
XV
1st ARMY
Fromelles
Hazebrouck
Vieux Berquin
XI
2nd ARMY
Laventie
Estaires
Aubers
Line 9 April 1918
Line 13 April 1918
Line 26 April 1918
25 Division
74 Brigade
XXII Corps
Corps boundary
Army boundary

been shot in the stomach by some Boche but that he had got him back to an ambulance in Bucquoy. We afterwards learnt that he had died almost immediately. He was a very great loss, being one of the best signalling officers I ever came across and his death really quite unnecessary.

I rode round at once to find our Battalions and to cancel the orders previously sent for the Brigade to take up a line east of Essarts, as there now was doubt whether we should have time to prepare it, and I told them instead to rendezvous west of that village. The jumble of traffic on the road and the general confusion just west of Bucquoy village was indescribable. I met Lord Hampden who commanded a Brigade of the 62nd Division on the western outskirts of Bucquoy, arguing with the gunners whether the people we saw coming over the Ridge a short distance to the south were our own or the enemy. The gunners had lost their heads and were shelling them but through my very strong binoculars I could see quite clearly that the men in question were British and Hampden got the artillery stopped.

The 62nd Division did not at all impress me during these operations. Just after leaving Hampden I saw General Braithwaite,* their Divisional Commander, come up and I believe that complete disaster was averted only by his personal efforts to pull them together.

Meanwhile Bethell had been round to get in touch with the situation and at 12 noon met COs and ordered the Brigade to take up a position in the old Boche front system of trenches between Gommecourt and Essart. These dispositions were complete by about 2 p.m. and we spent the afternoon reorganizing and preparing the position.

That evening, however, we got orders to withdraw and to concentrate at Couin, which was about seven miles back. I hung about until 4 a.m. before I had seen all the Brigade past the starting point at Fonquevillers, and got into Couin about 5.30 a.m. on *27 March*. I there got a real sleep, five solid hours, the first I had had for six days. I was awakened by an order that we were to march back about ten miles to Puchevillers on our way to entrain for another Army. The roads were so congested with troops and especially reinforcements going south in motor lorries and buses that we didn't get in to Puchevillers until after dark.

28 March

The Brigade having spent the night in the open, marched on to St Ouen and St Leger-en-Domart.

After a real rest the Brigade was again a going concern. Our casualties appear to have been something over a thousand but it was still difficult to get the final figures, as some of the missing might be with other formations. Having for the first time information as to what had happened further south, it became clear that the repeated withdrawals without being allowed to fight were absolutely necessary to avoid the danger of the Boche driving up behind us from the south. The Boche must have used up tremendous energy in re-occupying the wasted area as we gradually drew back to conform to the break of the 5th Army on our right. The 4th Corps, in which we were, certainly deserved great credit for having prepared emergency lines behind the front system. Owing to everyone's anxiety about their flanks, without such points in which to reform, a retirement is almost bound to become a rout, as it did with the 5th Army on our right, who had none of these prepared lines behind, which would have enabled them to fall back short distances without the danger of disorganization.

I spent much of the day going round to COs and Adjutants so as to get the fullest possible information of what really happened, with a view to writing the narrative of operations. That night the Brigade began to move off to entrain from a station a short distance south-west of Doullens.

Having seen the Brigade off on its march to the station, Brigade Headquarters motored off at dawn on *31 March* to entrain ourselves at about 8 o'clock. Just as we were going to get into the train, Hamilton, the GSO2, and Simeon, the Intelligence Officer of our Division, arrived in a motor and saw that we were all right. They were on their way with requisites and telephones to open up in the Bailleul area. Bethell, however, made them dump their baggage and telephones in the train and take me in the motor so that I could get on to Waterloo Camp and have a few hours before the arrival of the Brigade to finish work on the history of our operations. We reached our destination in the afternoon and, after dropping Hamilton and Simeon at Divisional Headquarters, I went on to Waterloo Camp just east of Bailleul intending to buy some candles in the town with which to get on with my work. I found, however, that Bailleul was completely ruined. During the previous fortnight the Boche had shelled it so continuously that hardly a house was left with a roof on it. It was very sad to see the havoc in Bailleul, which, when I had last been there, was a prosperous little town of about 15,000 inhabitants containing a very good Officers' Club and offering a respite from trench life which was much appreciated by the Division holding the line in the neighbourhood. As I could not do my work without the candles, I had to drive a good many miles to the north-east before finding a tiny little village shop at Locre where I was able to buy a packet of candles. I found the huts at Waterloo Camp quite deserted and very cold but got in a good many hours' work before Brigade Headquarters arrived in the small hours of *1 April*.

On arrival I was met with the startling news that Bethell had been ordered away to command a Division (66th), and I heard from our Divisional Headquarters that Bainbridge was asking that Craigie Halkett should be appointed in his place to command the 74th Brigade. Craigie Halkett is a very nice person and a most dashing leader of men, but completely ignorant about all Staff work and the detail of running a Brigade. During Bethell's leave he used to keep me busy setting him march tables and other routine orders etc. to practise on, and always ended by getting me to do them while he looked on. Life promised to be much less strenuous in many ways with the prospect of considerably more responsibility being thrown on the Brigade Staff.

As to Bethell, I wrote on *1 April*: 'He is only 35 and will be by many years the youngest Major-General in the BEF. If he doesn't get into trouble for trying to run everybody else's business besides his own he should go very far.'[24] Altogether he was a most difficult person to get on with, and I finally had some very straight talking with him on the morning of our retirement from Bucquoy when he flew into a rage about nothing. I told him that in this he paralysed everyone with whom he came into contact and by putting sand in the wheels only got 25% value out of his staff. He took it all very well but matters have been a little strained ever since, chiefly owing to his forced and unnatural good manners.

On *2 April* we took over the Le Touquet sector. The line had, however, advanced a little since I had held the same part over a year before while commanding the 11th Cheshires during Evans' absence.

In the afternoon Bethell turned up in a motor and said he was going to apply for both Marriott and me, and that he had already taken steps to get me transferred to him as GSO2, as that would be the more difficult matter to fix up. My feelings about the proposed move are rather mixed. I hate the idea of being a GSO2, as to my mind it is nothing like such interesting work as Brigade Major. In the ordinary way of promotion, however, I shall probably be moved up in any case in about four months and I should then of course have to go to some strange Division where I should probably know nobody. In any case it was extremely doubtful whether Bethell would be able to get the matter arranged, but he is so determined and unscrupulous in such matters as almost invariably to get his own way. His new Division (the 66th) is a Second Line Territorial Division which was commanded by Ian Malcolm's* brother until he was wounded a few days ago. Two of the Brigadiers and eight of the COs have also been knocked out and there are only 1200 fighting men left. I gathered that the old Division was pretty bad and that a very big reorganization would be necessary to turn its remains into a going concern.

3 April

Edward Greene came over to dine. It is curious how we continually meet in the Bailleul area. Bramwell Jackson, also in the Suffolk Yeomanry, is still up here with Sir Alexander Godley and wants me to go over one evening to dinner.

5 April

The Brigade moved out of the line and Brigade Headquarters moved back again to Waterloo Camp. Sir Guy Bainbridge had been over to the Army about Marriott and I being sent to the 66th Division. He was there told that he needn't think any further of the matter as it had just been decided to disband the Division in question.

This is a beastly country, nothing but drains and stagnant water. The trenches which we took over give one the impression of a Whitechapel slum owing to the neglect of our Australian predecessors. Everyone except me has a cold in the head or a sore throat and I feel as limp as a boiled rag from the combined effect of quinine and the relaxing climate.

7 April

We now hear that the 66th Division is after all *not* to be disbanded. Bethell had no doubt gone to GHQ and worried them out of their original decision. Now that we are out of the line, life is very quiet. Craigie Halkett leaves the Brigade much more to run itself. One therefore gets to bed quite early nowadays and, two days running Marriott and I have been so short of work that we have actually gone out for walks to get exercise. Plumer came over to see us and told us all the news. Bethell writes to Marriott that he now has a vacancy for GSO3 and has applied for him and that 'Guinness will be OK a little later'. In any case my transfer must take longer to fix up as GSO3s are appointed by Armies, but GSO2s have to go through GHQ.

9 April

During the morning a considerable noise was heard to the south of us and Craigie Halkett went over about 10 o'clock to Divisional Headquarters to find out what it meant. The only news they had was that the Boche had been very active on the Portuguese front,[25] and they understood that it was only in the nature of a very big raid. Craigie Halkett and I therefore rode on to see the Battalions entrain at Bulford and Aldershot camps. A great deal of bombardment continued throughout the morning and on our return about 1 o'clock we found that orders had been received to the effect that the enemy had broken through the Portuguese and reached the line Laventie–Fleurbaix, and that we were to move at one o'clock to Steenwerck where we are all to be at the disposal of the 34th Division. As we were all out, Brittorous, our Intelligence Officer, had sent out a warning order, and at 1.30 p.m. we ordered the Battalions to move off at once to Steenwerck, COs to meet us on arrival at the church. As the Brigade was scattered over the country training, and several COs were doing musketry on the ranges, and it was impossible to move off without considerable delay, Craigie Halkett and I rode off at once to the Headquarters of the 34th Division at Steenwerck where we learnt that the Boche was already across the Lys to the south of us. We met COs at the church and pushed forward patrols at once to find out the position and if necessary to drive the enemy out of Bac-St-Maur.

We found the enemy to be holding Croix-du-Bac and the general line of the road running north-east and south-west through that village. We established our Brigade Headquarters in Le Secquemeau in some huts which had just been evacuated by heavy artillery belonging to the Corps on our right. We immediately attacked with a view to pushing the enemy back over the river but were not able to do much before dark. The whole position was at first very obscure. Our Battalions had never previously seen the ground, and, the country being very much enclosed, had great difficulty in getting through. Brigade Headquarters was only about half a mile from the Boche and I had a tremendous argument with Craigie Halkett before I could induce him to draw back to Steenwerck. In view of the uncertainty of our position it seemed quite likely that at any time we should find our Headquarters attacked and that we should be cut off from all possibility of controlling the Brigade. Finally he agreed to go back to Steenwerck, where we established our Headquarters in a house looking on to the garden which contained the 34th Divisional Headquarters, reaching there a little before midnight. At 8.30 p.m. the 11th Lancs Fusiliers, in the middle of our line, attacked and made a considerable advance, but the General commanding the 34th Division insisted that we should immediately repeat the effort and push the Boche back across the Lys before the morning so as to recover and destroy the bridges.

At 2 a.m. on *10 April* we therefore renewed the attack and made good the village of Croix-du-Bac and a considerable amount of ground on either flank. Owing to the darkness and the unknown ground, either parties of Boche were overrun during the attack or some of them got through because of imperfect touch between the flanks of our own units

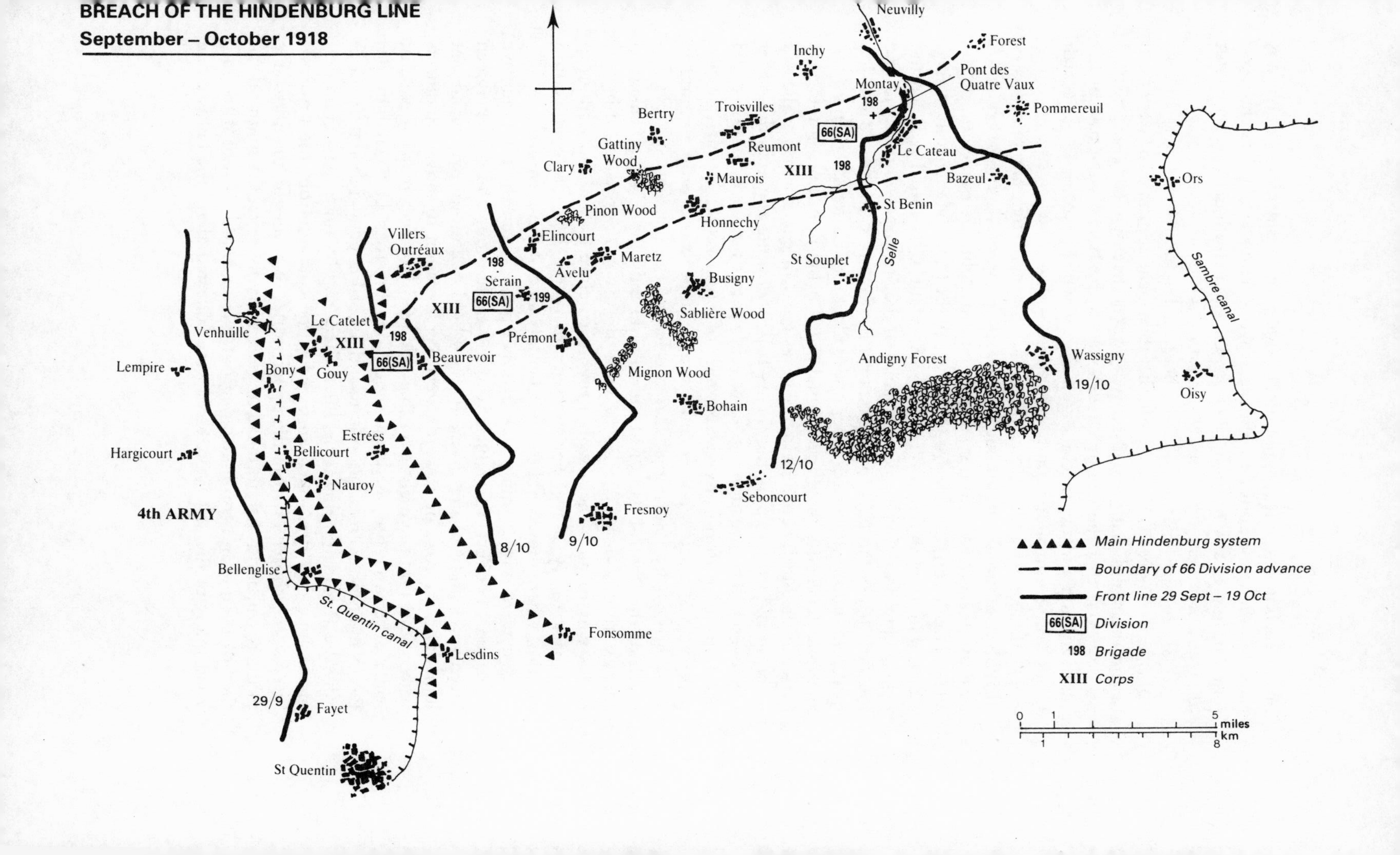

BREACH OF THE HINDENBURG LINE
September – October 1918
Neuvilly
Forest
Inchy
Montay
Pont des Quatre Vaux
Pommereuil
198
Bertry
Troisvilles
66(SA)
Gattiny Wood
Reumont
Le Cateau
Clary
Maurois
XIII
198
Bazeul
Ors
Pinon Wood
St Benin
Honnechy
Elincourt
Villers Outréaux
198
Maretz
St Souplet
Selle
Serain
Avelu
Sambre canal
66(SA)
199
Busigny
XIII
Sablière Wood
Le Catelet
Venhuille
XIII
198
Prémont
66(SA)
Beaurevoir
Andigny Forest
Wassigny
Lempire
Bony
Gouy
Mignon Wood
19/10
Oisy
Bohain
Estrées
Hargicourt
Bellicourt
12/10
Nauroy
Sebonucourt
4th ARMY
Fresnoy
8/10
9/10
Bellenglise
St. Quentin canal
Fonsomme
Lesdins
29/9
Fayet
St Quentin
Main Hindenburg system
Boundary of 66 Division advance
Front line 29 Sept – 19 Oct
66(SA) Division
198 Brigade
XIII Corps
0
1
5
miles
km
1
8

or between us and our neighbours. In this way considerable trouble was caused in the rear of our own units and we were uncertain as to the exact position. In the early morning the 34th Division Headquarters cleared out of Steenwerck, leaving us under the 40th Division.

At 8 a.m. Carter, the GSO of the 40th Division (who were on our right), came to see us. We told him that the Boche appeared to be between us and them and that we had thrown back a defensive flank. He assured us, however, that the troops we believed to be Boche were part of the 40th Division and the machine-gun fire of which our 9th Loyal North Lancs were complaining must be coming from somewhere else.

The Brigade by this time, owing to the hard fighting under very difficult conditions throughout a very dark night, was getting very much used up. Reassured as to the position on our right, we pushed on on the left and made considerable progress towards the Lys. The enemy, however, attacked in strength down as far as Bac-St-Maur–Croix-du-Bac Road and managed to break in between the flanks of the 9th Loyal North Lancs and the 11th Lancs Fusiliers. At 10.35 a.m. the enemy came round our left flank and shortly afterwards it became evident that Carter had been wrong and that the enemy were firmly established behind our line on the right between the Steenwerck Switch. Things got worse and worse as the day went on and by 3.30 p.m. the enemy began working round both sides of Steenwerck. The situation was now very critical and we obviously could not hope to re-form anywhere south of Steenwerck, as our line was penetrated at various points and the only hope was to stop a complete breakthrough by reforming what was left of the Brigade on a position north of the town. I had great difficulty in inducing Craigie Halkett to agree with this view. The Boche were already in the town, and he was on his way to meet them with a revolver before I could induce him to turn back to try and gather the remains of the Brigade together in a position where they could stop further advance of the enemy.

Men were now coming back in small parties from the town and we managed to collect a few men whom we put along the road between Steenwerck and Cabaret-du-Saule. I got hold of a motor cyclist and sent him along the road up towards Steenwerck station to show any officers who might find themselves on that side of the town a map on which I had marked our proposed new line along the road between Pont-de-Pierre and Steenwerck station just south of Stil Becque. I then rode off to rally the Brigade on this actual line. There was by this time a good deal of machine-gun fire which appeared to be coming from the tower of Steenwerck church or from the upper stories of houses on the north side of the town, and I therefore had to get off my horse on the south side of the Stil Becque and continue along our line eastward on foot. I found a good many of the 3rd Worcesters were collected along the railway line to the south-east of Steenwerck station. I had crossed the Stil Becque by the bridge on the station road and when I returned to collect my horse I found that the Boche was already holding the houses along that road. I therefore had to work along the north side of the river and vainly tried to find a way across. It was a muddy stream about 6 or 7 feet deep with very boggy banks and at least 12 to 15 feet wide. Finally in desperation I had to jump right into it and scramble out the other side.

I had been very angry with Baxter at Achiet-le-Petit for departing with my horse when they began to shell the place where I had left it, and so on this occasion he had remained on the spot where I had dismounted, a bit of sunken road, quite under cover, but by that time evacuated by all our men. I had arranged with Craigie Halkett that we should meet at Pont-de-Pierre and I therefore galloped along the open field just north of the road from Steenwerck station to Pont-de-Pierre to rejoin him. I saw him and a handful of men lying out behind a railway embankment which crossed the road about 50 yards south of Pont-de-Pierre. They made frantic signals to me when they saw me riding up which had the effect of making me cover the ground as fast as I could. It turned out that the Boche had been shooting straight up the road apparently from a few hundred yards range to the south and they naturally expected that he would open on Baxter and me. For some reason he never fired a shot, perhaps because he had run out of ammunition or was at the moment moving his gun to some other position. I found that our Signaller had 'T..d' [tuned?] into a line running along the ditch by the road towards the right turning from Bailleul towards Pont-de-Pierre. I got down into the ditch and told them to get me through to the 34th Division in Bailleul. While they were trying to do so, the operator got shot through the shoulder, which convinced me that the road was a very undesirable place, and made me get right down into the ditch, which didn't matter, as I was already soaked through to the skin from my swim through the Stil Becque. The General came on to the telephone himself and was infinitely relieved to hear that we had blocked the hole in the line. Up till then he had apparently heard absolutely nothing of what was going on, and didn't know what had happened to his own Division.

About 6 p.m. the enemy came along the railway from Trois Arbres and attacked the 3rd Worcesters who, owing to the retirement of the 34th Division on their left, were here holding a position almost at right-angles to the general line. The 3rd Worcesters were compelled to get off the railway beyond Steenwerck station by enfilade machine-gun fire. We put our Brigade Headquarters into a little farm a couple of hundred yards to the north of the Pont-de-Pierre and I then rode off to try and get in touch with the 34th Division on our left. I worked up to the Armentières–Bailleul Road, which was in a state of fearful congestion, being the bottleneck through which the troops had to evacuate that country which had been made untenable by the break of the Portuguese. Finally I found General Freyberg's* Brigade about La Creche and fixed up that we should be responsible for the line on the south of the railway and that they should hold to the north. On getting back to Brigade Headquarters I found that Freyberg's Brigade Major had been over and seen Craigie Halkett. We were still uneasy about our right flank, as, when the 9th Loyal North Lancs had fallen back from the Steenwerck Switch line, they had got out of touch with the 11th Lancs Fusiliers, whereas while we had fallen back in a northerly direction they had conformed to the movement of the 40th Division on their right which had diverged from us and gone more to the north-west. The gap in our line was partially filled by two Field Companies RE of the 40th Division.

11 April

At 4 a.m. the 5th Battalion Yorks and Lancs Regiment (49th Division) reported to reinforce our line, and we put them in between us and the 9th Loyal North Lancs. As we were now connected up Craigie Halkett insisted on making an attack to clear the Boche out of Cabaret du Saule. At 9.30 a.m. the 11th Lancs Fusiliers and the 5th Yorks and Lancs moved forward and after some very hard fighting cleared the enemy out of the enclosed country round Cabaret du Sole. The operation, however, was a great waste of energy, as the left of the 40th Division had meanwhile given way and this left our newly gained ground as a very dangerous salient.

In such operations sectional counter-attacks are absolutely useless as they only use up one's resources with no results. In this case the attack left us with nothing further in hand, and, as a result, when the Boche shortly afterwards attacked the 3rd Worcesters on our left, they had to give ground as we had nothing left to put in as reinforcements. In the attack on Cabaret du Saule we collected a certain number of Boche prisoners. They seemed to me extremely good troops; most of them wearing the Iron Cross, they were members of machine-gun detachments which had been pushed forward independently and had worked with an initiative that one could hardly expect from any but soldiers of very long service and experience. At 7 p.m. we received orders from the 40th Division that both they and we would be relieved by the 31st Division and that we were to rejoin the 25th Division at St Jeans Chapelle. The 31st Division were to attack with the 92nd and 93rd Brigades and, having passed through our position, the reliefs were to take effect. Although the 93rd Brigade carried out this programme, we never heard anything further about the 92nd Brigade, who were to relieve us. After the disappearance of the 40th Division we were left entirely on our own, under no one.

12 April

At 4 a.m. Brig-General Gore, commanding the 101st Brigade, with his Brigade Major (Gilbey), turned up saying that he had been sent up to support us. Both the Brigade Staff and all their troops seemed in the last stage of exhaustion and we arranged that they should stay just behind us on either side of the Pont-de-Pierre–Bailleul Road, ready if necessary to move up in support. We again became very anxious about our right flank. It turned out that the 93rd Brigade had counter-attacked before relieving the 40th Division and had failed. They had fallen back, leaving us in a most awkward position.

At 8.50 a.m. the 5th Yorks and Lancs reported that the enemy were massing on their right. We, however, couldn't possibly give up the bridgehead over the Stil Becque at Pont-de-Pierre and we therefore had to prolong our flank until our line was most dangerously thin in our attempt to get in touch with our neighbours. Our Brigade Headquarters meanwhile was much too far forward for the efficient control of our Battalions as we were within 300 yards of the front line and even less from our exposed right flank. The enemy also appeared to be coming round on our left judging by a bullet which scattered the glass of the window by my side all over the paper on which I was writing. The Boche artillery too was beginning to devote their attention to the farmhouses along the road, and the 101st Brigade Headquarters and ourselves therefore decided to move to the Bailleul–Armentières road where after a very unpleasant walk we managed to tie into a telephone line and get into communication with our Battalions through advance Headquarters which we had just left. We were very anxious about our right flank as we had not yet been able to regain touch. Meanwhile the Bailleul–Armentières road was an impossible place for Brigade Headquarters, as the Boche was continually putting shells on to it and, even if we were to escape, it was quite clear that we couldn't hope to keep our telephone lines uncut. We therefore moved our Headquarters about a mile north of the Bailleul–Armentières road to a farm on the northern part of the Mont de Lille. At 4 p.m. the 5th Yorks and Lancs were heavily attacked and forced back on their right flank. After dark they managed to get safely across the northern branch of the Stil Becque and to take up a position on the north bank, an operation which they could not possibly have done without disaster in daylight.

13 April

Another very anxious day. Ceaseless fighting and our line wearing very thin. The 11th Lancs Fusiliers were forced back at the Pale Pier but reoccupied the bridgehead with the help of an artillery barrage. During the day it became probable that owing to the Boche having worked round to the south-west of Bailleul, a further retirement would become necessary. We therefore made all arrangements in daylight for the Brigade if necessary to rendezvous on the Mont de Lille under cover of darkness. About 6 p.m. we learnt that the Brigade on our left had the Boche practically in behind them and General Freyberg sent his Brigade Major over to say that they were obliged to fall back. This meant that when our neighbours threw back our troops to close the gap, we should be left in the air. General Gore, however, who was now holding on our right, was told by General Nicholson that he was on no account to go back. This was all right for him as we covered his left, but put us in an impossible position as, had we conformed to Freyberg's movement, there would be a hole in the line on our left. After some desperate discussions with the Division on the telephone, they finally agreed to our withdrawal and under cover of darkness we came back about a thousand yards along the Armentières–Bailleul road and making our line of resistance the high ground on the Mont de Lille immediately south-east of Bailleul.

Meanwhile our Headquarters was getting unpleasantly shelled. The night before we had sat for hours in our gas masks owing to gas bombardment and tonight the Boche was right on to us with 4.25s and 5.9s. It was a good-sized farmhouse and when the tiles began to fly we went down to the cellar. I was very reluctant to do so as it was a very poor one with so thin a ceiling that in the room overhead one could hear every word which was being said there. Also I had hoped to get a couple of hours' sleep while the troops were carrying out orders to withdraw. When therefore I got down, Craigie Halkett told me I was to sit in the one wicker armchair and go to sleep. I refused to do so and while we were quarrelling over it, Colonel Shakespeare, who commanded the Pioneer Regiment attached to General Gore's Brigade, came down and sat in it, while I got into a corner and settled down to try and sleep, leaning up against some barrels. We hadn't been there five minutes when the whole place was blown in by a shell which fell in the road and blew a hole in the side of the cellar. All the lights were of course blown out, and instead there was an arch of starlit sky. Luckily I had an electric torch and found a candle which we lit (people poured downstairs at once to see what had happened). General Gore and his signalling officer were killed and the old Colonel sitting in the chair where Craigie Halkett wanted me to sit was blown across the cellar and so shattered that I believe he died afterwards.

Marriott (our Staff Captain) and Gilbey, Brigade Major of the other (101st) Brigade, were both knocked out, the former being pinned by brickwork on to the broken leg of the old Colonel, to the great pain of both, and the Brigade Major having his leg broken. Our Signal Officer has never been seen since and must have lost his reason from shell shock as the evidence shows that he rushed up through the hole in the wall saying that his leg was broken, which was obviously absurd.

13 April (Extract from letter to his wife)

We're still holding practically the same ground. Since then time after time it has looked as if we must be broken or retire, and yet somehow when things looked most hopeless they have always been re-established and after losing a hundred yards or so we've got it back again except for bending back a flank to join up with a readjustment of our neighbours. It has been intensely interesting as we've for the most part been cut off from any Division and simply had to play our own hand without any chance of reinforcement. When the swaying line is anchored again, they must pull us out as we've never been reduced in strength to the degree we now are. The Boche cannot conceivably go on throwing in Divisions at their present rate, and I am glad of these days as I know that each one as it passes must be shortening the war by months.

14 April

We spent the next three or four hours trying to disentangle the position and whereabouts of the 101st Brigade (of which Craigie Halkett now resumed command). We moved to new Headquarters in another farm near by. The Staff Captain of that Brigade was fortunately unhurt, but various orders had been given by telephone to his Brigadier of which he knew nothing, and for a long time I was trying to hear by a hopeless telephone line what the 34th Division had told him. This effectually prevented any attempt to get even a moment of sleep, as I had to go out at dawn to see in what kind of lines the Brigade were digging in on their new positions.

The attack developed pretty quickly and for the first time during these operations the Boche put down a really terrific bombardment. All day we were at it, and after dark the Boche actually crept up along some hedges to the top of the hill. Bombardment had by that time greatly weakened the garrison but fortunately fifty men of the 9th Loyal North Lancs who had been separated from us since the 10th, and with another formation, had turned up and been sent to reinforce. They arrived just in time to catch the Boche on the flank and crumple him up with great loss.

During the morning of the 10th we had moved our Brigade Headquarters back to a farm at La Bourse. I chiefly remember this farm for an enormous barrel of cream which had been left by the inhabitants in their hasty flight and I suppose it was due to the fact that we had had very little to eat for a good many days that I was able to consume several cups full of thick clotted cream without any ill effect.

15 April

We were relieved in the early morning on Mont de Lille by the 176th Brigade of the 59th Division. We took up a line two miles back, about a mile south of Croix du Poperinghe facing south. The General and I went to meet the Brigade as they assembled. They were a very small band, only a fifth of those who had gone in six days previously. All, however, seemed in wonderful heart and agreed that they had killed very large numbers of Boche, especially the previous day when they had been pressing on across the open to take Mont de Lille, the keystone of the Bailleul line.

We moved our Headquarters to a large house just behind but it was heavily shelled in the afternoon so that we cleared off into a cottage near by. In the afternoon the men had had to stand to owing to heavy attack on line in front, so what with digging new line (with very insufficient tools) and the order to stand to, the Brigade got little rest after their six days' incessant fighting. In the evening we were informed that the 59th Division had broken in front of us and that we must hold on at all costs to our new line.

16 April

Brigade Headquarters moved to Headquarters at Mont Noir, formerly occupied by Godley's Army Corps where I had dined only ten days before, little expecting the conditions under which I should next see it. The Boche came up to our line but we were not seriously engaged, enemy concentrations being very effectively dealt with time after time by the French artillery who came up this morning in support of us. It was a very pleasant sound to hear the quick barrages of the .75s, and our Battalions told us that their shooting had been extraordinarily accurate.

17 April

Heavy bombardment of our quarters at Mont Noir drove us to ground deep in dugouts in the morning. Since these were appallingly crowded, and thinking it had died down, I ran the gauntlet to get some lunch and recover the papers I had left in the hut occupied last night. Shelling, however, was still such that I have rarely eaten a quicker lunch and we decided that we must henceforth live the life of herrings packed in a barrel. General Nicholson had moved up to share the dugout and besides the Headquarters of his own three Brigades there were those of five others who are attached to his Division. Ours is far the weakest, having lost four-fifths of our strength, and as they had a very heavy shelling all day it was arranged that we should move back into support ready for immediate counter-attack, and this was carried out during the night.

18 April

Went to see Battalions. Men very cheerful but say yesterday's shelling was damnable. There is, of course, no cover for them and they have in many cases neither blankets nor greatcoats. I wish we could get them relieved but unfortunately, although our own Division are trying hard to get us out, the 34th Division say we cannot possibly be spared until they are relieved. We remained in this position until 4 a.m. on April 21st, when the 34th Division were relieved by the 133rd French Division. On relief we moved back to a concentration area at Hoograaf Camp and then on to join the 25th Division at Dirty Bucket Camp.

It was a great relief to get out of the close quarters at Mont Noir. There was literally no room to move in there and the work was made ten times harder by the physical inconvenience of overcrowding. Although each formation had cut down its personnel to the lowest possible limits, and had sent all surplus back to the transport lines, nothing could relieve the congestion caused by having Divisional Headquarters and eight Brigade Headquarters, not to speak of a lot of French officers from other artillery units or concerned with their forthcoming relief, packed into the one dugout. All the service cooks etc. had to find shelter somewhere, most of course in the passages; as it was, Borley had got the heel of his boot cut by a fragment of shell and of the other three servants whom we had kept at Brigade Headquarters, one was killed and another wounded. Near Hoograaf Cabaret on the way out I found Edward Greene, who seemed very well and in most comfortable quarters with lots of young flowers growing in boxes. They were, however, thinking of moving, as the line had come back inconveniently close to Corps Heavy Artillery Headquarters and some big shells had been dropping round their farm.

We spent from *22* to *25 April* in huts at Dirty Bucket Camp, well concealed in a wood on the north side of the road from Ypres to Poperinghe. We received drafts to replace our casualties and got to work on a new line which was to be dug approximately north and south a couple of miles to the east of Poperinghe. My own future was again uncertain. Furze, who, much against his will, had been transferred from Brigade

Major of the 7th Brigade to GSO2 of the 25th Division, had at last persuaded Bainbridge to let him take a Battalion and Bainbridge was asking for me to be appointed in his place. At the same time I heard from Bethell that he had seen General Lawrence* (the Chief of the Staff) and fixed up that I should be sent to him as soon as the present GSO2 was placed elsewhere.

24 April

I learnt from Furze that Bainbridge had been to GHQ to fix up about my replacing Furze but was firmly told that Furze must stay where he was as Staff Officers could not be allowed to go to other jobs. I should have preferred to stay with the 25th Division as I have got a great belief in Bainbridge and know the whole Staff very well. While at Dirty Bucket Camp we got a lot of new officers to replace casualties, new COs including Ward-Macquaid to replace Martin, who commanded the 11th Lancs Fusiliers until missing on 10 April. Ward-Macquaid was sent to us by Bethell but proved absolutely useless and had to be got rid of after a very few days. There was quite a lot of friction about this time at the way Bethell was snatching officers from us and unloading in return the people he didn't want. Marriott, who had been evacuated on the night of April 13th after being knocked out in our cellar, never returned, having been collected from hospital by Bethell and kept as ADC. As soon as he recovered he was appointed GSO3 to the 66th Division.

25 April

At 11.45 when most of the Brigade were out at work on the new line we received orders to be in readiness to move at an hour's notice to support the 22nd Corps (now commanded by Sir Alexander Godley with practically the same Staff as he used to have when his Corps was known as the 2nd Anzac). I sent out at once to collect the Brigade and at 1.15 they moved off to a position of concentration near Hoograaf Cabaret. They had to go a very circuitous road round the west side of Poperinghe to avoid the congestions of traffic caused by the French troops who seemed to be all over the road, whether it was allotted to them or not.

As soon as we saw the Brigade off, Craigie Halkett and I reported at Divisional Headquarters, a long ride to a Château north-west of Poperinghe. We arrived there very wet, as it was raining in torrents and found that Bainbridge was away concerting a counter-attack with the French who were to be on our right. We eventually managed to get an outline of the plan by telephone and rode off as quickly as we could to Hoograaf Cabaret to decide on the exact spot on which the Brigade was to concentrate. The roads there were already very unpleasant and shell-holes and dead animals made us look for a place as far as possible from crossroads or likely lines of traffic. We finally chose a patch of ground nearly a mile east of Hoograaf Cabaret and established our Headquarters in a farm a couple of hundred yards from the Poperinghe–Reninghelst road. All we then knew of the position was that the French had lost Mount Kemmel and that we were to counter-attack the next morning with a view to its recovery. No one knew where the line was and the first thing to be done was to send out patrols to find out.

In view of the uncertainty of the position the great difficulty was to know where to put down our original barrage. It had to start a long way in front of where our troops would be at zero and the danger was that they would run right into it. We were not on the telephone at our Brigade Headquarters and we had to go about a mile away to the Headquarters of the 7th Brigade to talk to the Division. After various amendments I was only able to send out the final barrage programme at 2.45 a.m. The artillery were to open at 3 a.m. on the Kemmel becque which the infantry had to reach by 3.30 a.m. We felt very anxious about the attack as, apart from the very short time available for troops to get to know the orders, the ground was very heavy and, if there proved to be any Boche west of the Kemmel becque, it was pretty certain that our people would never get there in time. As soon as we had got everything fixed up, we rode to an elephant iron shelter north of the Zevecoten-La Clytte road, about half-way between those places. We had, of course, to walk the last part of the way and the rain was so heavy that it ran down into my field boots and overflowed at the top.

The attack went astonishingly well. The French artillery never opened and the barrage was so thin that the enemy must have thought it to be only mild harassing fire and in consequence put down no SOS barrage. In spite of the Kemmel becque being so flooded as to delay the advance, the Boche machine-gunners were rushed and our attack got right on into Kemmel village. Meanwhile the 39th French Division on our right never moved; our 7th Brigade, who were attacking on our left having had very heavy officer casualties including all three Battalion Commanders, mistook their direction and lost touch with the 49th Division, who were on our left. The result was that before we had got our final objective and captured many prisoners and guns, we were left completely in the air and had to come back. I don't think any one would have got out of it if it had not been for a thick fog. As it was, they lost very heavily from enfilade fire owing to the Boche being on each of their flanks. Fortunately too we were up against a very poor lot of Germans, the prisoners being from the 118th and 186th Regiments of the 56th Division. The operation had, however, cost us many of our best officers owing to the fact that we had been filled up with half-trained recruits who didn't know their job and had to be shown. It was a very bad performance on the part of the French not to have warned us that their attack was abandoned. The 7th Brigade, who had suffered even more heavily than we, were taken out during the night and we took over the whole line. I spent most of the night trying to find my way about the new line. Some of the machine guns in the rear seemed to have got their calculations wrong and on my way back I came through unpleasantly heavy machine-gun fire which was being put down by mistake 100 yards behind our line.

27 April

We were relieved by the 75th Brigade and went into close support but our Brigade Headquarters did not move. We had chosen our Headquarters extremely well. The French Brigadier insisted on remaining at Hoograaf Cabaret right on the crossroads and wanted us to join him there. As we expected, however, a shell arrived and knocked him and most of his Headquarters out.

28 April (Extract from letter to his wife)

In our attack the day before yesterday the French never even started because they said their guns weren't up in sufficient numbers for the necessary artillery support. No explanation of their failure to let us know. We also had no barrage partly because the gunners didn't get their orders until after zero and partly because those that did shoot had only one round per minute instead of the usual four per minute. Luckily it was a misty morning, otherwise hardly anyone would have got back.

29 April

Owing to a report that Mont Rouge and Mont Vidaigne had been captured we were moved up again to form a defensive flank to the French troops. We found the ground already thickly occupied by the French who did not at all welcome our arrival and early on the morning of the 30th we returned to our support positions.

On the night *30 April/1 May* we relieved the 148th Brigade (49th Division) in the line rather to the north of where we had already previously held. It was an unpleasant relief as the night was pitch dark and we had to go in during an abortive French attack 1000 yards to our right which brought down a barrage of gas shells on our line. We had seen a good deal of General Greene-Wilkinson, commanding the 148th Brigade and his Brigade Major, Moxie. They were living in a little felt hut close to

Goetmoed Windmill. Greene-Wilkinson believed that this windmill drew Boche fire and, very foolishly as we thought, blew it up the night before we went in. We thought that the Boche would naturally realize that the windmill would not have been destroyed by us if it were not in a tender spot, the bombardment of which we were anxious to prevent. One of the many aeroplanes that came over no doubt took a photograph of the surroundings of the mill, showing our little felt hut about six foot square with its side sunk about three feet in the ground. The corrugated iron coverings for the trenches nearby would also look suspiciously like a Brigade Headquarters.

Accordingly at 4 p.m. the Boche began a regular 'area shoot', mixing up gas shells with HE. Craigie Halkett, his Orderly Officer (Godfrey) and I were sitting in the little hut wearing our box respirators. I was not personally taking much notice of the shelling as I was reading the newspaper which had just arrived, when suddenly Godfrey for no apparent reason got up and looked out of the door. He said, 'They're not shelling away to the right but seem to have got this trench taped and I think we had better go.' Fortunately I didn't argue because we were not twenty yards from the hut when a shell landed on the edge of it and we saw the whole place go flat in a cloud of dust. We remained at a safe distance until the shoot had ceased and on returning found the felt sides had been absolutely riddled with bits of shell and that if we had stayed another twenty seconds we should have been blown to bits. The sad part of the episode was that my mackintosh, wash basin and spare boots were all torn to shreds. Craigie Halkett's experience of cellars and felt huts now made him refuse to go into any Headquarters except a house, and we moved into a little cottage about half a mile further back, standing a little way west of the river out in the open fields. The direct hit on our Headquarters unfortunately buried many of the papers and maps which I had collected on the subject of our recent operations.

On the night *2/3 May* we were relieved in the line by the 148th Brigade and on the evening of the 3rd moved back close to the neighbourhood of Hopoutre siding, close to Poperinghe. On *4 May* we moved back near to St Eloi Cabaret close to Steenwoorde. I have found the recent operation far less of a strain than it used to be with Bethell, as Craigie Halkett is much easier to deal with and always took steps by arranging our duties so that one did not get more than about two sleepless nights running.

5 May

We moved close to Esquelbecq, near Wormhoudt, a nice farm with lots of eggs and butter, where I lived in a tent specially pitched so that I could see nothing but the meadow and the duck ponds beyond and could forget all about war. I motored over one day to Dunkirk and another day General Godley came over to see us and to say goodbye as we were now definitely leaving his Corps and going down south. He told me here that it was quite certain that I should be sent off to join Bethell as the correspondence had been sent to GHQ a few days previously.

8 May

We entrenched at Wayenburg.

10 May

Early in the morning after a very circuitous round by Dunkirk, Étaples, Beauvais and Paris, we arrived at Fère-en-Tardenois. It was a delightful change after the dull monotony of Flanders. We had breakfast in a little wood alongside the station carpeted with bluebells and lilies-of-the-valley and we then marched to billets in Coulonges. The Brigade was in French huts in a large French hutment camp just outside the village. We had a good deal of trouble with the French Military authorities who appeared to be extremely rapacious and were always demanding compensation on the ground that the wood of the huts had been burnt or that damage had been done to some farm. As usual on arriving in a new area, we at once got to work to construct rifle ranges and it was strong evidence of the little importance which the French attached to rifle shooting that there was no range within reach of what had for years been a large military camp. At Coulonges we were just behind the Chemin des Dames and though the Higher Command considered this to be one of the quietest bits of the line. Bainbridge, at an inspection of the Brigade on the 11th, made a very strong speech as to the necessity to get going as quickly as possible because in his opinion there was no part of the line more tempting for an attack from the German point of view than this which was very thinly held and was so close to Paris. We were sandwiched in among the French and we took over a bit of line from them. We become thus a British Corps in a French Army. The attack prophesied by Bethell took place shortly after I had left the Division and so little was left that the old 25th Division, as I knew it, was finally broken up. We were one of the four Divisions who had been sent down south on account of their exceptionally heavy casualties in the recent fighting. The other Divisions had arrived a few days ahead of us and it was thus probable that we should have a week or two of quiet during which to receive our drafts and to get reorganized.

[On this day the diarist wrote to his wife that he had heard unofficially that Bethell had recommended the award of a bar to his DSO: 'something about leading troops forward to re-establish the line at Achiet on 25th March'.]

Just when I had settled down comfortably to our new condition they telephoned from Division that orders had come for me to join the 66th Division. Apart from my exchange, Bethell had grabbed Nares who was perhaps the best CO we had in the Brigade, and was sending us some unknown man in exchange. Craigie Halkett spent most of my last day with the Brigade composing a letter. I did not see it, but Godfrey told me that it was most violent and that when it was finished he tore it all up so as to begin it again in order to leave out the 'my' before 'dear'. When Bagshaw [Guinness' replacement as Brigade Major] turned up we gathered that there was just as much feeling about all Bethell's cross-postings in the 66th Division as there was in the 25th.

The 66th Division had now been organized on a Cadre basis [i.e. a nucleus to which miscellaneous units would be drafted] and were waiting for the arrival of American troops whom they were to train. As they were not doing much work for the moment I fixed up to have a few days in Paris on my way to join them. Though I left the 74th Brigade on 15 May I did not therefore reach the 66th Division until the afternoon of the 19th. I found on arrival that most of the 66th Division were away on leave pending the arrival of the American troops. From Eu I motored to join the 198th Brigade in Bagshaw's place [in fact to become GSO2 of the Division] at a village about 10 miles to the north-east.

General Hunter (60th Rifles) who commanded the Brigade was away on leave, as also was Bethell. They both returned, however, the following day. The American troops were just arriving, and after riding round with Hunter we finished up at Divisional Headquarters at Feuquières and I stayed to dinner to have a talk with Bethell afterwards. He told me that the 66th Division were of a very low standard and that he had had to make a lot of changes with a view to getting them on to more satisfactory lines. When it was decided that the 66th Division were to become a Cadre Division he had been offered another one, but, having taken a lot of trouble to collect a lot of people, he did not like to have to go off to another Division where he would have to start all over again. He intended to keep the Cadre Division for the moment and then to work to get it made up with other troops. He had in mind particularly the 4th Battalion of each Brigade in the Near East which had become surplus under the reorganization scheme decreasing the number of Battalions in each Brigade to three and which would shortly arrive in France. Many of these Battalions were regular Battalions and the men were veterans in comparison with those then on the Western Front, most of them having gone out to Gallipoli, Egypt or Salonika at least two years before.

On *23 May* I joined the Division as GSO2 in place of Parry Jones who was sent off to become GSO2 to the 74th (Yeomanry) Division which had recently arrived from the Near East. There are a very nice lot at 66th Division Headquarters. [To his wife he wrote that day: 'Damned nuisance – beastly job and I was settling down comfortably here and much like General Hunter.'] Nosworthy,* the GSO1, is a very brilliant young Sapper with a DSO and bar and a Military Cross and bar. He originally came to France with the Indian Army and is the classical example quoted in all the hospitals of about the only recovery of a man shot plumb through the heart. Marriott is the GSO3 and the other occupant of the General Staff Duties Office is the Intelligence Officer, Durham. The Division is by no means a happy family, and there is very much discontent at Bethell's restlessness and high-handed methods. Bethell had just got as ADC Dudley Pelham,* a brother of Lord Yarborough and quite fifteen years older than himself.† Pelham is a very nice little person, a professional soldier who had served all his life in the 10th Hussars. He looks fearfully worried and says that his life is turned to bitterness because he can't read a map quickly in a motor car driven at 50 miles an hour. He tells me that I am always held up to him as the great instance of good powers of map reading, I suppose like the governess who always used to tell one that her previous pupil was perfect.

We remained at Feuquières until the *20 June* training Americans. Most of the time we had two Divisions, one of the first ones being the New York National Guard commanded by General O'Ryan. O'Ryan is a typical Irish soldier of fortune who had much to do with starting the National Guard Movement in America, which more or less corresponds to our Territorials. Like our early Territorials and New Army the New York Division had many men in the ranks who certainly ought to have been officers. One of the mess waiters, when Bethell went over to dine with O'Ryan, was the son of Cornelius Vanderbilt, and his father was commanding what corresponds to our Divisional Battalion. The other of our original Divisions was commanded by a very old man who, unlike O'Ryan, was much too weak to keep his end up with Bethell. Generally speaking, the senior American Officers were very poor indeed. Many of them were old Regular Army Officers, physically and mentally unfit for responsible commands under the strenuous conditions of modern war. They necessarily had to be given the command of Divisions and Brigades

†An overestimation of Pelham's age; he was forty-five, but that was indeed remarkable for an A.D.C.

because there was no one else with any military experience whatever and even they of course had never previously had experience with large bodies of men. Generally speaking the officers up to and including the rank of Battalion Commander (Major) were temporary soldiers and some of these were quite first rate. Whereas the Regular Army officers were not unnaturally rather disgruntled at being put under the wing of British advisers, the new Army officers were extremely keen to learn and as a rule both they and their men showed remarkable aptitude especially in those branches of training which needed mechanical knowledge, such as Lewis and Vickers guns. The general system was that each American formation or unit should have a corresponding British cadre to look after it, but as most of the time we had a couple of Divisions to look after with merely our own Divisional cadres and perhaps three or four Battalion cadres extra thrown in, we had of course to stretch our organization and to make, for instance, one of our Brigade Staffs look after a couple of American Brigades, or perhaps an American Divisional Headquarters and also an American Brigade Headquarters.

Our work was very much complicated by Pershing's* stupidity. He was generally said to be the stupidest man in France and showed quite remarkable narrow-mindedness and obstinacy. He worked out a so-called 'Schedule' of training which laid down almost hour by hour what the American troops were to do. In many respects this Schedule was perfectly absurd. For instance, it made no provision whatever for route marching, and although in our weekly confidential reports on the American troops which we had to furnish to our GHQ we continually emphasized this omission, nothing we could do was able to get it remedied. The result was that at very short notice we had to take the American troops up to take over the Reserve line and found the men physically incapable of marching. Then again the Schedules made no allowance for the training facilities available in various areas. All troops, wherever they were billeted, had to do exactly the same programme for each week of their course. We were obliged to organize the area so as to afford special facilities near the coast for long-range musketry and in the southern part for manoeuvres of, say, a whole Brigade at a time. The third area was only suited for elementary training owing to the difficulty of getting large tracts of land for manoeuvres and the impossibility of making safe rifle ranges. Nothing, however, would induce American GHQ to remodel their 'Schedule' so as to conform to the necessities of the training ground. Much as the American Divisions would no doubt have liked to take advantage of our organization and advice, they were too often afraid to do so because they had a vicious system under which the Inspector's Staff used to arrive unexpectedly, look at troops at work and send in a report direct to American GHQ, instead of going through Division or Corps, complaining, for instance, that instead of being at work on 'terrain exercises' at the particular time shown in their Schedule, the troops were often engaged, say, on musketry.

Some of the American professional soldiers were also fearfully zealous in carrying out the orders that no British Officer or NCO was under any conditions to command American troops, and they interpreted this to mean that a Sergeant Instructor couldn't even drill a platoon but must stand by and see the American officer making a hash of it. Owing to this system it was extremely difficult for the Americans to get the full benefit of their attachment. In theory our cadres were to teach them in the afternoon and evenings the lessons which they were to pass on to the American rank and file in the mornings, but in practice it proved very difficult to carry out this method.

My own work at Division proved to be much less interesting than it used to be at Brigade and consisted chiefly in fixing up all details about training, and being responsible for the starting and running of schools of instruction in Lewis gunnery, physical training, trench mortars and signalling. Besides this there were incessant moves. The Americans wanted, of course, to keep the same cadres with their units throughout their course. Bethell, however, was always thinking much more of training his own Division than of training the Americans and, as the Americans were prevented from moving round the area in the way he wanted, he was continually moving about our cadres and sending everyone exactly where they could only possibly go on the expenditure of the greatest possible amount of ingenuity and labour on the part of the Staff.

Lemon [Assistant Adjutant and Quartermaster General – a Divisional Staff Officer], used to supply us with an enormous amount of amusement, being extremely lazy and very much under the influence of red tape. Every night when Nosworthy and I came home to bed we used to find Lemon sitting in the Mess by the light of a flickering candle drinking whisky and soda and groaning at Bethell's latest atrocities. Bethell never took the slightest notice of any regulations and when Lemon made difficulties or pointed out that something was entirely contrary to all orders, Bethell used to shut him up and be extremely rude. Lemon was always waiting when there would be a day of reckoning for all the misdeeds which he was obliged to commit. During the time we were a Cadre Division there were very drastic orders about cutting down personnel. Furious letters used to arrive from the AG Department which used to give sleepless nights to Lemon but be flatly disobeyed by Bethell. While we were training Americans we were plagued with continual inspections, several visits from Haig, also Lloyd George, Milner* and Pershing and British Generals innumerable. The more important inspections used to give us no end of trouble as the Americans had very little idea of punctuality and their Staff arrangements were most primitive.

On 30 May I wrote: 'Milner inspected our Americans the day before yesterday, Pershing yesterday, Haig this morning, Rawlinson [Commander of 4th Army] this afternoon, Corps Commander tomorrow; I hate all generals. Classes to be fixed up, courses arranged, no time for anything except to fix up details about these infernal inspections.' I was also for ever sending off batches of Americans from Brigade Commands downwards to be attached to corresponding British formations in the line. This was a most infernal nuisance to everybody concerned. One had to get buses to collect the Americans who were always late and most of them were so undisciplined that they used to get lost on the road. When they arrived for their attachments they always made difficulties about going where Corps and Divisions in the line wanted to send them, and I had incessant trouble trying to smoothe things out.

Our A Mess where I feed consists of Bethell, his ADCs, Nosworthy, Lemon and I. It is a most uncomfortable life as Bethell is always bringing in impossible numbers of people to lunch or dinner without notice, and I much envy Marriott who lives in B Mess.

My time with the Americans very much shattered my illusions as to their powers of organization and quickness. Their reputation for hustling seemed to be quite unfounded, or only to apply to exceptions who just because they were exceptions had been so advertised as to make foreigners imagine them to be the rule. My impression is that Americans are far slower-thinking people than we, very bad organizers, very bad too at making up their minds and even worse at carrying out their decisions when arrived at. I daresay, however, much of the trouble is due to their very vicious Army system, very highly centralized and most cramping to all initiative.

21 June

Owing to fears of an early German attack we moved up at short notice with two American Divisions who were to be spread out in reserve to the 3rd and 4th Armies. During this move the neglect of Pershing to allow his troops to do route marching involved much unnecessary trouble and discomfort. Quite apart from their physical unfitness, the Staff work was perfectly appalling. On the evening before we moved up Rawlinson, who commanded the 4th Army, telephoned to say that he would like to see the American troops on the road. I therefore got through to the American Division to find out their marching arrangements. I found the Division had no idea when any of their Brigades were moving or by what roads but advised me to ring up the Brigades. I then got through to the Brigades who said that they hadn't yet received any copies of the Regimental orders and would I ring up the Regiments. On getting through to the Regiments they said they really didn't know when their Battalions were moving as they had got no telephones and there was no possible means of finding out before they closed their offices at 8 p.m. It was typical of the American frame of mind that time after time when there was important work to be done we found that they had rigidly adhered to their rule of closing offices at 8 p.m. If one rang up after that hour one generally found that there was no one but a telephone orderly who invariably said that it was against their rules for any officer to come back after dinner. Our work used always to go on well past midnight, and we used to wonder what would happen to the Americans when they got into the line if the Germans failed to observe the American rule of suspending all military operations at 8 p.m. Anyhow on this occasion there was no way of telling Rawlinson when the Americans would be moving and I rang up 4th Army and explained that the whole of the American Division had to get through the bottleneck over the Somme between St Valerie and Noyelles. Marching tables and proper arrangements for allotting roads and times are, of course, always imperative to avoid unnecessary waits and discomfort for troops, but under such conditions as these where one whole Division had to go up one road it was simply mad to let them march according to their own sweet will, because it meant that some of them had got to the bottleneck before others and had to wait hours before they could move.

On *24 June* as soon as all the Division had trekked up to the 3rd and 4th Armies, I went off to Camiers for a fortnight's special machine-gun course, it being proposed to do away with Corps machine-gun officers and to give the responsibility for Corps machine-gun defence to GSO2s at Corps Headquarters. I motored over accompanied by a French interpreter named Levy who had been attached to us for Intelligence at the suggestion of Nosworthy who used to know him at the (British) 2nd Corps. Levy is a terrible type of French Jew but very intelligent. He insisted on coming with me when he heard that a motor was going to Camiers as he wanted to call at Bercke Plage on the way back to see whether a little house that he had there was still standing.

On our way we called to see the Suffolk Yeomanry who were somewhere to the north of Doullens. Their Division (the 74th) has lately come from Palestine and is said to be very good. Having had very few casualties in comparison to the invariable mortality on this front, the officers certainly seem much more civilized than those which one finds in Battalions who have been long in France. The men, too, are both better educated and far finer physically than the new levies to fill the cadres of the BEF. I found there were still NCOs who had served in the Regiment when I knew them. At the same time the whole of this Dismounted Yeomanry Division, who have adopted as their Divisional Badge the very suitable sign of a broken spur, are naturally very raw to conditions on this Front. Their work and training for the past three years has been directed to open fighting and though they would give a very good account of themselves under such conditions, I feel rather anxious as to what would happen to them under the unaccustomed conditions of trench warfare. The whole look of the Division was rather amateur and their general turnout far behind the standard enforced out here. I got to Camiers just in time for dinner, and found a good many acquaintances among the GSO2s who had been sent to attend the course.

The course turned out quite a pleasant change after the incessant telephoning and rush which we had lately been having. At the same time I felt it rather a waste of time, as unless one is a professional soldier or a machine gunner it is not much use knowing all about the internal mechanism and technical details of machine guns; besides, we could only get a smattering of the subject, as they were trying to compress into a fortnight a resumé of a course which generally takes a couple of months. I always did hate machinery of all kinds and felt very much at sea the first day or two, trying to follow the mechanical part of the machine gun.

After the first couple of days we devoted ourselves to working out schemes for placing machine-gun batteries among the sand dunes and laying down their barrage tables and night firing. Much of this work was very interesting. The system of indirect fire has been largely borrowed from the Artillery and has been so simplified that even people like myself who are very bad at mathematics were able after a few days to work out how to shoot by the map and to find that the bullets were actually going in the right direction. Camiers would be quite a nice place if it wasn't for the wind. We lived in an isolated hotel on the sands and most days had to breathe and eat sand which blew in everywhere. The wind has one terrible effect in making us all feel very sleepy and we had much difficulty in keeping awake during the lectures.

After we had been at Camiers a couple of days an epidemic of influenza broke out and shortly afterwards all three of the instructors who had been allotted to our Staff course were laid up with it. As a third of us had also got it we were given a holiday of four days and told to go away. Paris unfortunately proved impossible at such short notice and so I took refuge at Boulogne where I lived on quinine in the hope of escaping the epidemic.

Owing to the break caused by influenza we stayed on at Camiers until *10 July*. I did get a slight attack of influenza with a temperature of 101°, but was only laid up for one day. On leaving Camiers I went home on leave, as Bethell wanted to get us all away before we gave up the Americans and started work training our new Division. On arrival Nosworthy met me and gave me details as to what had been happening. He had only been waiting for me to return before going off on leave himself. After dining at Montreuil at a very nice Club that has been opened there by GHQ. I went to Gaillefontaine, about half-way between Beauvais and Dieppe where I arrived late at night. Bethell was away at American GHQ. We had got a dozen malaria-infected Battalions from the Near East to look after, but things were pretty quiet as they were taking huge doses of quinine, beginning with 30 grains a day and gradually working down and in the early stage of the treatment were only allowed to do four hours' work a day. Divisional Headquarters were in a most magnificent Château belonging to a descendant of the Republican General Hoche. Bethell didn't turn up until three days after my return. He was very full of the Americans who seemed to be doing very well now they have started serious work. There was not much to do at first except to go round and find places for schools of instruction, ranges, etc., and to make acquaintance with our new Battalions. These are very promising material as they include many of the men who originally went out to the East in 1915 and who nowadays are veterans beside the short-lived levies of the BEF.

Dudley Pelham, who was quite miserable as Bethell's ADC and as incapable as ever of quickly finding his way on the map, had been asked to go as ADC to General Kavanagh* who now commands the 10th Hussars. Bethell told Pelham he could go as soon as he produced a substitute, which Pelham had so far failed to do. I can imagine very few people keen on becoming his successor, as Bethell's temper in a motor car is quite impossible. He expects his driver never to slacken speed at any crossroads and uses the most violent language if his ADC has not previously instructed him which turning to take. It is no easy matter to find the way going 40 miles an hour with imperfect maps.

[Guinness had expressed a poor opinion of the raw American troops he had trained in the Spring of 1918, but on 27 July he wrote to his wife: 'Bethell returned yesterday having seen the Americans who did the counter-attack. He says that the whole success was due to them entirely and that the French did hardly anything.']

2 August

There is still very little to do because as soon as our Battalions finish their first month of quinine treatment they are sent home on leave in very large batches, which means that training except under Battalion arrangements remains impossible for the Division. Poor Pelham is fearfully worried because Bethell says he is going to take him home on leave to look for an ADC. This would mean a choice between perjury or a continuance of his slavery and if he adopts the first alternative it probably involves losing a friend for life. Besides he had hoped when on leave to see his wife and to get some shooting, and he now lies awake at night picturing his life spent in calling taxis and carrying parcels for Bethell. Just before Nosworthy was to return Bethell telegraphed to give him a further fortnight's leave. We were doing very little at Divisional Headquarters beyond inspecting our new troops. Bethell is inspecting them very thoroughly and I found it very tiring work standing about so many hours a day and trying to fix so many new faces and names in my mind. We were often inspecting troops for four hours in the morning and transport for a couple of hours in the evening.

I had a certain amount of motoring these days in connection with the new Divisional Schools that we were starting. One day, for instance, I went over to see about taking over a Trench Mortar School on the sea coast near Dieppe. I took Pelham with me as he had a holiday, Bethell having taken Marriott out with him for the day. Though Pelham is nearly 50 he was like a schoolboy on holiday.

During this time GHQ had apparently made up their minds to make us up into a permanent new Division with the troops from the East whom we were training, and the original cadres of the 66th Division were gradually broken up and dispersed. Pelham now seems as if he would never escape from Bethell and was frightfully worried because the latter had said to him he expected we might move up in about six weeks time and 'of course you wouldn't like to be away then'. 'What could I say but "Oh! no",' exclaimed the miserable Pelham who now feels sure that he is doomed to remain in his slavery for the rest of the War.

11 August (Extract from letter to his wife)

I don't think there will be an election before December owing to the impossibility of taking soldiers' votes while operations are going on. It is therefore unlikely that I should come home before the beginning of November....

I think there is a great danger of an unsatisfactory peace leaving Germany in control of Russia in spite of treaty obligations to the contrary which we should not be in a position to enforce.

A year ago it seemed as if neither side could hope to obtain a decisive victory, that it would continue a see-saw in which, while both sides wasted away, neither would be strong enough to smash the other. Now, however, it is a mathematical certainty that we can so smash Germany as to cure her for a long time to come of 'militarism'. The fact that the United States can produce practically unlimited numbers of troops of an entirely different quality from anything else now in the field, troops of such physique that they can march (carrying their sixty pounds in battle order) far further than the dregs of humanity to which other armies are being rapidly reduced, makes it certain that if we stick to it we can in time get a real decision.

This ought certainly to be preached to people at home, but, whereas they might listen to one if in khaki, I fear they wouldn't if one were to return to civil life as suggested.

On *20 August*, however, Pelham's affairs came to a head, Bethell having proposed to take him on leave. From what he told me it was clear that he had no intention of looking for anyone else while on leave. Indeed he said he would not take him on leave at all unless he had decided to keep him because Pelham had been too short a time out in France to have earned his leave. I told Bethell that I didn't think this was fair either to Pelham or Kavanagh and a quarter of an hour afterwards he telephoned down to the office telling me to cancel Pelham's leave warrant. Poor Pelham was then in an awful state of doubt, torn between the temptation of immediate leave and the opportunity of getting away from Bethell and I really couldn't make out whether he wanted to go or stay. However, finally Bethell fixed up with Kavanagh that Pelham was to join him after a week's holiday which he was to spend with me. Pelham told me that he couldn't ever again be blown up for making 'another muddle'. As it turned out, Bethell started for his leave without his keys and had to come back about twenty miles to fetch them. Pelham told me triumphantly afterwards that he had happened to meet him on the door-step and had said, 'Well, General, it's not my muddle this time'. Bethell then sent for and cursed his servant who told him that he had himself told him to leave the keys on the table, which he had done.

On Bethell's departure I stopped the infernal Irish piper who used to come and catawaul under my window in the early morning, and we all in consequence slept the next morning until 7.30 a.m. A day or two after Bethell's departure Nosworthy turned up from leave. A question now arose of my going back to the Suffolk Yeomanry to succeed Jarvis who, owing to his age, was shortly to go. In answer to his letter suggesting my return I wrote that I would of course go back if of any use but that Grissell had stuck the monotomy of three years in the East and that it would not be fair to keep him out of the command if there was any chance of his getting it, and also that I had very little regimental experience in France and was necessarily ignorant of details of internal economy and training. He wrote and asked me to come over and see his Brigadier, and this I did on 28 August, but found that he had unfortunately to go away that day, so I missed him. I found the Regiment just going to entrain, as it turned out, on the way for the battle which was then raging. Jarvis said that the Military Secretary in France had drawn attention to the age of certain COs in the Yeomanry Division and that both Lord Kensington and Lord

Sackville had in consequence to go and that he was shortly to do the same. Jarvis did not think that their new Brigadier would consider Grissell fit for the command and that he himself was not particularly keen on getting it, having been a good deal shaken by having had both his brothers killed and recently losing his father. I told Jarvis that I would come if wanted, but in any case I would rather do nothing for the next two or three weeks. Meanwhile Nosworthy had written about it to Bethell and the latter had answered, 'It is the dickens about Guinness. Tell him that he might write and that I will do anything he may want at the War Office. It wants a lot of consideration and I suggest his writing to the present incumbent to hang on for another six months.'

There was so little work to do that on 29 August I went for a week to Paris, Nosworthy relieving me there in his turn on 5th September. He then brought a letter from Bethell saying that he had changed his mind about the Suffolk Yeomanry; 'No, he won't go whether he wants to or not'. On the whole I was rather relieved.

6 September (Extract from letter to his wife)

Another advantage is that I may now get free of the Territorial Force altogether as soon as the present slavery ends. Having done twenty years' service in Volunteers and Yeomanry I have just been given the Territorial Decoration so there's nothing further to wait for! Need hardly say I shall never wear the Territorial Decoration out here where it is an invitation for ungumming [i.e., being sent home] and shows to all and sundry that one is a back number. It is, however, worth having for after the War when people may remember again that Territorials did their best to become efficient under very uninviting conditions.

8 September

I got an urgent telephone message from GHQ to take over to them various information as to the strength, etc. of our units. I went over there with General Williams, one of our Brigadiers who was commanding the Division in Bethell's absence. We saw General Burnett-Stuart* who told us that owing to the shortage of recruits it would be necessary to breakup one of our Brigades and for the moment at least to take away another Brigade intact for use in the forthcoming cavalry manoeuvres. Burnett-Stuart made it pretty clear that we were not at all likely ever to see them back. General Williams and I gathered that the Division would have to be broken up altogether and before leaving GHQ we both wrote letters to Bethell explaining the position. I had told Williams that I was certain that Bethell did not want his Brigade broken up and so we offered up the 197th Brigade which was commanded by Wheatley. The day following our return a DAAG [Deputy Assistant Adjutant General] from the 3rd Echelon at Rouen arrived, as he said, to act as broker's man and helped us to work out the transfers of officers and personnel from the units that were to be broken up. This man told us that the manpower position made it out of the question to keep the present number of Divisions up to strength and that they must in the near future reduce the BEF from the then number of 60 Divisions to about 40 if Divisions were to be kept up to anything approaching their normal establishment.

13 September

Bethell returned from leave in the morning and on the 14th went off to GHQ to get news of our situation. I went with him and motored on to Etaples where I had to sit on a Selection Committee the next morning. The President of the Committee was Lord Ardee who commanded the Base Depot at Etaples. After lunch he took me over in his motor to the machine-gun base depot at Camiers which is now commanded by Gilbert Wills whom I wanted to see as he and I were almost the only MPs now remaining in France. We both felt that after the next election we should inevitably have to come back to the House of Commons but that until the Election was definitely about to take place it was best to stay out here. I was, of course, very uncertain as to my own plans, as it looked like the 66th Division coming to an end and my being sent off as GSO2 at a Corps. On my returning to Gaillefontaine I found that as a result of Bethell's visit to GHQ things had again changed and that the Division again appeared to be as permanent as any Division could be under present conditions as to manpower.

On the *15th* Bethell, Nosworthy and I went off to act as umpires in the cavalry manoeuvres with our Headquarters at the Training Department of GHQ at Crécy, and which lasted three days. We had quite an interesting time but I thought the cavalry work and turnout extremely poor. The troops showed extraordinarily little dash and the communications were appallingly slow. It is not altogether surprising that the cavalry should have lost their efficiency during these years of war during which other arms have been learning day by day and they have been waiting behind for an opportunity of going through the gap if a break in the German line should ever come. The manoeuvres were under the control of Sir Ivor Maxse,* the Director of Training, and the Commander-in-Chief was present and presided at the subsequent Conference at Anxi-le-Château. He is a very poor speaker and was almost inaudible, but as there were a lot of motors, lorries, motor cycles, and cavalry continually passing, it was perhaps rather difficult to make himself heard.

On returning to Gaillefontaine we were very busy arranging for our move up to the forward area. General Hunter's Brigade went through straight from the Cavalry manoeuvres and we were also to be joined there by the South African Brigade who had been put into the Division in place of the 197th Brigade when that was broken up. The 199th Brigade went up with us by train. Our Divisional Headquarters were established at Le Cauroy on the *21st*, belonging to Comte Hervé de Kergorley. The husband is attached to the French Naval Mission in London but there was rather a nice wife who was living in the Château. It is an attractive house outside but, having been used as a Divisional Headquarters almost incessantly from September, 1914, onwards, the inside is in a state of extreme dilapidation. We remained at Le Cauroy until the *27th*, spending the time in hard training.

Mme de Kergorley proves to have a very wide acquaintance among British Generals and every day at least two or three Divisional or Corps Commanders arrived to see her. Levy was an old acquaintance of hers and by chance repeated to Nosworthy what she had said about forthcoming operations. Nosworthy having worked for a long time as GSO2 Intelligence at Corps Headquarters took a very serious view of the leakage of information which was shown by her knowledge and we had a terrific controversy as to whether or not a report ought to be made and sent in to Army, Nosworthy holding that we were not justified in considering a lady's feelings too much in view of the tremendous issues at stake, and believing that if it was brought out that one of her highly placed friends was shown up for having given her secret information as to the forthcoming operations it might well teach the Higher Command to hold their tongues in future. Levy was distracted at Nosworthy's desire to make use of information which he had got from our hostess in conversation and said that he would be ruined. Finally Nosworthy was induced to leave the matter alone and to content himself with an interview with the lady. She was quite an attractive person, nice and amusing, but not really good-looking‡ and I should imagine that her military information was largely a matter of piecing together the knowledge which came to her as to the movements of our various formations.

While at Le Cauroy we first saw our new South African Brigade, magnificent troops, far ahead of any Canadians or Australians that I ever came across. Many of their officers and NCOs are old British Regulars who settled down in South Africa after the War and the result is that in discipline they are in a class by themselves among non-British troops, besides being splendid men physically.

‡Guinness seems to imply that, had she been really good-looking, the Generals would have told her everything!

27 September

We moved at very short notice down to the 4th Army area from the 1st Army in which we then were. The Division was moved by tactical train, a means of transport ensuring a maximum of discomfort for troops as it only takes personnel and transport has to go by road, which means that units have to do without their cookers, baggage and proper feeding arrangements for at least a couple of days. When most of the Division had started Nosworthy and I motored on to our new Army Corps and found that orders had just arrived on the morning of the 28th for a further move. As the advance billeting parties had already gone on to their areas we had a lot of trouble to get things pretty straight. It was shockingly bad staff work on the part of the Army not to let us know in time, and they expected our people, who had marched in some cases ten miles to the station, to march another ten miles straight off on getting out of the train. Eventually, however, we got things straight by getting through to Army by telephone and explaining the position. The end of this train journey landed us down on the Somme with our Headquarters at Corbie, on the *28th*. The whole district was very bad for billeting troops as the area had all been devastated by the Boche during the British retirement last Spring. From now onwards we ceased ever to see a door or a window and after our luxurious quarters in the back areas, all very much felt the cold at first.

On the 29th Divisional Headquarters moved on to the ruins of Mercourt, the 198th Brigade going to Harbonnières, the South African Brigade to Chuignolles, and the 199th Brigade to Proyart. While our troops were on the move Bethell and I motored over to 4th Army Headquarters. We found them in the middle of a battle doing very well. 4th Army were in huts and dugouts south of the Somme in one of the most bleak and desolate areas through which I had ever motored. The ground had been fought over time after time and nothing but ruins were left, and the roads were still almost impassable although the worst shell holes had been roughly filled in with rubbish.

30 September

Divisional Headquarters had moved on to the ruins of Mercourt and we did not move. Bethell and I went over to see the 25th Division. Since the final break-up on the Aisne their remnants had been sent home to England and had come out under a new Divisional Commander, General Charles.* None of the old Battalions were left and a few of the Brigade and Divisional Staffs were the only remnants of the Division as I used to know it. We found them in some dugouts near what used to be the village of

Montauban and on our return we found orders to move in and take over from them the following day. As they were mostly housed in old Boche dugouts, we were very glad again to have the prospect of shelter and warmth, the weather having turned very wet and cold.

1 October

We moved to Montauban, the South African Brigade being in the same area, the 199th Brigade at Mercourt and the 198th Brigade at Cappy.

2 October

The 198th Brigade moved to Guillemont and I spent much of the day reconnoitring the country round Montauban with an exercise by the Division in open warfare during the following days. This area is very much devastated by the continual fighting and it has become very difficult to find one's way by the maps as nothing is left of Mametz Wood and High Wood except the remains of one or two tree trunks which look in the distance merely like telegraph poles and the mounds which mark the sites of the villages are indistinguishable from thousands of other mounds which have been thrown up by the repeated trench excavations, gun emplacements and bombardments which have scarred the country since the First Battle of the Somme.

The dugouts in this area are warmer than the windowless walls in which we have lately been living. The Germans in their retirement have, however, left a good many delay action mines and other booby traps. Our Battalions have already found a good many and caused them to explode harmlessly. While at Montauban I wrote that 'though it is true enough that the Boche retirement will shorten their line and enable them to carry on longer with their failing manpower, the very large numbers of prisoners taken during the last two months (120,000 by the British alone) will do much to neutralize this advantage. The German morale is now very bad and many of their Divisions cannot be relied on to fight at all. Though, however, they seem tired of war there is no evidence that they are thinking of mutiny and without the Army on its side no rebellion in Germany can have any chance of success.'

3 October

Spent most of the day working out schemes of training which, however, had to be cancelled in the evening as we got instructions that we should be moving the following day.

4 October

Marched to Combles where we occupied some German dugouts. I had a busy afternoon writing instructions as to equipment, 'B' teams and the dumping of all but battle order in anticipation of taking part at once in the fighting. In the evening Bethell and Nosworthy returned from the Army; they had been to look at the ground where the fighting is now taking place.[26] We spent the early part of the night in conference with Brigadiers, CRE, Artillery, etc., and arranged for the various people concerned to go off early in the morning by motor to reconnoitre those parts of the country which were particularly to concern them.

5 October

We moved to Ronssoy, calling on the way to see the 25th Division from whom we shall be taking over. Accommodation is a great problem as there is nothing in Ronssoy and we shall have to live in bell tents. The weather is very bad and a scanty supply of bell tents is very inconvenient for the continual conferences which must now take place. After giving instructions about our camp on Ronssoy, Bethell and I went on to the high ground to have a look at the fighting which was going on around Beaurevoir. On getting back to camp Nosworthy and I had a hectic night drafting orders which we didn't get finished until after 4 a.m.

On the morning of *6 October* the Brigadiers arrived for a Conference and we went through the draft orders. Fortunately the attack had been put off from the 7th until the 8th and this enabled us to work out plans in greater detail after consultation with Brigadiers and others concerned. The 6th was again a day of great pressure and we didn't get finished with the revision and amplification of our orders and instructions until about 4 a.m. on the 7th. There was a vast amount of detail work to be got through, owing to the fact that tanks were to work with us and the whole thing was made much more complicated owing to the uncertainty as to the exact line from which we should have to start. On the evening of the *7th* we moved up to our battle Headquarters at Bony in a deep German dugout in the Hindenburg line.

8 October

We attacked about dawn at 5.20 a.m., the South African Brigade on the right and the 198th Brigade on the left on a first objective 3800 yards deep and about the same width. On these two Brigades reaching their objective the 199th Brigade were to go through on the whole Divisional Front and make good the village of Serain, a depth of a further 2300 yards. During the early stages of the battle Bethell and Nosworthy remained in the dugout and I had gone up about 4 a.m. to Forward Headquarters from which I could see the early stages of the attack. Our left flank became rather hung up and at 9.45 a.m., when Nosworthy joined me, the situation did not seem very satisfactory. I therefore went off on horseback with the CRE (Davies) accompanied by some cyclists whom I hoped to send back with information. We got through Beaurevoir but the road was so appalling that the bicycle wheels became discs of mud and the cyclists were quite unable to keep up with us. I therefore parted company with them and with Davies and rode off to see what was happening on our left flank. I found a good deal of shooting going on and, having left my horse in a fold of the ground, pushed on to our extreme left where I found we were at a standstill owing to some Boche who were holding a strong position in a farm. I went past, however, and talked to the advanced Battalion of the 38th Division (5th Corps) who were attacking Villers Outréaux on our left. They did not go for the actual town of Villers Outréaux but swung round it on the high ground. When they were well to the north-east of that place their position was threatened until the Boche in the farm which was hanging us up cleared away. I then made for a telephone wire and sent back word what had happened. This took me some time as it was quite impossible to speak and I had to get my message buzzed through. While I was doing so the 199th Brigade were pushing on towards Serain and many of the French population who had been left there came back through our line. They seemed supremely miserable, most of them having lost everything they possessed in the world. I got a certain amount of information as to the German dispositions and especially as to the position of their Artillery which I was able to send back for the information of our gunners. Having got my message through, I went on about 1000 yards to where the 199th Brigade were fighting on the outskirts of Serain. The clearing of that village gave a good deal of trouble and was not really completed until about 7 p.m. By the time I had seen what was happening and had found General Williams and Wyatt, it was getting on in the afternoon and I didn't get back to Divisional Headquarters until about 4 p.m. I there found Nosworthy in a very bad temper at having been kept all day with the General. On hearing my report, he was left there again while the General took me up in a motor to meet our Brigadiers. After going nearly up to Serain we finally came back and spent the night in a farm just west of Beaurevoir, that village being very unpleasant owing to the bombing of Boche aeroplanes. There was a fearful block of traffic going forwards just as it was getting dusk and while we were held up on the road by Beaurevoir we had rather an unpleasant time from a Boche machine which came and dropped bombs on the crowded transport.

We spent the night of the 8th in very close quarters, as the greater part

FINAL ADVANCE 7 November – 11 November 1918

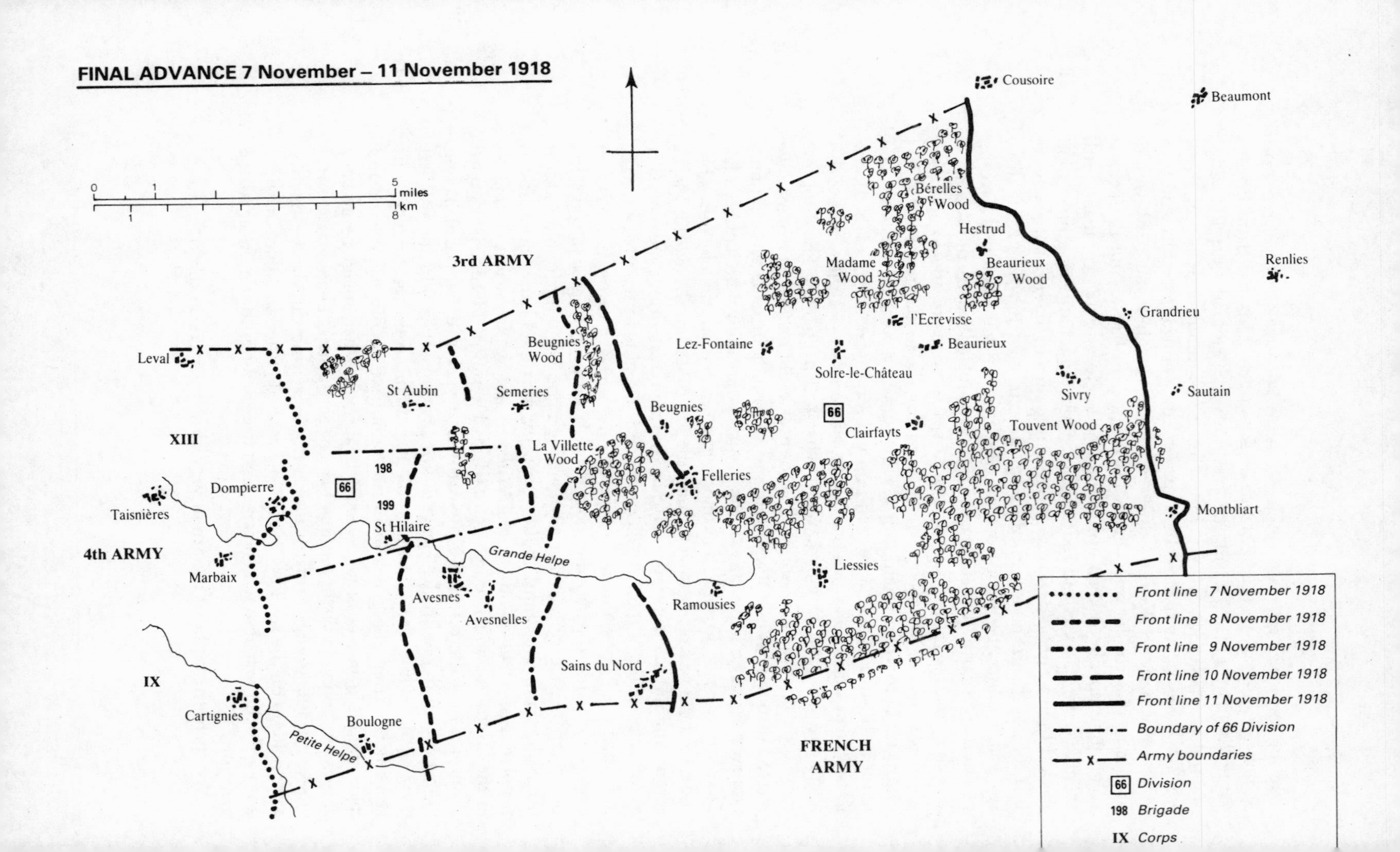

of the farm was taken up by a Clearing Station and there was not even room for the hundreds of wounded that were pouring in and who had to lie on the ground outside until ambulances could be got up to take them back. I spent the night in a tiny little room and got out orders for the further attack which was to take place at 5 a.m. the following morning. There was very little time to get things straightened out as it was necessary to get the 198th Brigade in to relieve the left half of the 199th Brigade. We had, of course, no typewriter or clerks, and Nosworthy and I had to get out our orders in manuscript. I only got one hour's sleep this night and, having averaged only about three for the previous three nights, my brains were beginning to get woolly.

9 October

I remained with Bethell during the early stages of the attack, Nosworthy having gone forward. The Corps Commander came up to see us and after he had gone we moved our Headquarters to a farm just west of Serain. The German resistance today was much less than yesterday and they retired so quickly that we were not able to take so many prisoners. The 199th Brigade on the right and the 198th Brigade on the left secured a first objective 5000 yards deep and 1000 yards wide by 10.45 a.m. The South African Brigade then went through for a further 4500 yards, reaching their final objective about 2 p.m. The total advance by the Division this day therefore included the villages of Elincourt, Avelu, and Maurois, and also the greater part of Maretz.

10 October

The Division again pushed forward another 3½ miles and took Le Câteau and Montay. By 5.30 p.m. the 5th Connaught Rangers had actually secured a footing on the railway embankment east of the town. The American Division, however, which was to have been responsible for the high ground known as the Railway Triangle just south-east of Le Cateau, never got there, and as the 5th Corps on our left were also hung up the 199th Brigade were obliged to come back to the west side of the Selle River. I went up in the morning to see about opening Divisional Headquarters in Reumont. When I got there I found a good many roofs nearby were being blown off, so had hastily to pack up and send our lorries back to the little cottage at Epinette just outside Maretz. We spent the night in a filthy little room with an appalling stench coming from indescribable remnants under the bed which we unfortunately did not discover until the morning of the *11th*. At Epinette I found a man of the 11th Hussars who had been cut off in the retreat in September, 1914, and had lived here ever since hidden in the woods or in the houses of the French peasants. He is an Irishman and I first thought he might be a spy, but subsequent evidence seemed to show that his story was quite genuine and that through all these four years he had feared to give himself up because he knew that others who were captured in this way behind the German line had been shot. This was the first night that any of the Division got sleep. The strain on the Brigade Staffs during the last few days must have been appalling as they have fought all day and spent each night in the frantic preparation of orders for the morrow. It has been bad enough for us but nothing to the strain they must have had as we have three staff officers as against their single Brigade Majors.[27]

11 October

We moved our Headquarters a few hundred yards into the village of Maretz. Now that we have received reports to show how the line runs it appears that our Division was the extreme point of the advance and that we are up against a hastily prepared Boche line where we shall have to wait until the Corps on our flanks catch up. When they get up level with us there should be little difficulty in beating the enemy back to the Valenciennes–Mauberge line. During the three days' fighting the Division advanced fourteen miles on a two-mile front, the actual time taken up being only 53 hours. We took prisoners from eight German Divisions, 26 officers and 1031 other ranks; also material, sixty-two 7.7 cm guns and four 21 cm Howitzers, three 8.8 cm Howitzers, three 5.9 cm Howitzers, one anti-aircraft gun, fifteen trench mortars, six anti-tank rifles, 126 machine guns and two motor cars.

12 October

The 5th Corps tried unsuccessfully to get forward on our left. I went up in the morning as, if they had been successful, our flank was to move in conjunction. On my way up in the motor just north-east of Reumont I caught up one of our RE Officers, causing his horse to shy and back on to the motor. He got a fall on the road and hurt his knee, but, although he was a good deal hurt, said that he really must go forward to reconnoitre the work, and went on while I called in at our Brigade Headquarters which were in some pits to the south of the road. I was only there for a few minutes and then went on to the Pont des Quatre Vaux, an important crossroad on the Le Cateau–Cambrai, Reumont–Bavai roads, from which it was under observation. I therefore sent my motor back under cover. The buildings at this crossroad were being continually shelled and I found the RE officer lying there dying with both his legs blown off. There were some sappers with him whom he had met there and there was nothing whatever to be done for him. I therefore pushed on along the low ground which runs northwards from the crossroads and then bends round east towards Montay. It was a most unpleasant walk as the Boche knew that our troops were sheltering in pits along the edges in this low ground and they were putting over bursts of artillery fire. I was not able to get to Montay since as soon as one showed round the bend of the valley to the north-east there was a burst of machine-gun fire and I found several wounded men lying at a stretcher bearer's post in a hole who could not be got back in daylight. These stretcher bearers have about the most horrible job that exists, as they are continually in contact with the result of that fire to which their duty compels them to expose themselves. They are always picked men and no praise can be too great for the way in which they generally carry out their work.

I have kept no record of our doings in detail during the following days, during which we were arranging for the capture of Le Cateau, a complicated operation which had repeatedly to be postponed owing to the Americans and others who were on our right not having been able to make good the necessary ground from which to jump off. Le Cateau was all this time inhabited by a good many unfortunate French civilians, and was so overlooked that neither side found it worthwhile to occupy it. As these French civilians are quite cut off from the world and were believed to be starving, Bethell ordered a dozen cases of food to be dropped into the place by parachute from aeroplanes with an encouraging message for the inhabitants.

Our attack finally took place on *17 October*. Owing to our previous experience when we got right through Le Cateau but had to come back owing to the high ground to the north-east and north still remaining in enemy possession, the plan on this occasion was to leave the town alone and in the first instance to attack on both sides of it. This operation was most complicated to carry out as it involved our starting 2½ hours after the Division on our right as they had much further to go than ourselves who were the pivot of the advance. Under these conditions it must always be a matter of great difficulty and anxiety whether the two inner flanks can make a junction at the right time and place. At 4 a.m. I went up in a motor, through inky darkness with no lights of course, to the combined Brigade Headquarters of the 50th Division on our right. All their three Brigadiers were congregated in a little house on the Busigny–Le Cateau road. This was only a few hundred yards from the river which they had to cross. Their attack, as also ours, involved getting bridges across the Selle River which was about 25 feet wide. I was to have learnt by a rocket which was to be fired as soon as anyone had got across after this important part of the attack had been carried out without a hitch. There was, however, so dense a fog that one couldn't see 50 yards, so rockets were absolutely useless. The only news I could therefore get as to the progress of the attack of the 50th Division was from their 'walking wounded' who reported that the leading Brigade were all across the river with very little opposition. I sent this news off by motor-cyclist to our own Brigades and then rode off to our advanced Divisional Headquarters. It was still very foggy. Our barrage came down as arranged at 7.30 a.m. Under its protection bridges were to be thrown across the river and troops of the South African Brigade were to assemble on the far side in readiness to advance at 7.50 a.m. Up till 8.30 I was unable to get any news whatever. The telephone lines were all cut and no messengers got through. I therefore motored up along Le Cateau–Reumont road so as to get information from the 'walking wounded'. It appeared that the South African Brigade had been stopped by very thick Boche wire on the far bank of the river and that while it was being cut they were having very heavy casualties from machine-gun fire. The wounded, however, all told me definitely that they were across the river. When I got back to advanced Divisional Headquarters the South African Brigadier was telephoning to ask us to bring the barrage back on to the wire so that he might start afresh. Fortunately we did not do so, and he telephoned a few minutes afterwards that a good many of his Brigade were across the river. The delay in starting caused by concealed wire on the eastern bank of the river caused our troops to lose the barrage and at 12 noon we brought it back to a line running from 300 to 500 yards behind the river so as to give our troops a fresh start. By midday we had captured one Battalion Commander and about 200 men, but it was evident that the South African Brigade had suffered very heavily in crossing the Selle.

I had a very strenuous day at Advanced Divisional Headquarters in intermittent telephone communications forward with our Brigades and back with Bethell in Divisional Headquarters in Maretz. All through the day and most of the night we were trying to co-operate with the changing phases of the attack by the 50th Division and there were masses of orders to be issued. The 'Railway Triangle' which dominated Le Cateau from the east was only captured by the 50th Division at 6.30 a.m. on 18 October and by midnight our South African Brigade had made good their final objective and the 198th Brigade had completed the mopping up of Le Cateau. I had a lot of trouble through these operations owing to a misunderstanding with the South African Brigade. Previous to the attack, General Bethell had been up to see General Tanner and had shown him the various objectives marked in various colours on his map. When we finally issued the orders these lines were shown in different colours. Tanner, however, still went by the colours which he had sketched on to his map at the original interview with Bethell, with the result that he attached a different meaning to the green or red lines to what I did in our telephone conversations.

On the *18th* Bethell got a wire saying that a vacancy was shortly occurring on the General Staff at the Supreme War Council – (Qualifications necessary are knowledge of French and general situation in Eastern Theatre besides Staff experience). After some hesitation I accepted Bethell's offer to recommend me and I afterwards heard from Versailles that my appointment had just been sanctioned when the end of the War cancelled the whole matter.

On the *19th* we moved our Divisional Headquarters to Reumont where I rejoined the remainder of the Staff after my two days and two nights at Battle Headquarters.

20 October

I made a thorough examination of the ground over which our South African and 198th Brigades had fought. The performance of the South African Brigade was wonderful. They forced their way over the river and cut a line through the wire by hand under the most murderous machine-gun fire at short range from a commanding position. They then rushed the railway embankment. This cutting was about sixty feet deep and gave the most perfect protection to the Boche who were holding it. The South Africans captured it by hand-to-hand fighting and the bottom of the cutting was full of dead Germans. I don't think I have ever seen so many dead as those for whom the South Africans were here responsible. From what the inhabitants of Le Cateau said, the Boche expected to hold their line for months and thought that it was practically impregnable. The performance of the South Africans who pushed on and held the high ground east of the railway made the actual capture of Le Cateau by the 198th Brigade comparatively easy, though even here there was a good deal of nasty fighting, as the town was full of cellars.

In the evening we were relieved. Everything had been fixed up, but at 12 midnight Bethell suddenly took it into his head to change all the plans. Instead of one Brigade remaining in Le Cateau until the next night and then moving back, he insisted on ordering both Brigades back into the Reumont–Maurois area, in spite of the fact that there was only room for one, and that with the relief taking place within a couple of hours it was impossible to alter the arrangements without the most appalling confusion. I have terrible recollections of the night of the 20th, though the inconvenience was chiefly suffered by Otter, the DAQMG (Deputy Assistant Quartermaster General) who had to spend the night wandering about in the pouring rain trying to do the impossible.

After, on the *21st*, we moved back to our old quarters in Maretz and we remained in this area resting and refitting until we moved up again to Le Cateau on *3 November*. The villages were full of French inhabitants who for four years had lived under the German occupation. It was curious in view of the boasted German hygiene that they had everywhere left us a plague of flies. Whereas in our own back area there had been no noticeable numbers, the ceilings were now black with sleepy swarms and the tea leaves at the bottom of one's cups consisted chiefly of their corpses. We had glorious autumn weather during this period which was very helpful to the success of the operations which were taking place by the Division now in the line.

I got my War Diary finished and had a fairly peaceful time. Nosworthy was away on a week's leave and Marriott was laid up with influenza. We had a lot of this plague among the Divisional and Brigade Headquarters and the South African troops, but our other two Brigades who had come from the East and who were still on a quinine régime were entirely free. During these days I reconnoitred the ground on our front by air. I particularly wanted to see the site of the Bois l'Eque and the Forêt de Mormal which were likely to concern us in the near future. Visibility, however, was very bad and there were continual showers of rain which made it impossible to see whether other planes in the air were ours or Boche, with the result that I could not go as far as I had hoped.

During this time my letters showed that we did not realize how close we were to Peace. I wrote on the 28th October; 'Already the Boche had shortened his line by ninety miles as compared with its length after he held Château Thierry and threatened Amiens. If he goes back to the line of Antwerp–Brussels and the Meuse he can effect a further shortening of forty miles. This would make it possible for him to accumulate enough reserves to go on fighting for a long time if his morale holds. As to the probability of revolution forcing on him peace from within it is impossible to judge. My own expectation is that the last rejoinder of President Wilson will pull the German people together for another great effort before their final defeat. The American Army is not pulling its weight. Their strength is being frittered away in the push towards Mezières by terrible incompetence which had probably caused them three times the casualties which should have been incurred for the results achieved. If you look at the lateral railways which our push here threatened you will understand why the enemy could not walk back in their part of the line as they did in the north, where, as a matter of fact, their evacuation had taken place except for insignificant rearguards, three weeks before the Allies realized it was taking place.

2 November

Our Brigades moved up to Reumont, Maurois and Honnechy and from now onwards were kept moving everywhere in close support ready to take over as soon as the Divisions in the line got worn out.

[On 4th November Guinness wrote pessimistically to his wife 'Unless internal conditions in Germany are much worse than we know I cannot believe they will yet accept our terms.' But the next day his mood changed dramatically: 'The battle is going so extraordinarily well that we are not in it. The Boche is running away and we have followed up so close that our Divisional HQ are only about three miles from the line.']

By 5 *November* we had moved up to Les Etoquies just north-east of Landrecies. We had torrents of rain all day which was extremely bad luck, as it made the pursuit almost impossible. The new 25th Division happened to be in front of us, with their Headquarters in Landrecies and their line about three miles to the east.

6 November

We again had downpours of rain and the roads were almost everywhere impassable with the lorries in the ditches or stuck in deep shellholes. I rode out in the afternoon across the Sambre to reconnoitre the crossings over that river and the Petit Helpe over which our sappers are hastily repairing and improving the bridges. I found much difficulty in distinguishing between the shallow puddle and the shellhole four or five feet deep and it was quite impossible even to ride at more than a walk. The difficulty of getting up food is becoming very acute. Last night even at our advanced Divisional Headquarters we had to wait four hours after arrival before we could get hold of our dinner of bully beef and dry bread, as our mess lorry had taken six hours to come six miles and had ended up hopelessly ditched a quarter of a mile away from our little farmhouse at Les Etoquies. Everyone in the battle is soaked to the skin which of course stops things even quicker than bullets.

7 November

We moved up to Taisnières and on the 8th we went on to Dompierre. We had now taken over the line and I had a very strenuous day while our Brigades pushed forward in our first experience of real open warfare. We made a considerable advance but there was again a lot of rain and things were made very difficult owing to the clever way in which the Boche had not only blown up bridges and railway crossings at the moment of his retirement but had also left delay action mines which again broke the railway communication weeks after the original mine craters had been repaired and when the troops dependent on them for supplies were several days march ahead. Our fighting on the 8th was just north of Avesnes and during the night the German rearguard cleared out and we were able to push forward early on the 9th and make good our final objective.

After we had made good our objective I went off to discuss matters with the Division on our left and on my return to Divisional Headquarters at Taisnières found that a wire had arrived constituting Bethell's force (a Cavalry Brigade, Infantry, 2 Squadrons RAF etc.) to act as an advance guard and keep in touch with the German rearguard. I spent a hectic afternoon and evening getting out orders. Finally, when all was settled and we had divided up our front between the three Cavalry Regiments of General (Neil) Haig's (Sir Douglas Haig's cousin) Brigade, and just when I was expecting a couple of hours' sleep, General Haig's Brigade Major arrived to see me in a motor car and explained that he had come fifty miles and that his available cavalry on which we had been reckoning only consisted of one and a half Regiments – the remainder being miles back. I therefore had to wake Bethell and explain the position which of course necessitated a considerable change in our plans.

Long before dawn on the *10th* we were on the move and went up to Beugnies where we found Nosworthy who had been trying to get things straight and was much worried at the continual changes of plan which we had had to send up to him. I left Bethell with him and went on in a motor to see how the advance was going. I found that the cavalry had got on through Solre-le-Chateau, and I pushed on to the east. By this time there was nothing but a screen out along each road, and owing to the block of the traffic and the necessity of a big detour through a muddy field, I got on to the Beaurieux road instead of the main road towards Beaumont. In a few minutes I unexpectedly found myself in Beaurieux, where I found the inhabitants in a great state of excitement, saying that there were still Germans in the village, and that moreover they had not seen any signs of our troops. I then turned to the left to l'Ecrevisse where I found the 12th Lancers pushing forward against considerable resistance along the Belgian frontier through the Bois de Warennes north and south of Hestrud. Having seen their CO I went back through Beaurieux and towards Sivry to see what was happening there and then returned to Divisional Headquarters.

About 7 a.m. on the *11th* Bethell ordered our Infantry to push on and make good Sivry and Grandrieu. Fortunately, however, before they had had time to do so we got a message shortly before 8, to announce the Armistice, and I quickly sent out the following message to the South African and 199th Brigades and the 12th Lancers. It was a curious coincidence that the message on my Army Form Block received the number GA11

THE WESTERN FRONT IN OUTLINE 1914 – 1918

'Hostilities will close at 11th hour today November 11th. Troops will stand fixed on line reached at that time which will be reported immediately to Headquarters 4th Army Advance Guard. Defensive precautions will be maintained. There will be no intercourse of any description with the enemy until receipt of instructions.'

Besides sending this off by motor cyclist I went round immediately in a motor to prevent any possibility of our Brigades sustaining any further casualties by pushing on. At the moment of the Armistice I was up at Hestrud with General Tanner. Up till the hour of 11 there had been a tremendous noise as if both sides were trying to get rid of their ammunition, and at 11 o'clock it suddenly became silent. On the front of the 199th Brigade north of the road between Sivry and Sivry Station at exactly 11 o'clock a very troublesome Boche machine gun stopped firing and the German gun team crept out of their holes in the ground, took their helmets off and made polite bows towards their British enemy, picked up their machine gun and slowly retired.

A good deal of stress was laid by the Army on not moving our line from what it was at the moment of the Armistice and some trouble was caused by the impossibility of our getting any message back to tell them exactly how we stood. We sent them forward by motor cyclists but the roads were in such an awful state and broken by so many craters that none of them managed to get through. Finally on the evening of the 11th an aeroplane arrived direct from Army Headquarters with an urgent message that we were to let them have the exact line which we held. When this had been written out the aeroplane failed to start owing to engine trouble and it would have taken quite 24 hours before the Army were able to get the information for which they were asking.

We had a great deal of trouble during these days in getting our men fed, and we hurried on every available man to repairing the damage on the roads and filling in the huge craters which the Germans had blown at all cross tracks, embankments and streams. We spent the six days after the Armistice preparing for the advance to the Rhine which was timed to begin on Monday, 18 November.

My last days were chiefly spent on writing up the history of operations, of which I unfortunately forgot to keep a copy, and in reconnoitring the roads of our front. Although we were supposed not to go forward beyond the line which we held at the time of the Armistice it was impossible to observe this literally, without risking a fiasco as soon as we began to move forward, and in this way I was able to have a very interesting motor drive to reconnoitre the roads on the first day's march. I was the first British Officer whom the villagers had seen since the German evacuation and it is quite impossible to describe the joy and relief which they showed at their liberation. The Germans had not done much damage on the roads behind the front which they had been holding at the time of the Armistice, but every bridge was mined and our Sappers had a lot of work to do removing the charges. Between us and the French, however, who were separated from us by the Grand Helpe River, every bridge was blown and I spent one whole day trying to get down to the French Headquarters at Trelon. After being hopelessly bogged at two crossings where the bridges had been blown up, I finally had to give it up and return to Solve.

Most of us had abominably bad colds, partly no doubt from reaction after all our excitements, and partly because a train full of abandoned Boche ammunition had blown up and smashed every window in Solve with the result that we had to stand and do our work in a terrible draught. Most people were very pleased at our being selected as one of the nine British and Imperial Divisions for the advance. My own feeling was that it would be a very long and most uncomfortable journey as our particular bit of country was very deficient in billeting accommodation and owing to the railways being out of action there would be great difficulty in getting up supplies as much as 100 miles by lorry. Now that the War was over I had no desire whatever for any further military exercises and was infinitely relieved when about the 16th we got a wire that a General Election had been announced and that all candidates for Parliament were to be given a month's leave.

When I had been home a few days it became evident that I should have no opposition at my Election. I wrote and asked General Bethell to get me replaced.

Biographical Notes

Alderson, Lt.-Gen. Sir Edwin Alfred Harvey, 1859–1927. Entered Army, 1878. Commander Mounted Division, Central Force, Home Defence, 1914; Canadian Division, 1914–15; Canadian Corps, 1915–16; Inspector-General of Canadian Forces in UK, 1916. Inspector of Infantry, 1916–18.

Asquith, Rt. Hon. Henry Herbert (1st Earl Oxford and Asquith, 1925), 1852–1928. Liberal MP, 1886–1918;1920–24. Home Secretary, 1892–95. Chancellor of the Exchequer, 1905–8. Prime Minister, 1908–16.

Bainbridge, Maj.-Gen. Sir (Edmund) Guy (Tulloch), 1867–1943. Entered Army, 1888. GOC 110th Bde., 1915–16; GOC 25th Division, 1916–18. Retired 1923.

Baird, Gen. Sir (Henry Beauchamp) Douglas, 1877–1963. Entered Army, 1897. ADC to Sir D. Haig, 1912–14; GOC 75th Inf. Bde., France, 1916–18; GOC-in-C., Eastern Command, India, 1936–40; General, 1937. Retired 1940.

Balfour, Rt. Hon. Arthur James (1st Earl, 1922), 1848–1930. Conservative MP, 1874–1922. Prime Minister, 1902–5. First Lord of the Admiralty, 1915–16. Foreign Secretary, 1916–19. Lord President of the Council, 1919–22; 1925–29.

Beresford, Admiral Lord Charles William de la Poer, 1846–1919. Entered Navy, 1859. Conservative MP, 1874–80; 1885–89; 1897–1900; 1902–16. Knighted, 1903. Commanded the Mediterranean Fleet, 1905–7; the Channel Fleet, 1907–9. Retired 1911. Created Baron, 1916.

Bethell, Maj.-Gen. Sir (Hugh) Keppel, 1882–1947. Entered Army, 1901. CO 1st Northants Regt. (1st Division), 1915–16; GOC 74th Bde (25th Division), 1916–18; GOC 66th Division, 1918–19; Military Attaché, Washington, 1919–23; GOC 2nd Rhine Bde, 1924–28; Brigadier, Northern Command, India, 1928–30; GOC Presidency and Assam District, India, 1930–34. Retired 1935.

Bethune, Lt.-Gen. Sir Edward Cecil, 1855–1930. Second son of Admiral C. R. Drinkwater Bethune. GOC West Lancashire Territorial Division, 1909–12. Director-General of the Territorial Force, 1912–17.

Bonar Law, Rt. Hon. Andrew, 1858–1923. Conservative MP, 1900–23. Leader of the Conservatives in the House of Commons, 1911. Secretary of State for the Colonies, 1915–16. Chancellor of the Exchequer, 1916–19. Lord Privy Seal, 1919–21. Prime Minister, 1922–23.

Braithwaite, Gen. Sir Walter Pipon, 1865–1945. Entered Army, 1886. Director of Staff Duties, War Office, 1914–15. Chief of Staff to Sir Ian Hamilton, Dardanelles, 1915. GOC 62nd Division, 1915–18; GOC 9th Corps, 1918–19. Adjutant-General, 1927–31. Retired 1931.

Bridgeman, William Clive, 1864–1935. Unionist MP, 1906–29. Home Secretary, 1922–24. First Lord of the Admiralty, 1924–29. Created 1st Viscount Bridgeman, 1929.

Broadwood, Lt.-Gen. Robert George, 1862–1917. Entered Army, 1881. Served in Egyptian campaign and South African War. Retired, 1913. GOC 57th Division, 1916–17.

Burnett-Stuart, Gen. Sir John Theodosius, 1875–1958. Entered Army, 1895. GSO1 15th Division, 1915; GSO1, GHQ, 1915–16; BGGS, GHQ, 1916–17; BGGS, 7th Corps, 1917; DAG, GHQ, 1917–19; DMO, War Office, 1922–26; GOC British Troops in Egypt, 1931–34. Retired 1938.

Carson, Rt. Hon. Sir Edward Henry, 1854–1935. Conservative MP, 1892–1921. Solicitor-General, 1900–6. Leader of the Ulster Unionists in the Commons, 1910–21. Attorney-General, 1915. First Lord of the Admiralty, 1916–17. Minister without Portfolio in the War Cabinet, 1917–18. Created Baron, 1921.

Cavan, 10th Earl of, Frederick Rudolf Lambart, 'Fatty', 1865–1946. Entered Army, 1885. GOC 4th (Guards) Bde, 1914–15; GOC, Guards Division, 1915–16; GOC, 14th Corps, France and Italy, 1916–18; GOC British Troops in Italy. C-in-C, Aldershot, 1920–22; CIGS, 1922–26. Field-Marshal, 1932.

Chamberlain, Rt. Hon. Sir (Joseph) Austen, 1863–1937. Conservative MP, 1892–1937. Chancellor of the Exchequer, 1903–5. Secretary of State for India, 1915–17. Minister without Portfolio, 1918–19. Chancellor of the Exchequer, 1919–21. Lord Privy Seal, 1921–22. Foreign Secretary, 1924–29. First Lord of the Admiralty, 1931.

Charles, Lt.-Gen. Sir (James) Ronald (Edmonston), 1875–1955. Entered Army, 1894. GOC 25th Division, 1918–19. Commanded Waziristan Field Force, 1923. Commandant Woolwich, 1924–26. DMO, 1926–31. Master-General of the Ordnance, 1931–34. Retired 1934.

Cowans, Gen. Sir John Steven, 1862–1921. Director-General, Territorial Force, 1910. Quartermaster-General, 1912–19. A very able administrator.

Curzon, George Nathaniel, 1859–1925. Conservative MP, 1886–98. Viceroy of India, 1898–1905. Created Earl, 1911. Lord Privy Seal, 1915–16. President of the Air Board, 1916. Lord President of the Council and Member of the War Cabinet, 1916–19. Secretary of State for Foreign Affairs, 1919–22. Created Marquess, 1921. Lord President of the Council, 1924–25.

De Pree, Maj.-Gen. Hugo Douglas, 1870–1943. Entered Army, 1890. BGGS 4th Corps, 1916–18. GOC 189th Bde, 1918. GOC 115th Bde, 1918–19. Commandant, Royal Military Academy, 1926–30. Retired 1931. His mother was Mary Haig and he was a Trustee of Sir D. Haig's Estate.

Douglas, Gen. Sir Charles Wittingham Horsley, 1850–1914. Entered Army, 1869. GOC Southern Command, 1909–11. Inspector-General, Home Forces, 1911–14. CIGS, 4 August, 1914–25 October, 1914, when he died.

Douglas, Maj.-Gen. Sir William, 1858–1920. Entered Army, 1878. GOC, East Lancashire (42nd) Territorial Division, 1913–17 (Dardanelles, 1914–15). Retired 1919.

Freyberg, Bernard Cyril, 1889–1963. Served Hood Bn, Royal Naval Division, 1914–16 (Antwerp, 1914; Dardanelles, 1915; CO Hood Bn, France, 1916).

GOC 173rd Bde (58th Division), 1917. GOC 88th Bde (29th Division), 1918–19. GOC New Zealand Forces, 1939–45. GOC, NZ Division, 1940–44. C-in-C, Crete, 1941. Governor-General 1946–52. VC, 1916. Created Baron, 1951.

Godley, Gen. Sir Alexander John 'Lord God', 1867–1957. Entered Army, 1886. GOC New Zealand Expeditionary Force, 1914–18. GOC ANZAC Division (Egypt and Dardanelles), 1914–15. GOC 1st ANZAC Corps (Dardanelles), 1915–16. GOC 2nd ANZAC Corps (Egypt and France), 1916–17. GOC 22nd Corps (France), 1918–19. C-in-C, British Army of the Rhine, 1922–24. Governor and C-in-C, Gibraltar, 1928–33. Retired 1933.

Gough, Gen. Sir Hubert de la Poer, 'Goughie', 1870–1963. Entered Army, 1889. GOC 3rd Cavalry Bde, 1914. GOC 2nd Cavalry Division, 1914–15. GOC 7th Division, 1915. GOC 1st Corps, 1915–16. GOC 5th Army, 1916–18 (removed from his command). Chief of the Allied Mission to the Baltic, 1919 (relieved by Lloyd George, the PM). Not re-employed. Retired 1922.

Goulding, Edward Alfred, 1862–1936. 'Paddy'. Conservative MP, 1895–1906; 1908–22. Created Baronet, 1915. Created Baron Wargrave, 1922.

Grey, Sir Edward, 1862–1933. Liberal MP, 1885–1916. Foreign Secretary, 1905–16. Created Viscount Grey of Fallodon, 1916.

Grigg, Edward William Macleay, 1879–1955. Editorial staff of *The Times*, 1903–5; 1908–13. Served in Grenadier Guards, 1914–18. Bde Major of a Guards Bde, 1916–17. GSO, Guards Division, 1918. Military Secretary to the Prince of Wales, 1919. Private Secretary to Lloyd George, 1921–22. National Liberal MP, 1922–25, Governor of Kenya, 1925–31. National Conservative MP, 1933–45. Minister Resident in the Middle East, 1944–45 (succeeded Walter Guinness, Lord Moyne). Created Baron Altrincham, 1945. Editor of the *National Review*, 1948–55.

Gwynne, Rupert Sackville, 1873–1924. Barrister, 1898. Married W. S. Churchill's relative, Stella, eldest daughter of 1st Viscount Ridley, in 1905. Conservative MP, 1910–23.

Haig, Sir Douglas, 1861–1928. Entered Army, 1885. DMT, War Office, 1905–7. DSD, War Office, 1907–9. Chief of Staff, India, 1909–11. GOC Aldershot Command, 1912–14. GOC 1st Corps, 1914. GOC 1st Army, 1914–15. C-in-C, France, 1915–19. Field-Marshal, 1917. Created Earl, 1919. Founded British Legion.

Haking, Gen. Sir Richard Cyril Byrne, 1862–1945. Entered Army, 1881. GOC 5th Bde, 1911–14. GOC 1st Division, 1914–15. GOC 11th Corps, 1915–18. GOC British Military Mission to Russia and the Baltic, 1919. High Commissioner, League of Nations, Danzig, 1921–23. GOC British Troops in Egypt, 1923–27.

Haldane, Sir, Richard Burdon, 1856–1928. Liberal MP, 1885–1911. Secretary of State for War, 1905–12. Lord Chancellor, 1912–15 and 1924.

Halkett, Craigie, Brig.-Gen. Hugh Majoribanks, 1880–1952. Entered Army, 1900. OC 9th North Lancashire Regiment, 1917–18. GOC 74th Bde (25th Division), 1918–19. Retired 1928.

Hamilton, Gen. Sir Ian Standish Monteith, 1853–1947. Entered Army, 1872. Chief of Staff to Lord Kitchener, 1901–2. GOC Central Force, Home Defence,

1914–15. GOC Mediterranean Expeditionary Force (Gallipoli), March–October, 1915. Not re-employed on active service.

Hamilton Gordon, Lt.-Gen. Sir Alexander, 1859–1939. Entered Army, 1880. DMO, India, 1910–14. GOC Aldershot, 1914–16. GOC 9th Corps, France, 1916–18. Retired 1920.

Harper, Lt.-Gen. Sir George Montague, 'Uncle', 1865–1922. Entered Army, 1884. BGGS (Operations), GHQ, 1914–15. GOC 17th Bde, 1915. GOC 51st (Highland) Division, 1915–18. GOC 4th Corps, 1918–19. GOC Southern Command, 1919–22. Killed in car accident.

Hodgson, Maj.-Gen. Sir Henry West, 1868–1930. Entered Army, 1889. GOC Eastern Mounted Bde and 3rd Dismounted Bde, 1912–16. GOC SW Force, Egypt, 1916. GOC 3rd Dismounted Bde and 230th Bde, 1916–17. GOC Imperial Mounted Division, 1917–19. GOC 4th Cavalry Division, 1919–20. Retired 1927.

Horne, Gen. Sir Henry Sinclair, 1861–1929. Entered Army, 1880. B.G.R.A., 1st Corps, BEF, 1914. GOC 2nd Division, 1915. GOC 15th Corps, 1915–16. GOC 1st Army, 1916–19. Created Baron, 1919. Retired 1926.

Inglefield, Maj.-Gen. Francis Seymour, 1855–1930. Son of Rear-Admiral V. O. Inglefield. Entered Army, 1874. GOC 12th Bde, 1909–12. GOC East Anglian (54th) Territorial Division (Gallipoli and Egypt, 1915–16), 1913–16. Retired 1918.

Ironside, William Edmund, 'Tiny', 1880–1959. Entered Army, 1899. GSO1 4th Canadian Division, 1916–17. Commandant, Machine Gun Corps School, France, 1918. GOC 99th Bde, 1918. GOC Allied Troops, Archangel, 1918–19. Quartermaster-General, India, 1933–36. Governor and C-in-C Gibraltar, 1938–39. CIGS, 1939–40. C-in-C, Home Forces, 1940. Field-Marshal, 1940. Created Baron, 1941.

Jacob, Sir Claud William, 1963–1948. Entered Army, 1882; Indian Army, 1884. GSO1 Meerut Division, 1914–15. GOC Dehra Dun Bde, 1915. GOC Meerut Division, 1915. GOC 21st Division, 1915–16. GOC 2nd Corps, 1916–19. Chief of Staff, India, 1920–24. C-in-C, India, 1925. Field-Marshal, 1926.

Kavanagh, Lt.-Gen. Sir Charles Toler McMurragh, 1864–1950. Entered Army, 1884. GOC 7th Cavalry Bde, 1914–15. GOC 2nd Cavalry Division, 1915. GOC 5th Division, 1915–16. GOC 1st Corps, 1916. GOC Cavalry Corps, 1916–19. Retired, 1920.

Kiggell, Lt.-Gen. Sir Lancelot Edward, 1862–1954. Entered Army, 1882. DSD, War Office, 1909–13. Commandant of Staff College, Camberley, 1913–14. Director of Home Defence, War Office, 1914–15. Chief of Staff, GHQ, France, 1915–18. Lt.-Governor of Guernsey, 1918–20.

Lansdowne, 5th Marquess of, Henry Charles Keith Petty-Fitzmaurice, 1845–1927. Governor-General of Canada, 1883–88. Viceroy of India, 1888–93. Secretary of State for War, 1895–1901. Foreign Secretary, 1901–5. Minister without Portfolio, 1915–16. In 1917 he publicly advocated a negotiated peace with Germany.

Lawrence, Gen. Hon. Sir Herbert Alexander, 1861–1943. 4th son of the 1st Baron Lawrence. Entered Army, 1882. Retired Army 1903, and entered the City.

Rejoined Army, 1914. GOC 127th Bde, 1915. GOC 52nd Division, Gallipoli and Egypt, 1915–16. In the summer of 1916 he drove the Turks from Sinai. GOC 66th Division, France, 1917. Chief of Staff, GHQ, France, 1918–19. Both his sons were killed in the Great War.

Lloyd, George Ambrose, 1879–1941. Before 1914 travelled extensively in Near and Middle East. Unionist MP, 1910–18. Served in Egypt, Gallipoli, Mesopotamia and the Heidjaz. Governor of Bombay, 1918–23. High Commissioner for Egypt and the Sudan, 1925–29. Created 1st Baron Lloyd.

Lloyd George, David, 1863–1945. Liberal MP, 1890–1931 and Independent Liberal 1931–45. Chancellor of the Exchequer, 1908–15. Minister of Munitions, 1915–16. Secretary of State for War, 1916. Prime Minister, 1916–22. Created Earl, 1945.

Long, Rt. Hon. Walter Hume, 1854–1924. Conservative MP, 1880–1921. Created the Union Defence League, the leading anti-Home Rule Organization, 1907–14. President of the Local Government Board, 1915–16. Secretary of State for the Colonies, 1916–19. First Lord of the Admiralty, 1919–21. Created Viscount, 1921.

Macready, Gen. Rt. Hon. Sir (Cecil Frederick) Nevil, 1862–1946. Entered Army, 1881. GOC Belfast, 1914. Adjutant-General, BEF, 1914–16. Adjutant-General to the Forces, 1916–18. Commissioner of the Metropolitan Police, 1918–20. GOC the Forces in Ireland, 1920–22. Created Baronet, 1923.

Malcolm, Sir Ian Zacchary, 1868–1944. Diplomat and politician. Attaché at Berlin, Paris, and St Petersburg, 1891–96. Conservative MP, 1895–1906; 1910–19. Private Secretary to Balfour at the Versailles Conference, 1919. British Government Director of Suez Canal Company, 1919–39.

Malcolm, Maj.-Gen. Sir Neill, 1869–1953. Brother of Sir I.Z. Malcolm. Entered Army, 1889. Chief of Staff, 5th Army, 1916–17. GOC 66th Division (severely wounded), 1917–18. GOC 39th Division, 1918. British Military Mission, Berlin, 1919–21. GOC Malaya, 1921–24. Retired 1924. High Commissioner for German refugees from the Nazi Regime, 1936–38.

Marriott, Maj.-Gen. Sir John Charles Oakes, 1895–1978. Entered Army, 1914. Captain and Adjutant, 1st Northants Regt, 1916. Staff Captain, 74th Bde (25th Division), 1916–18. GOC 66th Division, 1918–19. Military Attaché's Staff, Washington, 1919–20. Served Middle East, 1940–42, as GOC 29th Indian Bde and GOC 201st Bde. GOC Guards Division, 1945–47. GOC London District, 1947–50. Retired 1950.

Martel, Lt.-Gen. Sir Giffard Le Quesne, 1889–1958. Entered Army, 1909. Bde-Major, 75th Bde (25th Division), 1916. GSO2 Machine Gun Corps and Tank Corps, 1917–18. GOC 50th (TA) Division, 1939–40. GOC Royal Armoured Corps, 1940. Head of Military Mission at Moscow, 1943. Retired 1945.

Maxse, Gen. Sir (Frederick) Ivor, 1862–1958. Entered Army, 1882. GOC 1st (Guards) Bde, 1914. GOC 18th Division, 1914–17. GOC 18th Corps, 1917–18. Inspector-General of Training, France, 1918–19. Retired, 1923.

Midleton, 9th Viscount, St John Brodrick, 1865–1942. Conservative politician. Secretary of State for War, 1900–3, and for India, 1903–5. Served on Irish Convention, 1917–18. One of the leading Protestants in Ireland.

Milner, 1st Viscount, 1902, Alfred, 1854–1925. High Commissioner for South Africa, 1897–1905. Created Baron, 1901. Member of the War Cabinet, 1916–18. Secretary of State for War, 1918–19, and for the Colonies, 1919–21.

Monash, Gen. Sir John, 1865–1931. Civil Engineer, 1884 (Specialist in reinforced concrete construction from 1900). Lieut., Australian Citizen Forces, 1887. GOC 4th Bde, AIF, 1915–16. GOC 3rd Australian Division, 1916–18. GOC Australian Corps, 1918. Vice-Chancellor, Melbourne University, 1923–31.

Mond, Sir Alfred Moritz, 1868–1930. Son of a Jewish, German chemist. Called to the Bar, 1898. Between 1895 and 1926 created the Imperial Chemical Industries (ICI). Liberal MP, 1906–28. Created Baronet, 1910. First Commissioner of Works, 1916–21. Minister of Health, 1921–22. An enthusiastic Zionist. Created Baron Melchett, 1928.

Monro, Gen. Sir Charles Carmichael, 1860–1929. Entered Army, 1879. GOC 2nd Division, 1912–14. GOC 1st Corps, France, 1914–15. GOC 3rd Army, France, 1915. GOC Mediterranean Expeditionary Force, October, 1915–January, 1916. GOC 1st Army, France, 1916. C-in-C, India, 1916–20. Governor and C-in-C, Gibraltar, 1923–28. Created Baronet, 1921.

Montgomery, Archibald Armar, 'Archie' (Field-Marshal Sir Archibald Montgomery-Massingberd), 1871–1947. Second son of Rt. Hon. Hugh de F. Montgomery, PC. Added Massingberd in 1926 when his wife inherited the Massingberd estates. Entered Army, 1891. GSO1 4th Division, 1914. Chief of Staff to Rawlinson, 4th Corps, 1915–16 and 4th Army, 1916–19. Adjutant-General, 1931–33. CIGS 1933–36. Field-Marshal, 1935.

Mudge, Brig.-Gen. Arthur, 1871–1958. Entered Army, 1895. GOC 162nd Bde, 1915–20. GOC Warwick Inf. Bde, 1920–24. Inspector of West Indian Local Forces and OC Troops in Jamaica, 1925–28. Retired, 1928.

Nosworthy, Lt.-Gen. Sir Francis Poitiers, 1887–1971. Entered Army, 1907. GSO2, 2nd Corps, France, 1916–18. GSO1, 66th Division, France, 1918–19. GOC 4th Corps, 1940. C-in-C West Africa, 1943.

Pelham, Major Hon. Dudley Roger Hugh, 1872–1953. Fourth son of the 3rd Earl of Yarborough. Eton; Sandhurst; 10th Hussars. South Africa, 1899. European War, 1914–19.

Pershing, Gen. John Joseph, 1860–1948. Entered the United States Cavalry, 1886. Served in the Apache and Sioux Indian campaigns, 1886, 1890–91 and in the Spanish–American War, 1898. In command of US Troops sent into Mexico, 1916–17. C-in-C, American Expeditionary Force in Europe, 1917–19, Chief of Staff, US Army, 1921–24.

Plumer, Herbert Charles Onslow, 1857–1932. Entered Army, 1876. GOC 2nd Army, France, 1915–17 and 1918. GOC British Forces in Italy, 1917–18. GOC Army of the Rhine, 1918–19. Field-Marshal and created Baron in 1919. Governor and C-in-C, Malta, 1919–24. High Commissioner for Palestine, 1925–28. Created Viscount, 1929.

Rawlinson, Sir Henry Seymour, Bart., 'Rawly', 1864–1925. Eldest son of Maj.-Gen. Sir Henry Rawlinson, Bart. Entered Army, 1884. Commandant, Staff College, 1903–6. GOC 3rd Division, 1910–14. GOC 4th Division, 1914. GOC 4th Corps, 1914–15. GOC 4th Army, 1916–19. GOC Forces in North Russia,

1919. C-in-C, India, 1920–25. Died after an operation on 28th March 1925, before he could take up appointment as CIGS.

Robertson, Sir William Robert, 'Wully', 1860–1933. Entered Army as a Private, 1877. Commissioned, 1888. Commandant, Staff College, 1910–13. DMT, War Office, 1913–14. Quartermaster-General, BEF, 1914–15. Chief of Staff, GHQ, France, 1915. CIGS, 1915–18. C-in-C, Home Forces, 1918–19. Created Baronet, 1919. Field-Marshal, 1920.

Salisbury, 4th Marquess of, John Edward Hubert Gascoyne-Cecil, 1861–1947. Conservative MP, 1885–1903. President of the Board of Trade, 1905. Lord President of the Council, 1922–24. Lord Privy Seal, 1924–29. Leader of the House of Lords, 1925–29.

Smith, Frederick Edwin, 'FE', 1872–1930. Conservative MP, 1906–19. Head of the Press Bureau, 1914. Lt.-Col. attached to the Indian Corps, France, 1914–15. Solicitor-General, 1915. Knighted, 1915. Attorney-General, 1915–19. Created Baron Birkenhead, 1919. Lord Chancellor, 1920–22. Created Viscount, 1921. Created Earl, 1922. Secretary of State for India, 1924–28.

Smith-Dorrien, Gen. Sir Horace Lockwood, 1858–1930. Entered Army, 1876. GOC 2nd Corps, France, 1914. GOC 2nd Army, 1914–15 (Removed by Sir John French, May, 1915). GOC 1st Army for Home Defence, 1915. Governor and C-in-C, Gibraltar, 1918–23.

Willoughby, Brig.-Gen. Hon. Charles Strathavon Heathcote-Drummond, 1870–1949. Second son of the 1st Earl of Ancaster. Married daughter of the 14th Earl of Buchan. Entered Army, 1890. Retired as a Major, 1908. Member of the London Territorial Force. GOC 6th London Bde (later 142nd Bde) of the 47th (2nd London) Territorial Division, 1912–15. GOC 120th Bde (40th Division), 1915–18. Brother-in-law of Hon. Walter Guinness.

Wilson, Henry Hughes, 1864–1922. Entered Army, 1884. DMO, 1910–14. Sub-Chief, GHQ, France, 1914. Chief Liaison Officer with the French Army, 1915. Knighted, 1915. GOC 4th Corps, 1916. CIGS, 1918–22. Shot dead by Sinn Feiners on the steps of his London house. Field-Marshal and created Baronet, 1919.

Woollcombe, Lt.-Gen. Sir Charles Louis, 1857–1934. Entered Army, 1876. GOC Highland Division, 1911–14. GOC-in-C Eastern Command, 1914–15. GOC 2nd Army, Home Forces, 1915–16. GOC 11th Division, France, 1916. GOC 4th Corps, France, 1916–18. GOC-in-C Eastern Command, 1918–19. Retired, 1920.

Notes

1 (Page 24). Although no invasion was ever tried by the Germans, the British Admiralty, until December, 1917, considered such a scheme practicable and refused to take responsibility for preventing the transit of 60,000 men across the North Sea. Thus, large military forces had to be retained for home defence. With only one Regular Division in Britain the Territorials were the main defence in August, 1914.

2 (Page 31). After the failure to force the Dardanelles with the Navy alone between February and March of 1915, General Sir Ian Hamilton landed at Gallipoli on 25 April, 1915. After a heavy cost in casualties a foothold was gained but the Straits remained in Turkish hands. The attack was renewed but the successful landing of the 9th Corps at Suvla Bay on 6th August was not exploited. By the time the Eastern Mounted Brigade landed on 8 October, 1915, a stalemate had ensued which was ended only by the evacuation of the ANZAC and Suvla bridgeheads on 20 December, 1915, and of Helles on 9 January, 1916.

3 (Page 32). On 6th September, 1915, Bulgaria signed a military convention with Germany and Austria-Hungary. Consequently Bulgaria declared war on Serbia on 12 October, 1915, but her mobilization had warned the Entente Powers who landed at Salonika on 5 October, 1915.

4 (Page 32). The British and the French landed at Salonika in order to help the Serbs and remained there in 'the greatest Allied internment camp' until the collapse of Bulgaria in 1918.

5 (Page 39). On the night of 6–7 August the ANZAC Corps attempted to capture the Sari Bair Ridge, consisting of Chunuk Bair and Hill Q, which dominated the Dardanelles, to coincide with the landing at Suvla Bay. The 1/6th Gurkhas under Major C. J. L. Allanson took but then lost Hill Q, owing to shell fire and a lack of reinforcements. The ANZACs failed to exploit a fleeting chance to take Chunuk Bair and a decisive success had been narrowly missed.

6 (Page 49). Since he disliked General Sir Charles Monro's recommendation on 31 October, 1915, that Gallipoli should be evacuated, Kitchener visited the Mediterranean in November, 1915. He cabled home on 22 November suggesting the evacuation of Suvla Bay and ANZAC Cove but the retention of Helles 'for the present'. In fact Helles was abandoned too and with it the Dardanelles operation.

7 (Page 102). The 11th Cheshires (75th Brigade, 25th Division) were launched from Aveluy Wood in an attack against Thiepval on 3 July, 1916. After hurried preparations owing to a night advance and the late arrival of orders, the battalion was mown down by the German machine guns as it attempted to negotiate the uncut wire. The assault failed with heavy losses including Lt-Col R. L. Aspinall, who was killed. This is an example of the inept planning and tactics employed by the British Army on the Somme in 1916. The 25th Division was in reserve on 1 July.

8 (Page 107). Field punishment number one involved public humiliation. A soldier might be handcuffed to a wagon wheel and spreadeagled for two hours daily. Field punishment number two, for less serious offences, involved forfeit of pay, sleeping under guard and extra fatigues and pack drills. See Denis Winter *Death's Men* (1978) page 43.

9 (Page 110). This and the next day's entry look like the 'live and let live' system in operation. See Tony Ashworth *Trench Warfare, 1914–18* (1980).

10 (Page 118). In the Battle of Morval, 25–28 September, 1916, Rawlinson's 4th Army renewed the offensive to take the objectives which had not been secured during the Battle of Flers-Courcelette. On 25 September, 14th Corps (Guards, 6th, 5th, and 56th Divisions) took Morval and Lesobeufs but 15th Corps (21st, 55th, and New Zealand Divisions) failed to take Gueudecourt, which was captured on the next day while 14th Corps took Combles. The position was then consolidated.

11 (Page 119). During the Somme offensive tanks were used for the first time in the Battle of Flers-Courcelette on 15 September, 1916. Thirty-six tanks reached their startlines before zero hour but less than a dozen played a part in the battle owing to mechanical breakdown and the inexperience of the crews. Thus, the tank's potential was underrated owing to its mechanical unreliability.

12 (Page 122). On 9 October, 1916, the 10th Cheshires (7th Brigade, 25th Division) stormed the north face of Stuff Redoubt completing the capture of this work. The Reserve (5th) Army had wanted it captured by the 29 September but the 11th Division had only been able to capture the southern face before being relieved. With the fall of Regina Trench and Schwaben Redoubt (39th Division) the dominating Ancre Heights had been taken despite bad conditions and heavy losses. This allowed the successful attack on Beaumont Hamel on 13 November.

13 (Page 127). Between 1 and 10 October, 1916, the 1st, 2nd, and 3rd Canadian Divisions failed, after heavy losses, to capture Regina Trench. The Canadian Corps were relieved and it was not until 21 October that Regina Trench was taken by 2nd Corps in a combined attack by four Brigades, namely: 53rd Brigade (18th Division), 74th and 75th Brigades (25th Division), and 11th Canadian Brigade (4th Canadian Division). They were supported by two hundred heavy guns and howitzers and the field artilleries of seven divisions. Sixteen officers and one thousand and forty-one other ranks were captured.

14 (Page 129). A reference to the Curragh Incident in March, 1914, when Sir Henry Wilson, then Director of Military Operations at the War Office, encouraged John and Hubert Gough and other Cavalry Officers to refuse to obey orders to enter or 'invade' Ulster.

15 (Page 129). Wilson, as Director of Military Operations between 1910 and 1914, was chiefly responsible for making the plan which enabled the British Expeditionary Force to be sent to France in August, 1914. Historians still disagree about the wisdom of these pre-war staff talks and whether or not they actually committed the British Government to war. Our opinion is that the staff talks were necessary but did *not* bind the Government. See also Trevor Wilson's article in *History*, October, 1979.

16 (Page 130). Guinness' evaluation of Horne was probably correct. Cavan did well as the British Commander in Italy in 1917–18.

17 (Page 130). Rumania entered the war on 27 August, 1916, on the Allied side but within three months had collapsed with the fall of Bucharest on 6 December, 1916, following Mackensen's invasion of the province of Dobruja and Falkenhayn's advance into Transylvania.

18 (Page 130). The Staff College at Camberley had, by 1914, prepared far too few officers for a major war but it was unwisely closed on the outbreak of hostilities. See Brian Bond *The Victorian Army and the Staff College* (1972) chapter 10 and Appendix V.

19 (Page 153). The Second Army commander, Plumer, and his Chief of Staff, Sir Charles 'Tim' Harington, have been much praised for the meticulous planning and preparations which led to the capture of Messines on 7 June, 1917. This account shows the same high standards of preparation at brigade level and below.

20 (Page 162). An important reminder that only two days before the ill-fated Passchendaele offensive began it was very hot and dry, by no means the swampy wasteland of popular imagination. See the entry for 1 August.

21 (Page 164). The first day, 31 July, 1917, of the Third Battle of Ypres, better known as Passchendaele, was designed by the Fifth Army to break through the German defences. The early attacks in August, however, failed because of the mud, generated by heavy rain and the long bombardment, and the offensive tactics which were unsuitable against the German methods of defence in depth. Control of the offensive was handed over by Sir Douglas Haig to Plumer's Second Army on 24 August. This necessitated a delay of three weeks to prepare for siege warfare, which aimed at a succession of limited, cautious advances in contrast to Gough's bold offensive plans.

22 (Page 181). The British Third Army (Byng) had attacked over the chalky downs at Cambrai on 20 November, 1917, without a preliminary bombardment relying on tanks and the element of surprise to break through. On the 21st the bells of London rang out in premature peals of victory. However, once again, the initial success was not exploited owing to the lack of reserves. The attack ended in near disaster when the Germans counter-attacked on 30 November and surprised the over-confident British.

23 (Page 189). On 21 March, 1918, three German Armies attacked on a forty-mile front with thirty-two divisions, and another thirty-nine divisions in reserve, with the aim of winning the war. The British, facing this massive offensive force had only seventeen Infantry divisions on Byng's Third Army front of twenty-six miles and three Cavalry and fourteen Infantry divisions on Gough's Fifth Army front of forty-two miles. Gough, after bearing the brunt of the attack, was made the scapegoat for this disaster, perhaps unfairly. Ludendorff had aimed to split the British and the French Armies by driving on Amiens and was nearly successful but Allied reserves arrived just in time to restore the line. Ironically, in this offensive on the Somme and in Flanders in April the Germans frittered away their reserves in heavy losses and the holding of large salients. This exhaustion and falling morale provided the opportunity for the victorious Allied offensive between July and November, 1918.

24 (Page 198). Bethell continued to serve until 1935 but never rose above the rank of Major-General. Presumably the impatience, irascibility and overriding of regulations which Guinness conveys so forcefully told against him in peacetime.

25 (Page 199). On 9 April, 1918, the Germans attacked the 2nd Portuguese Division on the River Lys and broke through. By 12 April twenty-four miles of front had been engulfed and Sir Douglas Haig issued his famous 'backs to the wall' order of the day. British and Australian reserves, however, arrived from the south to seal the breach as the German attack lost momentum.

26 (Page 230). This fighting had been the breaking of the Hindenburg Line, at St Quentin, by the 9th Corps, 13th Corps, Australian Corps, and 2nd American Corps of the Fourth Army (Rawlinson), which was one of the outstanding achievements of the war. Between 29 September and 5 October, 1918, the Fourth Army forced its way through the awesome German defences until the main Hindenburg position and the Hindenburg Reserve System had been captured and held against counter-attacks. Ludendorff and Hindenburg concluded that Germany had to ask for an armistice 'to save the Army from catastrophe', and the Kaiser agreed.

27 (Page 234). This entry illustrates the point that popular criticism of 'the Staff' – both during and after the war – was too sweeping. A distinction clearly has to be made between divisional and brigade staffs, whose work was exhausting and dangerous, and staffs of the higher formations, namely Corps, Armies and GHQ.

Index